FOREIGN LANGUAGE TEACHER'S GUIDE TO ACTIVE LEARNING

Deborah Blaz

EYE ON EDUCATION
6 DEPOT WAY WEST, SUITE 106
LARCHMONT, NY 10538
(914) 833–0551
(914) 833–0761 fax

ISBN 1-883001-75-7

Library of Congress Cataloging-in-Publication Data

Blaz, Deborah.
Foreign language teacher's guide to active learning / by Deborah Blaz.
p. cm.
Includes bibliographical references (p.).
ISBN 1-883001-75-7
1. Language and languages—Study and teaching. I. Title.
P51.B544 1999
418'.007—dc21
99-12549
CIP

10 9 8 7 6

Editorial and production services provided by
Richard H. Adin Freelance Editorial Services,
9 Orchard Drive, Gardiner, NY 12525 (914-883-5884)

About the Author

Deborah Blaz, a French teacher at Angola High School in Angola, Indiana, is a native of St. Charles, Illinois. She received her B.A. in French and German from Illinois State University, a *diplome* from the Université de Grenoble in Grenoble, France, and, in 1974, an M.A. in French from the University of Kentucky. Ms. Blaz has taught French and English to grades 7 through 12 for the past 20 years in Indiana.

Ms. Blaz, author of *Teaching Foreign Languages in the Block,* has been a frequent presenter on successful teaching strategies, most recently at the 1998 American Council on the Teaching of Foreign Languages (ACTFL) national convention, as well as at numerous universities and high schools. She was named to the All-USA Teacher team, Honorable Mention, by *USA Today* in 1998. She was also honored as the Indiana French Teacher of the Year in 1996 by the Indiana chapter of the American Association of Teachers of French (IAATF).

She may be contacted at Angola High School, 755 S 100 E. Angola, Indiana 46703.

ACKNOWLEDGMENTS

I would like to thank everyone whose encouragement and input have enriched my book: foreign language teachers Dellawanna Bard, Jocelyn Raught, Faye Conway, Sharon Kazmierski, Dr. Lucinda Hart-González, and Reggie Thomson, who contributed creative teaching strategies and resources; Linda Jane C. Barnette, Sari Kaye, Patricia Hattori, Kathleen Babbitt, and Richard H. Adin, whose comments on the original manuscript were invaluable; and my editor, Bob Sickles, for his patience and support throughout my second book. My warmest gratitude also extends to my family, Walter Best, Mary Blaz, my husband Michael, and my children Nathaniel and Suzanne.

TABLE OF CONTENTS

1

Incorporating Research on a Daily Basis

The five C's—Communication, Culture, Connections, Comparisons, and Communities—stated in the new *Standards for Foreign Language Learning: Preparing for the 21st Century* (1998) do not require a major change in foreign language teaching; after all, foreign language teachers wrote them! The standards are, however, a good reminder to construct lessons to include all five areas as often as possible. They also reflect a shift in what the public wants of us: communication has moved to the forefront. Parents want their children to be comfortable communicating in the language, knowing how, when and why to say what to whom, rather than simply knowing how to read and write.

To achieve this goal, we need to modify what we do every day in the classroom. We need to implement two very important goals:

- Be current.
- Use variety.

Chapters 1, 2, 6, and 7 of this book deal with the information that you need to be on the cutting edge of foreign language teaching. It is important to be familiar with current buzzwords such as brain research, multiple intelligences, block scheduling, and alternative assessment; implementation of these tools will contribute to your success as a teacher. Technology will also continue to develop, and we must learn to use it as fully as possible to prepare our students and maximize the learning potential it offers.

The other chapters in this book address the issue of using variety. Creating a great class requires imagination, creativity, and innovation—and taking advantage of every teaching opportunity. We must have a classroom that allows students to experience, experiment, fail, or discover without punishment. The teacher who can do this is prepared to meet the challenges of this era in foreign language education. Chapter 2, which presents the theory of multiple intelligences, has many ideas that you can use daily, and Chapters 3 through 5 provide some creative ideas for presenting information in different ways that will appeal to your students.

BRAIN RESEARCH

Recent improvements in MRI (magnetic resonance imaging) have changed our knowledge about how we learn: which parts of the brain are used for speech, short- and long-term memory storage, and other processes that are central to learning. Watching someone's brain while they are hearing a foreign language, or studying it, or trying to memorize something, has shown us that the basic strategies that we use to teach languages work, but can stand to be improved or modified (such as increasing the frequency of certain types of activities and decreasing the frequency of others) to facilitate better learning. Knowing how the brain processes information and learns is invaluable when deciding how to structure a lesson, and which materials you need.

The brain has priorities by which it stores material:

- The highest priority is for anything that is a threat to survival. Unfortunately, menacing the survival of students would result in the loss of our jobs. Failing Friday's test is not life-threatening, much as we teachers might wish it were.
- The second highest priority is for information attached to a strong emotion. When emotions such as anger, fear, or joy are evoked, the conscious processing of the brain stops, and the older limbic system takes over. This sort of effect is one that we can achieve in the classroom occasionally; for example, the thrill of discovery of a concept through inductive or deductive teaching would help maximize what material is stored. We all know the value of humor, too.

A lot of material is remembered because it has emotional associations attached to it. Think of a word such as "Mom," "holocaust," "abortion," or "Monday," and a lot of other words, ideas, or pictures will pour into your mind. Helping students make these associations increases learning. Memory Model, a method explained in Chapter 2, is good for encouraging this type of association.

After this, the brain gives priority to material that the working memory thinks is important. The working memory is what 10 years ago was called the short-term memory. Its capacity changes with age (a high school student has a larger capacity than does a young child, for example) and it has a definite time limit. Ebbinghaus (1885), in his research on forgetting, memorized long lists of nonsense syllables (what could be more like a foreign language, at first) and stated that the time limit for memorizing is 45 minutes. Sousa (1995) states that recent research has found that the time limit is actually between 10 and 20 minutes for adolescents and adults. (See Figure 1.1) A brain, it seems, is like a cup; you can pour information into it for only so long, 10 or 20 minutes, and either fatigue or boredom sets in. For a person to be able to focus his or her attention beyond that time, *change* must take place. By change, I mean that there must be a radical difference in how the material is taught; for example, changing from a thinking activity to physically dealing with the ideas, or making different connections between the material and other learning.

FIGURE 1.1. THE VALUE OF CHANGING TEACHING STRATEGIES OR TOPICS WITHIN A LONGER CLASS PERIOD

Retention During a 20-Minute Learning Episode

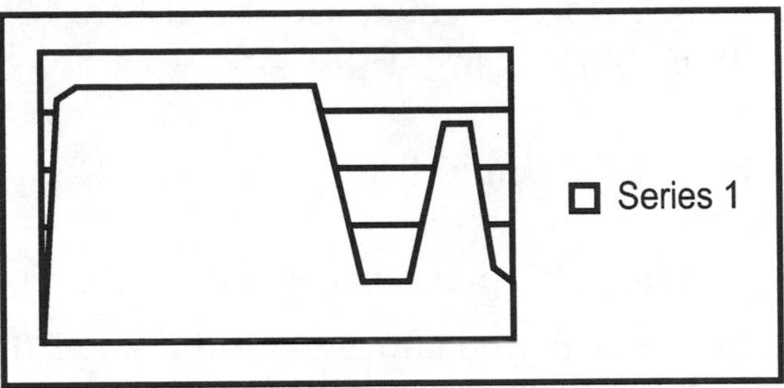

Retention During a 40-Minute Learning Episode with One Lesson

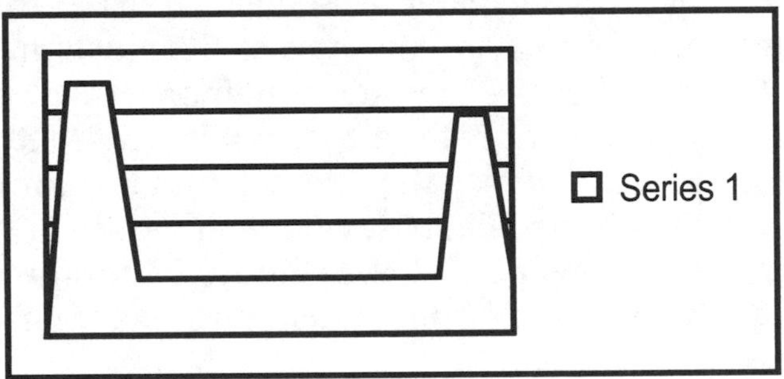

Retention During Two 20-Minute Learning Episodes (40 min.)

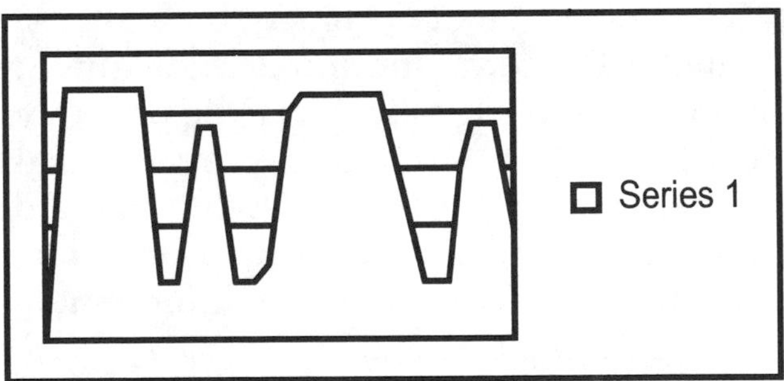

This has profound meaning for all of us whose classes last longer than 20 minutes, and especially for those on a block schedule, with 70- to 90-minute classes: variety is not only suggested, it is a necessity. Try appealing to a different intelligence (see Chapter 2) or alternate grammar, culture, conversation, reading and listening activities to maximize the attention spans of your students.

CRITERIA FOR LONG-TERM STORAGE

If you usually review material right before you give a test, you will never know whether a student has that material in his or her long-term memory. Reviewing the material reenters that material in a student's working memory (data that has been retained for immediate use). For data to go from the working memory into long-term storage, it must meet two essential conditions. Ask yourself:

- Does the material make sense? (Does it fit with what the student already knows?)
- Does it have meaning? (Is it relevant to the student's life and needs?)

For the information to be placed into long-term storage, the answer to both questions must be "yes." Relevance could be increased by simply requiring a student to recite something the next day, for the class, for a grade (the element of being on display and possibly embarrassed is a great motivator for most), but *not* by giving a quiz or test on the material. Relevance also increases when a student sees a need for something every day, rather than just once.

Data requires *time* to enter the long-term memory: time to process and rehearse the material. However, more time does not increase retention unless it is time in which the student can personally interact with the information. Ebbinghaus (1885) found that we remember best whatever we see or hear first, and we remember second best whatever is last. (See Figure 1.1 for the most recent findings that corroborate the work of Ebbinghaus.) With that in mind, Sousa (1995) suggests the following:

- Teach new material first

  Instead of beginning class with review, present something new. Remember to teach in 20-minute chunks—the new material should take 8 to 10 minutes at most. In the middle eight minutes or so, when the least amount of learning takes place, do your review of previously learned material, or check homework, or make announcements, or practice the new material. During the middle time, the brain is still capable of organizing the information for further processing, so that time is not wasted, but no information will be put in long-term storage during that time.

- Teach right to the end of class, and provide closure

  Giving the students five minutes' free time at the end of the class is an absolute waste of those five or so minutes at the end, which scientists say are the second-best learning periods. Save something new or important for the end.

SUCCESSFUL TEACHING PRACTICES

Questions such as "Why do we need to know this?" or "Do we need to know this?" reveal that students are having trouble seeing relevancy in the material that you are presenting. Dr. Madeline Hunter (1982) of the University of California has done a lot of research on the interrelationship between teaching strategies and student performance. She suggests, as Sousa did, that:

- Teachers select material to present during the first part of a lesson, condensing it to the smallest possible amount that will have maximum meaning for the students.
- Teachers model the steps to apply to deal with the particular situation being studied, such as putting the correct endings on verbs, making adjectives agree, selecting the correct verb tense, or using a dictionary correctly. A good model is very specific and accurate, and avoids any controversial or emotional issues or words that will distract or redirect the attention of the students.
- Teachers bring in examples from students' own experiences to bring previous knowledge into the working memory (for example, reminding them of another verb tense that is formed in a similar manner).
- Teachers can, if needed, help create artificial ways of giving meaning to the material. A good example of this is the use of mnemonic devices, or strategies such as Memory Model, found in Chapter 2.
- Teachers insist that students practice in their presence, in a focused manner. Focus them by standing near them, especially if they are off task. We have all seen how well this works.
- Teachers provide prompt and specific feedback for students during practice of a concept. If students receive quick corrective feedback, they are more likely to continue working. That is why computers are so effective in learning, by giving immediate, specific feedback and permitting students also to evaluate their progress.
- Teachers use every available minute of class time. This involves using "sponges," a concept that I have found very helpful.

SPONGES

What do your students do while you are taking attendance, writing on the board, rewinding a tape, talking to a student, parent, or colleague one on one, or when they are moving into groups? The probable answer is that they get restless, or start talking in English, or get off task (their attention wanders). If you have sponges ready to assign, you will be able to get students to use these bits of time to do something constructive in the target language.

SPONGE is an acronym for:

Short, intense, vivid activities, which provide

Practice of learned material, which students can do

On their own, and which will also include

New arrivals or those finishing an assignment early, by keeping the

Group involved, and designed to

Elicit an immediate response.

To write sponges, just think of the chapter in all four aspects: grammar, vocabulary, culture, and literature. Then, consider the five different types of sponge:

- Say to yourself
- Say to another
- Say in chorus
- Write a response
- Signal

In the "Say to yourself" type of sponge, you ask the student to tell themselves something. This type of quiet activity is good for settling down things at the beginning of class, after a fire drill or an announcement, while you are erasing the board or they are moving into their groups, or after a test while a few slower ones are still finishing. Here are some examples of this type of sponge:

- Describe to yourself what you see in this picture/poster/video with the sound OFF.
- Look at this handout, and underline all the words you already know (or, the ones you don't know).
- Think of how the character in yesterday's story/movie was feeling when...
- Locate the main idea in the third paragraph.
- Read the story/dialogue/paragraph and make up an appropriate title for it.

Notice that all sponges use action verbs in the command form.

A "say to another" sponge asks a student to do a short activity with a partner, such as:

- Alternate naming objects, verb endings, colors, favorite foods, etc.
- Take turns describing a family photograph they have brought to class.
- Practice the dialogue. Then switch roles.
- Tell each other the most important thing you learned in this class yesterday/today (very useful, especially if several were on a field trip or testing the day before).
- One of you name a category such as "clothing." The other will name as many items as they can that fit in that category.
- Ask your partner a question.
- Taking turns, one of you name a verb, and the other will conjugate it in the _____ tense. Then switch.
- Tell your partner something funny/sad/complimentary/insulting.

This sort of activity will involve the students in teaching/correcting each other, which according to the Glasser scale (Figure 1.2), is quite beneficial.

FIGURE 1.2. GLASSER'S LEARNING SCALE

We Learn . . .

10% of What We Read
20% of What We Hear
30% of What We See
50% of What We Both See and Hear
70% of What Is Discussed with Others
80% of What We Experience Personally
90% of What We *Teach* to Someone Else

William Glasser

The third type of sponge asks students to say, together, things such as the alphabet, months, or days of the week. They could also sing a song learned in class, chant the verb endings for the past tense, or count by fives to a thousand. Something I like to do is to make them do these things forward and backward, to make sure they understand what they are saying, rather than simply memorizing a string of sounds.

The "written response" sponge would ask the student to write something like the following:

- List the four seasons, and typical weather for each one.
- Record what you want your friends/teacher/parents to do for you.

- Make a list of foods that are served (or never served) at the school cafeteria.
- Produce a five-word description of the story/poem we read yesterday.
- Write a five-word description of your favorite place to visit/favorite sandwich/favorite class.
- Finish this sentence: The teacher is...
- Use the same noun in the nominative, accusative, and genitive cases.
- Name four famous people and tell what country they are from/what clothing they would wear/what they look like.
- Write eight commands or questions that you often hear from your parents.
- Indicate in writing three things you ought to do sometime soon.

"Signal" sponges appeal to almost any student learning style (oral, visual, kinetic, etc.). Examples of this type include hitting the desk, stomping feet, standing up, lifting a piece of paper, or some other physical demonstration to indicate if:

- A word is masculine or feminine, singular or plural, nominative or genitive, etc.
- A sentence (either written or spoken) is true or false.
- A verb is in the past or present, future or conditional, indicative or subjunctive tense.
- A given situation requires the passé composé/preterite or the imperfect tense

In summary, sponge activities keep you from wasting valuable class time as well as require that students continue thinking and performing in the language. Make every minute count, and test scores should go up, too. This is not a skill that you gain overnight, but don't give up, as you will see a big difference in classroom discipline and in learning.

Figure 1.3 lists some sponge activities that I use when doing a unit on families and family members.

SPIRALING

Dr. Hunter also discovered that "massed" practice is inferior to "distributed" practice. Massed practice means trying a concept in a variety of different ways, over a short period of time. Distributed practice is when material is practiced over time. According to Dr. Hunter, tests should not only test material in the current chapter, but should also allow/expect students to use material previously learned. This is called a "spiral curriculum" because the ideas and skills are used again and again. Too often textbooks teach a verb tense during one unit

FIGURE 1.3. FAMILY UNIT SPONGES

Note: These would normally be written in the target language

- Say to Self
  - The number of cousins you like, with a separate count of boy cousins and girl cousins.
  - How many brothers and sisters you have.
  - The name, age and relationship to you of your favorite relative.
  - The name, age and relationship to you of your least-favorite relative.
  - Look at the family tree on the screen. You are the person marked with an X. Tell yourself what each person's relationship is to you.
  - Look at the picture on the front board. Invent a name for each person in the family, and be ready to tell me their relationships to each other (e.g., Marie is the daughter of Luc and Claire, and the sister of Marc).
  - Pick the hardest word in this chapter's vocabulary and think of a creative way to remember it.
- Say to Another
  - Describe your family to your partner and help him or her draw a family tree based on your description. Correct your partner gently if they get something wrong.
  - Tell your partner who your favorite relative is and why.
  - Tell your partner who your least-favorite relative is and why.
  - Alternate naming people on the family tree on page ___. After one of you names a name, the other must tell what family member that person is. For example, Véronique is a daughter and a sister.
  - Alternate saying one of the family vocabulary words. After one of you says a word, the partner must supply the equivalent for the opposite sex. For example, if Person A says *uncle*, Person B must say *aunt*. Then Person B might say *husband*, and Person A must reply *wife*.
- Write
  - Draw your family tree. Don't forget the word *my* with each one.
  - Pick up one of the cutout magazine photos on the desk. Each is of a family. In writing, introduce me to the people in the photograph, including their name, age, relationship, and, if they are an adult, their profession.

- Write a postcard to a penpal in France. Tell them about your family.
- Read the story on page ___, and draw a family tree based on the information in the story.

♦ Say in Chorus

- List the male family members, from oldest to youngest (Grandpa – Dad – Uncle – Brother – Cousin), forward and backwards.
- List the female family members from oldest to youngest, forward and backwards.

♦ Signal

- Show me, by holding up fingers, how many aunts you have.
- Show me, by clapping your hands, how many uncles you have.
- Show me, by stomping your feet, how many cousins you have.
- Show me, by hitting the desk, how many husbands you have.
- Show me, by snapping your fingers, how many brothers you have.
- Show me, by nodding your head, how many sisters you have.
- Show me, by kicking your left foot, how many pets you have.

---

and then the next unit is primarily vocabulary, with no more use of the verb tense until several units later. Changing an activity in the book to require that particular verb tense, enabling students to continue to practice it, or supplementing the text with a reading in that tense or a composition that requires it would be an easy way to "spiral" ideas.

Motivational Factors

Another thing Hunter (1982) discovered was that motivational factors can increase the time that working memory can deal with language.

♦ **Interest:** If the learner is interested in the item, he or she is dealing with it in several ways, often making new connections to past learning. Interest significantly extends a student's attention span. We have all seen it happen: a student who can't listen for two minutes will raptly view a video for an hour, for example.

♦ **Accountability:** If students believe they will be held accountable for the material, processing time is increased. (Driver's education classes, for example, have both the interest factor and accountability.) To stimulate a feeling of accountability, show students how a skill might affect them later in life.

- **Level of concern:** If students are to care about learning, they need to have a little "helpful anxiety." Students who are concerned about doing a better job will try harder to learn more. Too much concern, however, is not good. Here's how to help students to feel some helpful anxiety:
  - *Give consequences*. Low-level consequences such as "Knowing this will help you in the next chapter" raise anxiety less than consequences such as "This will be on your semester exam."
  - *Stand near them*: We all know this works well if students are off task.
  - *Give the right amount of time to do the task*: Too little time raises anxiety, and extending the time lowers it.
  - *Help them quickly*: This is the most difficult one, as you don't want students to become too dependent on you.

USE OF GESTURES

New research by several American psychologists has shown that using one's hands while talking can unlock something they call "lexical memory." The latest studies show that they can help people retrieve words from their long-term memory storage.

We have known for years that gestures can be a language themselves, such as the ASL (American Sign Language) used by handicapped students. Many foreign language teachers on the FL-TEACH list on the Internet who are currently using the TPRS (Total Physical Response Storytelling) method report that they use ASL gestures while telling a story in the target language, which enhances students' comprehension of the vocabulary.

The new research (Begley, 1998) shows that gesture is like a key that unlocks a door in the brain, especially for words that connect easily with spatial ideas or movement, such as the word *castanets*. Researchers attached electrodes to people's arms, and found that people who didn't even think they were gesturing were actually activating their muscles in response to words (for instance, a "clench" movement for the word *castanets*). Doctors also notice that people whose memory is impaired after a stroke also tend to gesture more.

This makes sense when you think back to what was stated earlier: the more associations, especially using the senses, that we can link to a word, the more accessible it becomes. I often use gestures to practice reflexive verbs such as wake up, hurry, get dressed, comb hair, brush teeth, as well as the less spatially obvious ones such as remember, be nervous, have fun, and other emotions. I have my students decide which gestures we will use (this is important—if they feel responsible for the action, they learn it better. As we begin to practice them, I'll say, "this one was Mark's verb" to prompt them, and they all nod and do the action as they say the verb) and we rehearse using gestures. First, as I say the word they do the gesture, and later I gesture and they say the word. As they take the test later, I will see many of them gesture, nod, and write. It really seems to help.

Not only does using gestures help retrieve items from long-term memory, the ownership of thinking of the gestures, as well as the extrasensory stimulation of doing them, make the material more likely to go from the working memory into the long-term memory. In one study done at the University of North Carolina at Greensboro, subjects had to hold on to a bar so that they were unable to use their hands. These subjects often failed to learn the vocabulary, or took longer to do so, than a group who were allowed to use their hands.

Students should be encouraged to think in spatial terms for any vocabulary. Even abstract concepts such as "freedom" may be linked to some sort of physical idea that is easy to make into a gesture, and this enables students to learn it more easily and to retrieve it again more quickly.

Increasing Transfer

Transfer is the ability to learn something in a certain situation, and then to be able to apply it in other situations. Transfer is involved in problem solving, creative thinking, artistic endeavors, and other higher-level mental activities.

As new material is introduced to the working memory, it searches through the long-term storage for similar material. All of us have probably experienced hearing a song that brings with it a flood of associated old memories. This is another example of how emotion attached to information guarantees its storage in long-term memory. It is also an example of transfer in action.

But studies show that students are generally not good at recognizing how things that are learned in school apply to life outside school (Perkins & Salomon, 1988). To maximize transfer, teachers should help students look for two things when new information is introduced: similarities and differences.

Similarities means linking the past to the present: showing students how one verb tense resembles one that they already know, or how the Spanish/French use of the preterite and imperfect is similar to how it is used in English. It could be things such as talking about the ways Japanese food is similar to what they can get at the Chinese restaurant in town. Discovering similarities helps students' brains decide which material already in long-term storage this new material fits with and can be stored with ("chunking"). Positive transfer is especially easy when the two skills (new and old) are similar: learning one Romance language makes learning a second one easier, for example. When similarities exist with "old" material, the brain simply adds the new to the old, and stores it as a chunk of information.

Metaphors, analogies, and similes are especially effective ways to promote positive transfer. For example, telling students that conjugating a verb is like smoking a cigar: first, the tip is clipped off, which is like dropping off the -en, -ar, -ir, or whatever ending is on the verb as it is found in the dictionary. Then a match is needed (matching the new ending with the subject pronoun), and then, as the end of the cigar changes appearance as it is transformed into ash, a new ending appears on the part of the verb that was left when the end was clipped off. Or, for compound tenses, compare fixing a sandwich with conjugating a verb: trim off the crust/endings, put in some filling (helping verb, adverbs, negatives, and pronouns) and so on. Any colorful comparison such as these, especially if it is accompanied by a poster or drawing containing this same image (for the visual learners), will positively affect students' ability to remember the material.

Students also need help linking the present to the future. Although material is filed in long-term storage by its similarity, it is retrieved by its differences, called "critical attributes." An example from everyday life is finding a friend in a crowd of people. To find your friend, you need to think about what makes him or her different from everyone else, and look for those attributes. Here, again, is a place where the teacher can guide students to discover what the critical attributes of the new information are, so that they can find it when they need it again. If material is very similar, it will be hard to learn.

Another way to link the present to the future is to provide students with an activity in which they will have to use the current information to communicate: a simulation. Simulations are discussed in depth in Chapter 2.

PROVIDING VARIETY

Variety is the key to learning, but be careful! Too much variety is as bad as too little. Sousa (1995) warns us not to overload students with symbols, images, and input—the working memory in older students can only hold *seven* items at a time (Figure 1.4).

FIGURE 1.4. CHANGES IN WORKING MEMORY WITH AGE

Age Range	*Minimum # of Items*	*Maximum # of Items*	*Average*
Less than 5	1	3	2
5 to 14	3	7	5
14 and older	5	9	7

Students must have time to process, select, and file information before more is added. However, because students are usually either verbal or visual learners, providing information in both modes will not overload anyone, as a verbal student's working memory will retain verbal information, while a visual student will process what is taught visually. Use diagrams to discuss relationships between subject and object pronouns, masculine and feminine adjectives, or other concepts that are easy to organize into groupings. Show the smallest possible portion of a video, then stop it and discuss what was shown.

Here is a visual representation activity: After reading a story, have students draw a stick person and attach their notes to it. Have them write the character's ideas and draw a line to the brain, hopes and dreams with a line to the eyes, words with a line to the mouth, actions with a line to the hands, feelings with a line to the heart, movements with a line to the feet, and so on.

Diagram the plot of the story like a mountain: the causes on the left (upward) slope, the effects on the right (downward) slope, and the conclusions (theme/message/ moral) at the base.

Appealing to Upper-Level Thinking Skills

Using Bloom's taxonomy scale (Figure 1.5), let's examine the types of thinking skills that you can ask students to do. The bottom level, knowledge, is just rote recitation ("What is the word for 'cat'?"). The comprehension level asks students to summarize information, or to convert the information to a new form ("Why is Cecile's cat important in the story?"). The application level has the student use the information in a new situation ("If Cecile brought her cat to your house, what would you do?"). The analysis level and above are where you want to concentrate the majority of your classroom activity. At this level, students will be using the language to communicate more than just basic necessities. They may also notice a gap between what they want to say and what they are able to say, test hypotheses about the target language, and retain more of the language that they were successful in using. For example, an analysis question asks, "What happened in this story that is typically French?" or "What happened in this story that could really happen?" A synthesis activity is one that results in a product, such as having students retell the story, adding Cecile's brother or a dog to the cast of characters. An evaluation activity asks students to make a judgment based on given criteria: "Was it right for Cecile's cat to eat her sandwich?"

Another scale based on educational research is that of William Glasser (Figure 1.2, p. 7). His scale shows the outcomes of various teaching strategies in terms of the amount of information that is put into long-term storage. Again, we reach the same conclusion: students who work with the language on a personal, individual level (whether with a partner, a group, or one-on-one with the teacher) learn the most.

RIGHT-BRAIN/LEFT-BRAIN LEARNING

We have all read a lot of right-brain/left-brain research and information and know that girls tend to be more left-brained, and boys more right-brained. Whatever your beliefs about this research, it should be obvious that this is yet another reason to include as much variety as possible in your lesson to accommodate the different learning styles of your students. To briefly summarize in terms of foreign language learning, the left brain processes "text" and codes information verbally, and the right brain handles "context," nonverbal, visual information. The right brain is superior, according to Danesi (1990), in processing new information and stimuli.

FIGURE 1.5. BLOOM'S TAXONOMY SCALE

Note: No level can be done without also having done the levels below it.

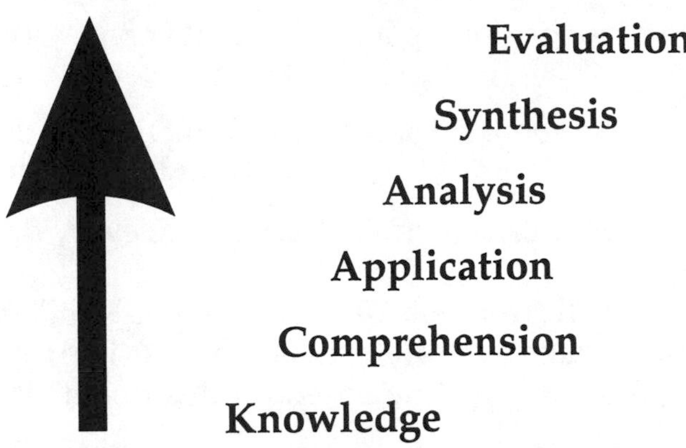

For foreign language and ESL teachers, it is *very important* to begin instruction following a right-to-left hemisphere sequence of strategies (Danesi, 1990). This means that you should initially teach students using brainstorming and concrete visual strategies, only later moving on to more organizational and formal types of instruction such as drill, translation, dictation, and so forth.

Do not rely heavily on grammar or vocabulary memorization during the early stages of instruction. Do more with contextual activities, incorporating trial and error, brainstorming of meaning, visual activities, and role playing/simulations such as TPR and TPRS, all of which give the right hemisphere time to establish the context of the activity. The right brain uses verbal and nonverbal cues to adapt speech to a specific person or social context, and enables students to use grammatical forms (i.e., *usted* vs. *tu*, *vous* vs. *tu*, *Sie* vs. *du*) in context.

After the right brain has the context it needs to grasp meaning and nuance, then apply left-brain activities (vocabulary memorization and grammar drills). This approach benefits left-brain as well as right-brain learners, because it increases the role their right brain plays in their language competence. The left brain does the analytical and sequential processing of information necessary for vocabulary, rules of punctuation, word formation, and sentence structure.

Conversational competence involves both hemispheres, say researchers, in order to combine form and thought into something coherent. The analytic ability of the left brain generates the grammatical features, while the right brain synthesizes them into meaningful, coherent wholes. Keep this in mind also when you construct a test (see Chapter 6).

You can also organize your class and room according to right-brain–left-brain ideas.

For Left Brain Skills	*For Right Brain Skills*
Make talkers sit apart from each other.	Use board and overhead frequently.
Erase everything before beginning a new topic.	Give oral versus written options on assignments.
Have students keep notebooks, use agendas.	Have bulletin board relevant to the current instructional topic.
Role-play and use hands-on material.	Use closure every day on lessons.

Both types will benefit from lots of metaphor and simile-creation activities, or "what if" questions, such as "how is this verb tense like (other verb tense)" or "What if we tried to draw a picture based on this poem? What would it look like?"

METAMEMORY TECHNIQUES

Metamemory is the area of study that deals with people's understanding of how their own memory functions. Students will often tell us how hard they studied, yet they performed poorly on the tests. Teaching them some basic metamemory knowledge about themselves may help them study more efficiently. Memory is based on three sets of variables: personal, task, and strategy variables.

To discover what your personal variables are, ask yourself what you remember best. Is it the words to songs (things set to music)? Things that rhyme? Things stated like a formula? Things that you hear, say, or see? If, for instance, you remember musical things, then put whatever you have to memorize to music. Sing it to a familiar tune, such as a commercial jingle, or a nursery song such as "Twinkle, Twinkle, Little Star." Another type of important personal variable is discovering what time of day is best: Are you a morning person? A night owl? and What mood do you need to be in to study well? Then, arrange your schedule as much as possible to make use of that time and that mood. If you study best late at night when the family is asleep, take a nap before or after dinner so that you can use the late-night hours without falling asleep in school. If you need to be in a relaxed mood, discover music that relaxes you, and play it softly in the background.

Task variables that affect learning are things such as the amount of information involved, essay tests versus objective ones, and the different approaches taken by different instructors. If you learn small amounts of information (such as chapter tests) better than large amounts of information (such as exams), plan to study a chapter a night until the exam rather than cramming the night before. Because objective tests require more knowledge of detail, a person good at trivia/details might prefer an objective test, while a person who likes to understand the "big picture" might prefer an essay format. Some teachers provide choices in test format. Often, in bigger schools, students also have a choice of teachers. If they have found one whose teaching style seems to suit their learning style, they should request that teacher for future classes, if possible.

Finally, strategy variables are important. Mnemonics are one strategy that works for almost everyone. One I recently learned was that "Caroline" contains all the letters that are doubled in Spanish. This could really help when, for example, spelling *gato* (cat)—because there are no t's in Caroline, the t in *gato* cannot be doubled. A variation of mnemonics is to make a silly sentence using the first letter in a string of words to memorize. Another Spanish example is to list the Spanish-speaking countries in South America (Venezuela, Colombia, etc.) as the sentence Victoria Can't Eat Peas, Beets, Carrots, and Uncooked Potatoes. Let the students, however, make up their own sentences, or have a class contest to do so, and they'll remember them better. The word "Caréful" is useful in French, as it contains the letters that are pronounced at the end of words; in most cases, all other letters are silent. I still remember inventing (and drawing a caterpillarlike monster) the "Be-ent-er-ver-zer" (one syllable on each section of the monster) in order to remember the beginnings of all the German verbs I needed to remember that don't use "ge-" in the past participle form.

ALTERNATIVE SCHEDULES

Another topic to know to be current is that "hot topic," block scheduling.

There are basically three types of block schedule: the A/B or alternate-day schedule, the 4/4 schedule, and the trimester (Canady & Rettig, 1995), but many schools have permutations of these schedules.

In an alternate-day schedule, rather than meeting every class daily, students and teachers meet every other day for a longer "block" period of time. Alternate-day schedules are also called A/B, Odd/Even, Day1/Day 2, and Week 1/Week 2 schedules. A typical 6-course schedule offers 3 courses each day in 120-minute blocks; an 8-course schedule offers 4 classes per day in 90-minute blocks. These classes alternate all year long.

In a 4/4 block, or semester/semester plan, or "accelerated" schedule, students enroll in 4 classes that each meet for approximately 90 minutes a day; teachers teach 3 classes and have 1 preparation period. A class that was formerly offered over a year's time is now condensed into one-half of the school year. Halfway through the school year, the student takes an entirely different four classes. The four classes the student is currently taking meet every day.

The trimester schedule is an attempt to address both the need for blocks of time in which to teach, and the need for time in which to provide extended learning opportunities for slower learners. The trimester plan involves shorter, more intense classes, with students taking six to nine classes a year. In a trimester schedule, students take 2 or 3 classes for a period of approximately 60 days, then a different 2 or 3 classes for another 60 days, and then a third set of classes to finish the school year. This option provides extended learning time in the following way: If a student is not doing well in a class, instead of assigning a failing grade at the end of the first trimester, the student just continues to take that class during the next portion of the trimester. The instant repeat without the stigma of an F seems to succeed, especially with ninth graders (Canady & Rettig, 1996).

Here are some advantages offered by this type of schedule for foreign languages:

- The teacher has a longer period of time in which to teach.

  Classes of 90 minutes or longer make it possible to do significant research, engage in a prolonged conversation or seminar, view a movie-length video, complete a whole set of learning centers, do a lengthy cultural simulation, and so forth. In short, teachers are motivated to use a variety of instructional activities other than lecture, which also makes the 90 minutes much less tiring for the teacher.

- Usable instruction time is increased.

  Because of fewer class changes and unavoidable class opening and closing activities, students will spend more actual time thinking, speaking, and so forth in the target language. More time on task, especially in such a concentrated fashion, should translate into more learning taking place. The block also offers time for a greater diversity of activities, such as field trips, guest speakers, student speeches and skits, and better use of audiovisual and computer-oriented resources, as well as time for getting involved in community service opportunities.

- If the block increases the students' options (number of classes they may take), they are more likely to continue taking a foreign language.

  If students had trouble fitting your class into their schedule when they had six choices, with eight choices, they now have room.

- Fewer class changes have unexpected benefits.

  Fewer times in the hall means less time to create conflicts that spill over into the classroom. There will be an automatic reduction in the number of tardies, and fewer disciplinary referrals. Experts recommend that students with attention problems, for example, should have a limited number of teachers, physical relocations, and disruptions throughout the school day. The block is ideal for these students.

- You will see more homework done than in the past.

  With fewer classes each day, students have less homework to do each evening and are more likely to do it, and to do a better job.

- Morale will improve.

  One teacher reported to me that she no longer felt as if she had been "hit by a steamroller at the end of the day." Teachers who have taught for over 30 years say the block has "energized" them. The combination of less stress (fewer students, less paperwork) and enhanced potential or creativity is a winner.

- On a 4/4 or trimester schedule, you only keep records on half the number of students, grade half the number of papers (and final exams) on any one evening.

  You have (usually) fewer preparations each "semester," because you only teach three classes at once. The students also experience the same drop in stress: only four teachers to adapt to at once, only four sets of homework to do. But most importantly, classes meet every day, an important factor when learning a foreign language: constant, regular exposure.

- On the 4/4 or trimester schedule, teachers and students have two or more "fresh starts" each year.

  If you have the "class from Hell," you can say goodbye to them at midyear, and start anew with a different group. Joking aside, there *are* some educational ramifications to the "fresh start" idea. First, if a student is failing the class, the student may audit for the remaining time and retake it immediately next semester, if it is offered, instead of having to wait until the following school year, or may drop the class and try again at the next possible opportunity.

- The 4/4 and trimester schedules also offer the opportunity for acceleration for students.

  An interested student can take as much foreign language as the student wishes; if there is a college or university nearby, the student could possibly proceed directly to its program and earn college credit while still in high school. The upper level classes will have more students enrolled in them, and there is the possibility of adding more classes (or more languages) to your school's curriculum.

One warning, however: the block schedule is merely a new way of setting the bells, a new structure for the class day. The most important part of the block schedule is what takes place in your classroom. You need to use a lot of variety, and reexamine what and how you teach to be able to take advantage of the longer class period. The first year is a lot of work, but well worth it. I am in my fourth year of teaching in a block schedule and it has given me the impetus (and the time) to increase the variety of activities I do in my classroom. I feel (and grades and performance show) that my students are learning better. Also, because I am on a 4/4 block (accelerated) schedule, I can offer six levels of French, whereas before we only offered four levels. Thus, the block schedule has opened up new opportunities for my students.

EDUCATION ABROAD

Japanese students traditionally score higher than American students on tests, and social psychologists have been studying their educational system and techniques to determine what the differences are between the Japanese and American systems. They hope to apply what they learn to education here in America. The University of Michigan in particular is writing a textbook for mathematics using the Japanese approach to learning.

The major differences lie in students doing less drill and seatwork—less repetitive practice—during class time. Instead, whole-class discussions are initiated that encourage students to find solutions and strategies and to explain their thought processes. Students are encouraged to give feedback to each other. Japanese texts also purposely use real-life situations to show the relevance of what is being taught, along with eye-catching pictures and many short story–type presentations of data such as vocabulary or grammar ideas.

The countries (including Japan) whose students score better on standardized tests than do our students use these ideas:

- More is not better. In-depth learning is preferable to quantity of material covered.
- Conceptual thinking is used much more often than rote memorization and drill.
- Problem-solving and sharing strategies and concepts are the best strategy.
- The person leading the discussion should not supply the answer right away, so all can participate.
- Learning should be made meaningful for students.

It is interesting that these five strategies are some that not only are sound according to the principles of the latest brain research, but that teachers on block schedules also often emphasize. When teachers going to a block schedule worry about "getting the material covered," perhaps they are overlooking the benefits of in-depth coverage. Learning that goes into long-term storage is the goal of educators, rather than a "spray and pray" approach.

The conceptual idea can easily be applied to foreign language learning by using methods I observed in math classes. When a teacher asks a student to write on the board, the teacher afterward asks the student to explain why he or she wrote it in that way. Walking mentally back through the thought processes that were used, such as "I decided to use the imperfect tense because this was description, and so I dropped X from the verb, and added Y ending" more firmly fixes the process necessary in the memory of the student performing the task. It also embeds the idea in classmates' minds, because of the frequency of hearing others go through the same processes that they themselves used. Taking class time to do this is important, and should show good results.

Using concept deduction and attainment strategies (based on observing data scientifically, drawing conclusions from it, and forming a hypothesis, or vice versa) fit perfectly with the idea of conceptual learning and discussion of learning.

CONCEPT ATTAINMENT

This activity, which begins on the individual level, proceeds to pairs work, and ends as a group activity, is used to introduce new material, replacing the traditional lecture method. Prior to beginning the activity, the teacher selects the concept to introduce and chooses and organizes the examples that contain characteristics of this concept. At least 20 pairs are needed, especially for more complex concepts. Few texts provide such lists, so creating the pairs involves a bit of work and thought. Concept Attainment works well for introducing concepts such as masculine/feminine/neuter endings, teaching students to identify a particular style of art or that of a particular artist, or learning how to form a new verb tense.

In Phase One of the activity, the teacher lists several examples, labeled as positive (good/yes) examples of the concept or attribute, or as negative (bad/no) examples. The teacher asks the students to contrast the positive examples with the negative (to themselves, not out loud), and to take notes on those differences. (This is a good sponge activity.) If he or she wants, the teacher could underline portions of the example to call attention to them. Then the teacher adds a few more examples, asking students to make a hypothesis about what the difference is between the positive and negative examples. A few more examples are given to test and refine the hypothesis. Then, a new step—unlabeled examples are presented, and students are asked (still working on their own, and not out loud) to guess, using their hypothesis, if the examples are positive or negative. (Students love this approach; it is challenging, yet gamelike.)

Phase Two begins when it looks as if most of the students have a workable hypothesis. (Use body language to identify this—nodding heads, smiles, etc.) Pair the students and have them share hypotheses with their partner and then test these new, combined/synthesized hypotheses with a few more unlabeled examples. The final step is to share these as a whole-class discussion. At this time, the teacher confirms the correct hypotheses, refining how they are stated if necessary, and supplies the name of the concept (i.e., "This is called the future tense, and you have correctly identified how it is different."). Finally, the student pairs generate their own examples of this concept.

Concept Attainment is also an excellent review tool or evaluation tool if you want to check to see whether some material that you covered previously has been mastered; by giving good and bad examples of the concept, you will determine the students' depth of knowledge by how quickly they catch on, and also reinforce their understanding of this concept.

CONCEPT DEVELOPMENT

There are three basic steps in this method, which was first used in scientific investigation. First, a set of data on the topic are created, either by the students or by the teacher; second, the data is grouped into categories based on similarities observed; and third, the categories are labeled, or named. When students identify the similarities, they are using many higher-level thinking skills (interpreting, inferring, generalizing) that lead to a greater ability to manipulate the category and apply it to new situations. This strategy is very often used to teach basic grammatical concepts such as how an adjective, adverb, phrase, or clause functions and how it is different from other parts of speech, *without* having to teach the concept in English, or use grammatical terms. For example., students who are provided with sentences with all the adverbs underlined would group them into categories such as location, time, or description, and then you could discuss, still using the sample sentences, how any words that would fit these categories are placed in a typical sentence (i.e., immediately after the verb) without having to use the word "adverb."

Some warnings: The more examples the better, and, even more important, the simpler the better. Beware of "false decoys" such as some sentences with noun subjects and some with pronouns, or sentences that alternate adverb clauses with simple adverbs. Make sure that the only element that varies is the adverb, or whatever concept you are presenting. Use the words in a sentence so that the students learn to handle them in context.

I like to use the Concept Development method in French for the simple "ir" verbs (*dormir, partir, servir, sortir,* etc.), which are rather confusing for my students when they are simply presented separately in the book. A similarly useful activity is to present students with sets of irregular verbs whose *nous/vous* forms closely resemble the infinitive (*vouloir* and *pouvoir*, followed by *aller, boire,* and *devoir*) and have students discover this pattern for themselves (using concept development), and then apply it to new verbs.

One small variation is to have the students create their own data file, perhaps by looking at a page in a text, and making a list of what they see/read. For example, in French, by making a list of fruits, they might discover that all fruits listed are feminine in gender, and end in "e," a useful generalization.

MAKING IT MEANINGFUL

Finally, with the new Standards for Foreign Language Learning, teachers are being asked to shift their emphasis on teaching foreign languages to a mode in which relevance is emphasized: Communication, Communities, Culture, and the other two Cs all promote student involvement with the language, which in turn, according to brain research, make that material more likely to go from the working memory to long-term storage. Interdisciplinary learning, another new trend, also helps students to make a lot of connections between material they are learning and material they have previously learned in other classes, making the material much more easy to retrieve from where it is stored in the brain.

2

Activities That Appeal to Multiple Intelligences

In 1983, Howard Gardner proposed his Theory of Multiple Intelligences, which is rapidly being incorporated in most school curricula today. He defines intelligences as "the capacity to solve problems or to fashion products that are valued in one or more cultural settings" (Gardner & Hatch, 1989). His theory is based on biological and cultural research, and expands the traditional view that there are just two types of intelligences (verbal and computational) to also include music, spatial relations, physical activity, and interpersonal and intrapersonal relations. His theory states that all eight intelligences: logical-mathematical, linguistic, spatial, musical, bodily-kinesthetic, interpersonal, intrapersonal, and the newest one, naturalist, are needed to function productively in society, and must be considered to be of equal importance. Therefore, teachers need to use more variety when teaching to appeal to a broader range of talents and skills, to engage most or all of the intelligences.

This need for variety when teaching is one foreign language teachers have recognized for years, but perhaps have not implemented as effectively as we could. During one grading period, we perhaps did something musical, something active, something communicative, something artistic, and so on, but not during one unit, or one lesson. This chapter will suggest types of activities for you to choose from for each type of intelligence. A varied presentation of material will not only excite students about learning, but will lead to a deeper understanding of the material because it reinforces the same topic in a variety of ways.

Using Multiple Intelligences in the Foreign Language Classroom

All students come into your classroom with different sets of developed intelligences. That they all have strengths and weaknesses is not a new concept at all, but that you, the teacher, need to appeal to many types of strengths is perhaps newly emphasized. One way to do this is to modify assignments to accommodate more learning styles. For example, last time I gave an assignment that had always been to write a short story, I offered options: short story, poem, postcard, song or rap, video, or PowerPoint presentation. Not only did I get a wider variety of output, but the general quality was better and the test scores improved.

Of course, it is foolish, and quite impractical, to appeal to every learning style in every lesson, but a little effort to offer more variety will pay great dividends, both in student performance and in their satisfaction with you and the language that you teach. An awareness of your students' varied learning styles will help you show them how to become better learners. For example, you could suggest that an especially musically intelligent student learn verb endings by making up a song about them, or that a kinesthetic student should associate each subject or verb ending with a different gesture or movement. Teaching students how to use their more developed intelligences to learn material outside the classroom will also free you from having to appeal to every intelligence every time, instead you will be able to work to strengthen their intellectual weaknesses.

Assessments need to be changed, as well. As you will see, the linguistic intelligence involves listening, reading, writing, and speaking a language—everything we do in a foreign language class. It's no surprise, then, that most standardized foreign language tests only appeal to this one intelligence. Assessments are needed that allow students to explain the material in their own ways using the different intelligences: student portfolios, independent projects, student journals, and creative tasks.

An especially interesting application of Gardner's theory, however, is its cultural aspect. Gardner's research (1983) argues that culture plays a large role in the development of intelligence, and that different cultures value different types of intelligence (see Figure 2.1). The cultural value placed upon the ability to perform certain tasks provides the motivation to become skilled in that area. As foreign language teachers, we should teach our students to look for these cultural differences and understand them better.

GARDNER'S EIGHT INTELLIGENCES AND THEIR APPLICATIONS

LINGUISTIC INTELLIGENCE

Linguistic intelligence, according to Gardner and Hatch (1989), consists of the mastery of a language. This involves the ability to read, write, and speak a language to express and appreciate complex meanings. It also involves the ability to use language in order to remember information (reading for understanding as well as taking notes). Linguistic intelligence–influenced teaching and testing dominates most Western educational systems (Lazear, 1992).

FIGURE 2.1. GARDNER'S EIGHT INTELLIGENCES

- *Linguistic:* Listening, speaking, reading and writing
- *Logical-Mathematical:* Using deduction, induction, patterning, interpreting graphs, and sequencing ideas
- *Visual/Spatial:* Using three-dimensional ways to perceive imagery, navigate, produce, and decode information
- *Kinesthetic:* Using the mind to control bodily movements and manipulate objects
- *Musical:* Using rhythm, tone, melody, and pitch
- *Interpersonal:* Communicating and collaborating with others
- *Intrapersonal:* Maintaining self-esteem, setting goals for oneself, and acquiring values
- *Naturalist:* Sensing patterns in and making connections with elements in nature

LISTENING

The first skill that is part of linguistic intelligence, and the first that foreign language students are asked to use, is listening. From the very first day of class, students will listen to the teacher speak in the target language. Listening is much more important than you may think. Postovsky (1981) found that focusing on training students in listening comprehension early in the first level had a much greater effect on the students' foreign language skills than did an initial focus on oral use of the language.

TIME LAG

What many teachers do not realize about listening is that this activity inherently involves a huge time lag that students rarely take advantage of: a speaker can only speak about 200 words per minute, but a listener can hear and process from 300 to 500 words per minute (Campbell et al., 1996). Students need to learn how to make use of that extra time. One easy way is to encourage the student to repeat, aloud or silently, all or part of what was heard. Repetition of passages appears to improve listening comprehension more than other techniques (Berne, 1995).

Teach your students to take notes that identify the main point the speaker is trying to make. When taking notes, also outline the main points, underlining the most important ideas and placing an asterisk (*) next to unclear concepts and/or particularly interesting items, as well as writing questions. Figure 2.2 is an example of a form given to teach note-taking as well as to elicit multicultural observations. It was used as a part of a learning center, where students listened to a conversation in which two students planned their evening activities: where to go, what time to meet, and who to invite with them.

Other things you could ask students about such a conversation, especially beginners, are: How many people are talking? How many are male/female? Are they arguing or friendly? What do you think their relationship is? Doing this sort of activity early will reassure students that they are not expected to know everything they hear, and that they do understand more than they think they did. Confidence in listening abilities is an important attitude to instill in your students!

A second important component of listening activities is the need for variety in the type of activity presented and the need for authenticity. Foreign language students are usually asked to listen to conversations, stories read aloud, and lectures by the teacher. These may be presented live by the teacher or classmates, or on video- or audiotapes, by native speakers with a variety of accents. Research on listening points to the increased benefits of video listening as opposed to audio only (e.g., radio); these findings argue strongly for the purchase of any videos that go with your text (Secules, Herron, & Tomasello, 1992). Authenticity

FIGURE 2.2. CONVERSATIONAL RECORD

Name ______________________________

Date ______________________________

Who is speaking? ______________________________

To whom? ______________________________

Where are they? ______________________________

What is the purpose of this conversation? ______________

List the topics discussed:

1.
2.
3.
4.

What was their final decision? ______________________

Did this increase or decrease your stereotype(s) of French students? Explain.

List any questions you may have about this conversation (vocabulary words not understood, cultural ideas, places named, and so on):

What was the most interesting thing about this conversation?

is also a strong factor in the quality of learning. There are strong arguments for using technology to provide a wide variety of listening activities through CD-ROMs, satellite broadcasts, target language films on video, as well as native speakers and music on audiotapes. The more different types of listening passages and different modes of presentation, the better the language is learned (Rost, 1991).

Finally, it is possible to teach your student to be a better learner, but you might be surprised at which approaches seem to work best. Research findings indicate that providing students with a list of vocabulary as a pre-listening activity has little benefit. Instead, researchers argue that it is much better for students to be provided with either a short synopsis of the listening passage or that they be allowed to preview comprehension questions that will be used afterward (Berne, 1995). Why make a secret of where the activity is headed? Real-life conversations always take place in a context. Too often taped activities or dictations lack this aspect, and students waste valuable time listening for the setting and purpose of a conversation that has been pulled out of context.

LECTURES

It is important to remember to keep listening activities short. A student is like a glass of water. Even the strongest student (biggest glass?) will overflow if you continue to pour in information without giving him or her time to process it. In fact, even the best student cannot absorb more than about 10 minutes' input all at once. Think of that the next time you lecture for more than 10 minutes! Do you have to stop lecturing? Of course not; just structure your lecture to include time to summarize and/or discuss what has been said.

Here is how to have students handle a lecture, ideally:

- *Before the lecture* have students write down
  - Everything they already know about the topic;
  - Questions they have about the topic; *or*
  - How they feel about listening to this talk.
- *During the lecture* have them list the main points you or the speaker make, but stop every five minutes or so and have them process what they've heard by:
  - Underlining the most important thing said so far;
  - Putting a star next to the most interesting thing;
  - Reading someone else's notes and marking them with a check mark if they agree or a question mark if they don't agree;
  - Looking back at the list of questions written before the lecture, and checking off any that have been answered.

The above activities, incidentally, are done completely without talking. The teacher should walk around the classroom to observe what the students are underlining. This is valuable feedback on what the students have or have not comprehended.

- *After the lecture,* ideally within the next eight hours for maximum learning to take place, have students jot down, or tell someone else (a classmate, or even a parent):
  - What they heard that was new to them;
  - How what they heard relates to what they already knew;
  - The relevance of the information in the lecture to their own life;

This can be done by asking the students to summarize the lecture or to discuss it, either inside or outside class.

Students love to be read aloud to, or told stories, even high school seniors. However, because, according to Glasser's scale (see Figure 1.2, p. 7), students only remember 20 percent of what they hear, you need to involve them more. Present visuals during the story (students remember 50 percent of what they see and hear), or have students discuss something during a break in the reading (students retain 70 percent), act out what they have just heard (according to Glasser, students remember 80 percent of something that is part of personal experience)—even if it's just something like "Show me with your face how this character feels." At the upper levels of foreign languages, have the students take turns reading to each other (we retain 95 percent of what we teach to someone else!).

The addition of visuals will also appeal to the students' spatial intelligence, acting will appeal to kinesthetic intelligence, discussion will appeal to interpersonal intelligence, and reading to each other will appeal to intrapersonal intelligence—you can easily see how you could use one activity, modified slightly, to provide more variety and to appeal to the strengths of different students. The TPRS (Total Physical Response Storytelling) method uses many props and visuals.

SPEAKING

Speaking may be formal or informal in nature, humorous or not; it may present data briefly or tell a story. But in a foreign language class, in the context of linguistic intelligence, speaking does not mean short replies to a teacher's questions, or repeating aloud what was heard. Speaking means producing communicative responses to a given situation. Speaking usually takes one of the following forms:

- Conversation/Discussion
- Circumlocution (description)
- Memorized speech
- Oral reports
- Interviews

FIGURE 2.3. EIGHT STEPS TO BETTER LISTENING

For better listening:	*Weak listeners:*	*Strong listeners:*
1. Find areas of interest.	Tune out "dry" subjects.	Ask "what's in it for me?"
2. Work at listening.	Fake attention; easily distracted.	Concentrate and show active listening posture and gestures.
3. Listen for ideas.	Listen for facts.	Listen for themes.
4. Judge content, not delivery.	Tune out if delivery is poor.	Judge content; skip delivery errors.
5. Hold your fire.	Give up if listening becomes difficult.	Listen for possible clues or answers later in sentence.
6. Be flexible.	Take intensive notes using only one system.	Take fewer notes; use 4–5 different systems.
7. Keep your mind open.	Agree with information only if it supports your ideas.	Consider all points of view before forming opinions.
8. Use a graphic organizer.	Get off task easily unless the task is well-defined.	Listen for key words.

Q AND A

The simplest form of conversation is the question-and-answer format. I have a game we play called Hot Seat, in which students prepare a set of questions to ask classmates. One at a time, they take a turn in the Hot Seat (a high chair set in front of the class) and answer 10 different questions put to them by 10 different classmates. In addition to taking a turn in the seat, each student is required to ask 10 questions. Make sure that these questions are not yes/no or either/or questions, and are not totally obvious (such as "What color is your hair?"). To make it a bit more conversational, let the person in the Hot Seat ask questions of the questioner, either asking them to explain the question a little more, or adding something like, "And how about you?" to their answer.

Another question-and-answer game is called Twenty Questions. Have some students think of famous people, places, or even just vocabulary words, and then have classmates ask them questions in the target language and try to guess what or who the students are thinking of. For example, if the topic is food vocabulary, students might ask questions such as, "Are you a fruit or a vegetable?" "Are you large or small?" "Are you eaten for breakfast?" and so on. The student who correctly guesses the word takes over the chair, and a new round begins.

Another question-and-answer game is called "Botticelli"—this one is for upper-level classes only! The person who is "it" pretends to be a well-known person, either living or dead, and tells the other players the first letter of his or her last name. The others ask yes-or-no questions to discover who "it" is. However, to earn the right to ask a yes-or-no question, the person must first ask "it" a question they cannot answer. For example, the questioner might ask, "Did you invade England in 1066?" If "it" answers, "No, I am not William the Conqueror," then the questioner may not ask another question. If, however, "it" is stumped by the question, and the questioner tells "it" the correct answer, then the questioner may ask a yes-or-no question about the person "it" is impersonating, such as "Are you male?" or "Are you alive?" If the questioner asks a question about the person "it" has chosen to be, "it" answers, "Yes, I am Mad King Ludwig" and the round is finished, and the person who asked the question is the next "it."

The next level of conversation is one in which additional information is given that has not been not asked for. This may be in the form of introducing a new topic or just expanding on an old one. My upper-level classes often do an activity I call Elaborations in which a question is asked that is a yes-no question, but to which students are not allowed to simply answer yes or no. Instead, they must provide at least one more item of information. For example, if asked if they like pizza, they could say that they indeed like pizza and prefer a certain brand, or tell what their favorite toppings are, or when and where they last ate pizza. More advanced classes could do longer appropriate dialogues, for example, "Say, Paul, how are the slopes?" "Great! I'm going back up right now." "Is the snow good? Yes, it's deep."

CONVERSATION STIMULATORS

If you have a group that is reluctant to talk, try one of these ideas:

- Hand around a bowl of M&M's to the class, instructing students to take a few and place them on the desk to await further instructions. After everyone has taken a few, tell them that they owe the class one sentence for every one they took on (name a topic—their summer vacation, their likes and dislikes, or something relevant to the chapter you are working on).
- A less expensive version, but one that high school students think is hilarious, is to hand around a roll of toilet paper, asking each student to take some. Again, for each square of toilet paper, they owe one sentence. It's fun to watch them move slowly down a strip of toilet paper from square to square, tearing off the squares as they complete them and tossing them into the air.
- Yet another enjoyable way to limit/force speaking is to give the student a jar of bubble liquid, and a topic to speak upon. Have the student wave the wand, and then he must speak until the last bubble has broken. If students don't produce enough bubbles and don't speak for as long as you would like, pair them and have them make bubbles for their partner.
- Take a ball of yarn or string. Tell something about yourself and, holding the end, throw it to someone else. They tell something and,

keeping hold of the yarn, throw the ball to someone else, until everyone is holding the yarn. Then, reverse the direction, with the class trying to remember what each person has said, aloud, winding the yarn back onto the ball as you go. This tests listening and speaking skills, and is a good team-building activity as well.

- If one person monopolizes conversations, consider using "talk tokens." Before the discussion, give each person the same number of tokens. Each time a person speaks, they must put one token in a container. When they are out of tokens, they may not speak.

THINK/PAIR/SHARE (T/P/S)

This is a very good activity to use in almost any classroom situation in which you would like to begin a conversation or discussion. First, ask a question of the class, telling them to think silently for a minute or so. Then pair them with another, and have them exchange opinions. If there is disagreement, they must explain further, until they reach an agreement. If you want the paired students to then share their opinion orally with others, there are several options. One is to combine the original set of partners with one other set and have them interact once more. This is really beneficial if they are practicing a structure or vocabulary that will come up on a test. The more times they must say the structure or the word, the more firmly it will be embedded in their minds, and the more different versions of it they hear from others, the more likely it is that one version will stick in their minds.

Another way to have them share with others is to call on selected students to say their opinion. This could be done randomly by the teacher (or perhaps based on good ones heard while walking around during the sharing sessions), or have each team pick their favorite to speak, or draw a name from the jar. However, my favorite way to have the whole class share is to ask the students to stand up when they have finished sharing with their partner. Not only can the teacher see clearly who is still working (or needs help) and go to that area, it is also one more chance for students to get out of their seats—student movement that is built into the lesson plans. Once everyone is standing, there is another benefit: the teacher will pick one student at random to say the phrase for the class. When he or she is done, and sits down, the teacher asks everyone else with that answer to sit, also. The whole class will look to see who has the same answer, and a little bit of "bonding" occurs, based on similar interests. The teacher will also get a very good idea of how similarly the class feels on that topic, and, by writing on the board what each person/group answers, will have a nice list for review (or for visual learners) by the time everyone is seated.

Some possible T/P/S topics might be: Why did you take this class? What would you most like to learn this year? What sport is the most interesting? What is your favorite holiday, and why? What is your stereotype of a Spanish/French/German/Japanese person? What city would you most like to visit and why? If you had a million dollars, what would you do? These generally are short-answer questions, and a Think/ Pair/Share activity doesn't take very long to do. According to Glasser's scale, discussion produces a high retention of material, so these activities are very worthwhile to do. The "think" portion is also a very good activity to use at the beginning of a class period, or as a transition activity (as students change seats, or hand in papers, etc.).

TELEPHONE USE

If you have voice mail at school, or an answering machine at home, you have a valuable conversational accessory. Assign your students to make telephone calls to you on various topics. Be very specific. Tell them they must greet you, identify themselves, and then tell you something or ask you something, and then say goodbye. Here are some things I have asked my students to do:

- Name three things they saw at a local store and want to buy. Ask me to lend them money.
- Tell me they saw another classmate, where he or she was, and what he or she was doing. Ask me to call them back, and tell me what number to call (uses imperfect tense, preterit, and commands).
- Pretend they are at a restaurant in Paris. Tell me the name of the restaurant and what they are eating. Ask me a question about a Paris monument or museum (a review of food and culture).
- Phone in a response to a note that I have sent them, asking them to do something with me. They are to tell me that they cannot accept, and why.
- Call and ask me to do something with them: Tell me what we would do, when to meet, when we would get home, and at least one reason why I would want to do this with them.

With very little thought, it should be easy to come up with a phone call topic for every unit.

CIRCUMLOCUTION ACTIVITIES

Circumlocution is a longer form of discussion. It involves talking about something without specifically naming it. An easy circumlocution listening activity involves the use of pictures from the text that have been enlarged, numbered, and posted on the front board. The teacher would say something such as, "I see an animal that likes to eat birds. It has green eyes, a long tail, and claws. It says, Meow." As the teacher speaks, the students note which picture is being spoken about. To change this to a speaking activity, you would put students in groups. Each group would have a smaller set of pictures. Students would take turns. Student A would describe one of the pictures in a similar way (without using the vocabulary word). When Student A is done, the other students say the vocabulary word. If the majority of the group identify the picture from Student A's description, Student A gets to take the picture. If not, the picture remains there for someone else to describe. The student with the most pictures wins.

BUZZ GROUPS

Buzz groups are cooperative student groupings that are designed to facilitate discussion, in the form of group brainstorming, followed by evaluation and selection of the best idea. This is a good activity for students to fill in open-ended statements (For example, "I wish..."), group brainstorming for possible answers for something that has many correct answers. It is also a good anticipatory activity before assigning a project or a paper.

One of my favorite buzz group activities involves a prop: a plastic key. I purchased keys that were originally hooked together as a combination rattle/teether for babies. After separating the keys, I gave one to each student, and, as homework, asked them what this key opened for them The next day, they sat in buzz groups and discussed. (Incidentally, the buzz groups found each other by the color of their keys, an easy way for them to sit together quickly.)

Each buzz group usually has a recorder/reporter for the group. As each person speaks, the recorder writes down their opinions or ideas. Sometimes all the teacher does is collect these; other times the group must choose the best one to report back to the class.

INSIDE-OUTSIDE CIRCLE

This activity can be used almost daily for any type of communicative exercise. First, divide the students into two groups. Have half stand and form a circle facing outward. Have the others stand in an outer circle, each with one of the inner circle students as a partner. Explain the activity: each should tell the other his/her favorite sport and greet the other appropriately, tell what he was doing at seven o'clock the previous evening, or what she would like her parents to give her for her birthday, or whatever concept you are working on at the time. After about 30 seconds, the teacher will interrupt, and instruct one or both circles to move over two or three places and do the same activity again with a different partner. In several minutes, a student will have had four or five different partners, at which point the activity is finished, or the teacher assigns a different topic of conversation.

Compare the efficiency of this to the traditional method of questioning each student individually, going up and down rows until each has answered: in Inside-Outside Circle, each student speaks many times (and will be gently corrected by classmates if there are any errors) rather than only once. Each student is actively involved at all times. The student must learn the phrase, sentence, or pattern being practiced more completely, in order to use it many times with partners whose answers may vary.

Here are some other Inside-Outside Circle topics I have used and liked:

- For a beginning level class, find out the partner's name, age, and hobbies.
- The inner-circle student (literally) runs into another, apologizes, and introduces a friend.

- The inner-circle student calls the outer-circle student to ask about a homework problem. The outer-circle partner helps and then is thanked politely.
- The inner-circle student is a clerk in a (type of store) and the outer-circle student is shopping for a party/picnic/new outfit/birthday present.
- The outer-circle student is walking down the street and meets the inner-circle student, who asks him or her to do something that evening. The outer-circle student declines, explaining that he or she has a test, and says goodbye.
- The outer-circle student is a salesperson who is selling dictionaries (or whatever). He or she introduces him or herself to the inner-circle student, and tries to sell them something. The inner-circle person doesn't want one, as he or she already has one. They, of course, remain polite, and end the conversation.
- The inner-circle person calls the home of a friend to tell him or her something important. The outer-circle person answers as a parent, to say that the friend is not home, and to take a message.
- This may also be used to review vocabulary. Have students prepare a card that lists several vocabulary words in the target language on one side and the same words in English on the other side. Each will quiz his or her partner, target language-to-English, or English-to-target language, giving hints in the target language if the partner doesn't know the vocabulary.
- Another way to review vocabulary that involves more discussion is to arrange for students to pair vocabulary words in a logical fashion. For example, the inner circle is given cards with the name of a room in a house. After stating what room they were in, the outside circle asks them if they saw a certain item, to which they would answer yes or no, depending on whether or not it was logical.
- Grammar can also be practiced using Inside-Outside Circle. The inner circle has a card with a situation on it (sort of a Dear Abby type), while the outer circle advises with phrases such as "I think that you…" or "In my opinion…" that they are required to use to begin their answer (which in French requires the subjunctive). Again, both students and cards are rotated; the advice is sometimes silly and sometimes serious, but this exercise is a very high-interest activity.
- Figure 2.4 shows another circumlocution activity my students enjoyed, which was suggested by a foreign exchange student. Each student would have a list of some typically American things. Taking turns, each student had to explain one item from the list to the partner in the target language, and the partner would guess what the

idea being explained was. When they were done explaining, they compared lists to see how well they had done.

FIGURE 2.4. CIRCUMLOCUTION ACTIVITY

Partner A	*Partner B*
1. Beanie baby	1. Barbie doll
2. Brownie	2. Jell-O
3. Cheerleader	3. Pep rally
4. Detention	4. Field trip
5. E-mail	5. Paper clip
6. Pajama party/sleep over/lock-in	6. Braces

- Inside-Outside Circle is just great for doing skits. Put the skit pairs facing another pair. Pair A does their skit, then Pair B, then they each rotate one space and repeat. If the teacher stands in one spot, in a class of 24, after 6 rotations, the teacher has heard every skit; every student has done the skit six times instead of once (more practice speaking *and* receiving gentle peer advice, or correction, or encouragement). This is much less stressful for shy students *and* it saves a lot of class time: If each team did a 3-minute skit, plus a minute to get up from and return to seats and a minute of teacher feedback, that would be 12 skits of 5 minutes each, for a total of 60 minutes. Using Inside-Outside Circle, two 3-minute skits plus feedback times 6 rotations takes 42 to 45 minutes; enough time is saved to do another activity or two! If the teacher doesn't have to hear every single skit, there is no need for six rotations; two or three are sufficient practice. So let's say this activity now takes 25 minutes, less than half the time, and students were active all the time, either performing or listening.

Kagan (1995) says that requiring the students who listened to provide feedback (praise or correction) after each performance is perhaps the most valuable aspect of this activity, so don't skimp on that portion. I have been known to give my whole class grades based on how perfect the skits were. If I heard serious errors that their partners should have caught and corrected, then the whole class lost points on the activity. This is an excellent way to teach and promote social language. Figure 2.5 is a list of feedback phrases to use.

MEMORIZATION

Memorizing and saying aloud phrases, poems, and other short bits of a foreign language is highly recommended. Have students learn a new word every day in class as well as over the holidays or weekends, and then practice them in conversation. There are two types of mnemonics (memorization methods) that work best: rhymes and reductions. Rhymes and jingles, especially ones that

FIGURE 2.5. FEEDBACK PHRASES TO USE IN CLASS

Español	*Français*	*Deutsch*
Sí	Oui	Ja
Es verdad	C'est vrai	Wahr
Es cierto	Bien sur	Jawohl
Lo creo/Creo que si	Je crois que oui	Ich glaube daß
¡Qué bueno!	Très bien!	Sehr gut!
¡Qué fantástico!	Fantastique!	Phantastisch!
¡Qué interesante!	Très intéressant!	Sehr interessant!
¡Qué formidable!	Formidable!	Wunderbar!
Espero que sí	J'espère que oui	Hoffentlich
¿Verdad?/¿De veras?	N'est-ce pas?/C'est vrai?	Nicht wahr?/wirklich?
¿Es cierto?	Tu es sûr(e)?	Bist du sicher?
¿Es serio?	Tu es sérieux/se?	Bist du ernst?
No estoy seguro/a	Je ne suis pas sûr(e)	Ich bin nicht sicher
A veces	On verra	Möglich
No me importa(n)	Ça ne me fait rien	Das macht nichts
No	Non	Nein
No es verdad	Ce n'est pas vrai	Das ist nicht wahrhaftig
No lo creo/Creo que no	Je ne te crois pas	Das ist nicht glaubhaft
¡Qué ridículo/ tontería!	C'est ridicule/bête!	Unglaublich!
¡Qué aburrido!	C'est absurde!	Unsinnig!
¡Pura mentira!/Mentiroso/a!	Tu mens! Menteur/euse!	Du lügst!/Lügner!

teach a concept, are worth a dozen lectures. They are easier to memorize if they rhyme, and even easier if they are set to music. (See Musical Intelligence later in this chapter for several suggestions.) For students who are aural learners, tape-record the rhyme and play it back. For visual learners, provide a written copy. For kinesthetic learners, add gestures. Poems, especially ones such as Mother Goose rhymes, not only provide practice speaking the language, and have high appeal to students, but can point out some cultural differences (or similarities) when translated. There are some very good sources for children's rhymes to be found on the Internet.

Reduction mnemonics are also a method of memorizing, in which information is clustered or chunked for the students by reducing a lot of information to a shorter form, with one letter to represent each shortened piece, making it easier to handle and remember. In French, we use BANGS to remember the rules on adjective order. Most adjectives follow the nouns they modify; the exceptions are the ones to do with beauty, age, numbers, goodness, and size. Spanish can teach the subjunctive by using the words WEDDING and DISHES (see Chapter 5 on teaching the subjunctive). The French subjunctive can be taught using UWEIRDO. Reductions can also be in sentence form. For example, the descending order of metric prefixes—kilo, hecto, deca, (measure), deci, centi, and milli—become the sentence "King Henry Doesn't Mind Drinking Cold Milk."

ORAL REPORTS

Public speaking is usually required in any class, but consider using Inside-Outside Circle (see the previous section of this chapter) for this type of activity, as it encourages active participation at all times and decreases the fright factor for shy students, as they don't have to face an entire room of people.

However, there are some very rewarding activities to evaluate student learning and progress orally. Here are some tips for a successful oral presentation:

- If possible, structure presentations so the student is not presenting alone. For example, in a unit about movies, do a Siskel and Ebert-type presentation as an oral report. Each student would give his or her opinion about the same movie, agreeing or disagreeing about various aspects. Let them show a short clip of the movie, and I guarantee your classes will beg to do this activity again.
- Incorporate props whenever possible. Posters are OK to use, but everyday items are more interesting. If a student is talking about himself or herself, have them bring in three items that show something about them. A student might then bring car keys, an award, a picture of a horse/pet/family, and so on. If students are giving reports on various regions of a country, have them bring a suitcase full of items and unpack it in front of the class, explaining each item: suntan lotion for the many beaches, a menu of typical foods, a charcoal briquette for the coal mined in the area, and so on. Not only do these items jog the memories of the presenter(s), but they take a bit of the focus off the person giving the report, helping shyer people, and, again, more directly involving the audience.
- Have the audience participate by reviewing the speaker. Ask your students to list the things they liked best about the report. Don't let them criticize, except perhaps to have a listing such as "I wish you had told more about...."
- Try to make reports more interesting by varying the setting. Instead of a plain report in front of the class, make a backdrop: For example, make the report a "special broadcast"—a famous person has just

passed away, and the student will recap that person's life for the class (who take notes, of course.) For a report on ecology or the environment, go outdoors. If the students are reading a poem or performing part of a play, go to the auditorium.

- Make oral reports more interesting by adding audience participation. Have students prepare a list of questions about a city/region/country/event/holiday or custom they have researched, and distribute these questions to their classmates. If the order of questions is important, they should number these questions. Then, have students ask these questions, which the reporter will answer. This is much more relaxing (and entertaining) than the standard speech.

INTERVIEWS

An interview can also be a great short communicative opportunity. Students love to learn more about each other. Pair students, and have them interview each other. You may give them a set of prepared questions on a topic such as family members and pets, food likes and/or dislikes, sports and hobbies, vacation plans, future plans (college, career, family), what makes them angry/happy/sad, chores they have to do at home. All sorts of topics lend themselves to this format.

However, many students prefer not to talk about themselves. If you have a class such as this,

- Have the partner take good notes, verifying what is written with the interviewee (writing *and* reading practice) and then report on the interview to another pair. This would practice changing the verbs from the "I" form of the interviewee to the "he or she" form for reporting, as well as changing any possessive adjectives ("me/mine" to "him/her or his/hers"), so I highly recommend it.
- Have students write questions and then interview native speakers of the language who live in your area and/or people who have traveled to an area where your target language is spoken: where they are originally from, how/when/where they came to the United States/foreign country, their initial reaction, cultural surprises and so on.
- Give your students the option of presenting live or on videotape.

Because there is usually no all-class presentation made, unless you need to grade these exercises, you will simply need to eavesdrop a bit. If possible, take notes and, the next day, provide your students with a list entitled "Find a Classmate Who...," have them locate the person described, and ask the person referred to in that item to sign or initial that space. Reward the first few who complete the activity, or all who get every blank signed correctly. Here are some examples:

Find a Classmate Who:

_____________ Plays football
_____________ Hates oranges
_____________ Lived in New York
_____________ Wants to be a teacher
_____________ Has a grandma who speaks Spanish
_____________ Spent last summer cooking at a local restaurant

This is a good "mixer" activity in an intermediate or advanced class.

SOCRATIC SEMINAR

A lot of groups want me to explain this technique, and the first thing I tell them is that I do not often use it. It is best suited for discussion of literature that has been read, or of political events such as World War II, or of abstract topics such as "What is culture?" It is, however, a highly effective way to get some real meaningful discussion going in your classroom, so I'd like to include it here.

When speaking, students need freedom to speak freely, to feel that their ideas will be accepted. They also need to feel some control over the discussion, as well as to have fun while doing it. Guidelines for a Socratic seminar:

- Sit in a circle.
- Everyone must have read the material to participate.
- Quiet is not bad; allow students to formulate their thoughts. The greatest skill being developed in the Socratic seminar is critical thinking.
- Allow the discussion to move on its own.
- Always make students connect their opinions to the text being discussed. This is the best way to make sure discussion doesn't stray too far from the seminar topic.
- It's important that the facilitator allows only one student to speak at a time. A Socratic seminar is not a debate.

The trickiest part of organizing a Socratic seminar is writing the questions. Here are my suggestions:

Focus on the goal:	The goal is to enlarge understanding by exploring ideas and issues, not to establish facts.
Use open-ended questions:	Avoid yes/no questions. Ask no fact questions.
Keep questions value-free:	Participants make judgments and connections. You remain neutral.
Use questions with meat:	Can the group explore this for 15–20 minutes ? Does it prompt thinking beyond the obvious? It should not be answerable without having read the text. The question should emerge from experiences, events, and language that are common to all participants.
Ask questions in order:	Begin with an opening question, then ask two to five core questions and a closing question.
Ask followup questions:	Questions should be asked of speakers to clarify and probe. These are not planned ahead, but should include things such as: "Are you saying that...?" "Where in the text do you find support for that?" "What do you mean by...?" "What is your point?" "Would someone take issue with...?"

Figure 2.6 is a sample sheet of questions I have used for one of my Socratic discussions. The usual followup to this discussion would be for them to write/ draw/ sing/rap (my assignments have a lot of options that accommodate different learning styles) a fable of their own.

I have rather strict student rules for Socratic discussions:

1. You are not allowed to give your opinion on the question you read aloud. Rather, lead others to your opinion by dropping hints, using quotes, asking for more varied opinions from other students, and so on.
2. You do not need to raise your hand. Simply allow the speaker to finish, and then state your opinion.
3. If you are called on by the teacher or a member in the group and you do not want to answer at that time, you can pass.
4. Respect all participants. If you disagree with what someone has said, don't moan and groan or roll your eyes. Wait for them to finish, then say that you don't agree with them. Improper body language will result in being sent from the room with an alternate assignment.
5. Be honest about your opinions. If you are playing devil's advocate, announce that you are doing so.

FIGURE 2.6. FABLES OF LA FONTAINE: SOCRATIC SEMINAR QUESTIONS

1. A fable is a story in which animals have human characteristics. Why?
2. What types of animals were used?
3. The fox is in every poem. Describe him.
4. What behaviors or characteristics were portrayed as positive/good?
5. What behaviors or characteristics were portrayed as negative?
6. Were "good" animals rewarded, and "bad" animals punished? Give examples.
7. Each poem has a moral that can be stated as advice ("Do this" or "Don't do that"). What was the advice contained in your poem?
8. What does this advice tell us about life during La Fontaine's time?
9. Why were La Fontaine's fables popular?

Figure 2.7 illustrates some of the differences between a Socratic seminar and a class discussion.

READING

The third aspect of linguistic intelligence is reading. Reading in a foreign language is difficult, so help your students by building in the following steps for *any* reading assignment, no matter how short:

- Step One: Prereading/prediction
- Step Two: Skimming
- Step Three: Careful reading
- Step Four: Applying what is read

STEP ONE: PREREADING/PREDICTION

Have students take inventory of their knowledge prior to reading a selection—vocabulary they expect to encounter, cultural aspects they are likely to find, attitudes or stereotypes they hold. For example, before reading an article on clothing, you could have students do the following:

- Board Race: review all the clothing vocabulary they know, or
- Graffiti: on paper or whiteboards, students write all the clothing-related vocabulary they can remember (prizes for those who remember the most in a preset period of time).

FIGURE 2.7. DIFFERENCES BETWEEN SOCRATIC SEMINAR AND CLASS DISCUSSION

Socratic Seminar	*Class Discussions*
Students and teacher in circle. All have eye contact; teacher is on same level.	Students are in rows. Teacher is set apart and often higher, on stool or behind podium.
97% student talk; students know teacher won't comment.	97% teacher talk, even if many questions are asked. Teacher elaborates and answers.
Average response for students is 8–12 seconds.	Average response for students is 2–3 seconds.
No verbal or nonverbal approval or disapproval is present. Affirming feedback by the teacher is taboo; only students provide feedback.	Teacher affirmation of correctness is critical. Sustaining feedback for incorrectness is critical.
Thinking, backed up with textual evidence, is paramount.	Rightness is paramount; thinking ends as soon as one is right.
Students listen primarily to peers.	Students listen primarily to teacher, who has the answer.
Students have ownership for much of the flow.	Teachers have ownership for most of the flow.
Students are held accountable for contributions based upon preagreed criteria.	Students see discussion as a frill, a "participation grade." If you miss class, you didn't miss much.

- Think/Pair/Share: think of your stereotype of a Mexican/French/German/Roman/Japanese person. Get together with a partner and draw the person. Label as many items on your picture as possible. Share your picture with another pair (or the class, lined up on the front chalk rail to see how many common items there are).
- Sponge: Look at the title and picture accompanying today's reading selection, and write down your prediction of the content and vocabulary that will be in the selection.
- Sponge: Read the first three lines of the story, and write down questions you think will be answered in the rest of it.

STEP TWO: SKIMMING/SCANNING

Have students scan through the selection quickly for additional information. Perhaps they could underline all the words they find easily recognizable. They should always be told to look for cognates (words similar to English words). After they skim the selection, have them revisit the prediction they made in Step One, modifying it if they found additional information while skimming. You could also have them run up and write their cognates on the board and look for *false cognates* (words that look like English ones, but have different meanings).

If the selection is very difficult or long, I sometimes have students underline or highlight unfamiliar words, and we brainstorm about what they might mean, based on their context. If reading time is limited, though, I have them choose three words to look up prior to reading the selection if I am not going to allow dictionary use during the reading.

Another way to use skim/scan and to make upper level students more accountable is to first provide them with several title-synopsis combinations, and ask them, by skimming, to match these to the actual article, poem or story. After checking their results, have each group then choose a story, article or poem to read.

STEP THREE: CAREFUL READING

Doing Steps One and Two will have given students a frame of reference as well as some confidence in their ability to handle the material they are about to read. Students who skip those first two steps often are frightened by the length of a selection, or get bogged down by unfamiliar vocabulary and quit. Encourage them to look for meaning through context: How is the word used in the sentence? Description? Action? Guess at what it means, or skip it and see if the sentence or paragraph still makes sense.

> The axtlzbn is worn primarily by meebs for the blurvle ceremony each kipto. It consists of a wlomb made of cygde and tied with a qorf. It is decorated with many hujas.

For example, in the above selection, axtlzbn is obviously an article of clothing worn for a special purpose. There is a very good chance that that unfamiliar word is explained later in the selection, or in an illustration, or may not be necessary to comprehend the rest of the selection. Teaching students to skip such words is good; too often they hit one unfamiliar word and quit, or get bogged down.

STEP FOUR: APPLYING WHAT IS READ

After reading, do *not* have students answer simple questions, or do cloze or fill-in-the-blank exercises. Go back to the boxed selection above, and see if you can do these:

Describe the axtlzbn________________________________

Who wears an axtlzbn? ______________________________

What ceremony is it worn for? ______________________________

Fill in the blanks: The __________ is worn by _______ for the ______.

Of course, you were able to answer these—but did you have to understand any of the new vocabulary words? No!

A good application is one that uses creativity and higher-level thinking skills. Have them draw a picture of an *axtlzbn* or a *blurvle* ceremony if none is in the book, or write a comparison between an *axtlzbn* and what they are wearing that day. They could tell you why or why not they'd be willing to wear one, or show you with their faces/bodies how an *axtlzbn* wearer feels. They could look through their text, or a different book or magazine, to find more examples of the clothing, the ceremony, or whatever else was in that selection. Have them rewrite the selection from the viewpoint of a *meeb* getting ready for the ceremony. Have them write quiz questions over the selection, and quiz each other. How about creating a postcard to tell the folks back home about the ceremony they saw (using various past tenses), or perhaps a one-sided telephone conversation about the reading selection? I suggest giving the class many such options of equal difficulty, so that they can choose one to suit their own strengths. Creative applications such as these test knowledge and require students to demonstrate their understanding of what was read.

To see some examples of how others have used a six-step reading program similar to the one above, try these Internet addresses:

Movies in Madrid:
http://members.aol.com/maestro12/web/johnson1.html

Kino in Frankfurt:
http://members.aol.com/classweb/activities97/kino.html

Shopping in Paris:
http://members.aol.com/classweb/activities97/paris.html

USING NEWSPAPERS AND MAGAZINES

Newspapers and magazines are great resources for reading selections. First-year students can usually read ads for restaurants, hotels, concerts, movies, etc. and tell you who/what/where/when information, and then create their own ads that are similar to the ones they saw. In addition to newspapers and magazines, don't forget that catalogs or telephone books, which also have ads and information that must be read, are also wonderful resources.

For second-year students, choose something more complex such as an obituary. Then have them do activities such as:

- Question each other about information from the article
- Construct the family tree of the deceased person from information in the article
- Write an obituary for a famous person

- Write their own obituary as they would wish it will be (millionaire, movie star, or whatever)
- Write a story about the death
- Role-play a funeral, having the family members and friends talk about the deceased

Another newspaper activity is to check the want ads for a job, house, or car that meets their needs (I like to give each student a "needs" statement, as it saves a lot of time by having that decided for them. A sample "needs" statement lists how much they have available to spend, whether they have other people to live or ride with them, and so on. Each student gets a slightly different set of needs. Because the needs statement is written, they get even more reading practice!)

Articles about natural or human-caused disasters are very high interest, also. So are those dealing with hobbies or special interests such as sports or music. Sports magazines usually have a lot of cognates, and are easily understandable with little need for a dictionary.

Why not have a scavenger hunt? Set up teams of students, give them lists (written in the target language), and a time limit. Have them cut out the items when they find them, and glue them to sections of the answer sheet. Items on the list could be things such as "a picture of a man wearing a tie" or "an ad for a one-bedroom apartment" (vocabulary), "a verb in the third-person singular preterite" or "a feminine plural adjective" (grammar), or "an ad for a bullfight" or "an ad for a New Year's party" (culture). In a telephone book, they could look for rates for calls to a particular city at a certain time, an area code for a city, an emergency number, the phone number of the fifth Smith in the book, or some sort of comparison with our own phone books, such as "what color are the Yellow Pages?" (in France, they are yellow!)

ROLE-PLAYING AND DRAMATIZATION

Role-playing is a good way to test for comprehension of a reading selection. The obvious sort of role-playing is for each student to become a character in the story and act it out. Dramatization involves rewriting a story into a play, creating more dialogue than the original story, and modifying verbs from the third person to the first person. Again, the end result would be to perform it. For upper-level classes, you could take a longer selection, and give each group a different section to present to the class. If you would like to do something a bit less obvious, have students try some of these:

- Produce a puppet play version of the story.
- Invent and insert a new character in the story. This could be to see if the class notices that this has been done, or it could be incredibly obvious, such as putting a movie star or other famous person in.
- Draw the events in the story in cartoon form on overhead transparencies.

- Make a storybook version and read it to the class, perhaps changing the ending, or insert errors in order to have the class correct them.

Role-playing does not have to be done live. Any of the above activities could be done in video form.

FAIRY TALES, FOLK TALES, AND CHILDREN'S BOOKS

These are good for any level of language study because of their repetitive nature. They can be read aloud, or used for pleasure reading. They provide background on cultural traditions and are usually heavily illustrated. The plots of fairy tales are usually already known to the students, who listen and look for familiar parts, quickly learning the key words ("bears," "porridge," etc.) and chiming in quickly on refrains such as the "Fee, fi fo fum" or "The sky is falling!" Read a fairy tale, aloud or silently, turning the pages, pointing to illustrations, or transparencies of them. Use props to retell the story—but with mistakes they must correct! For upper levels, give students the props, and have them reenact the story as you or a classmate tell it, encouraging humorous variations which the students with props must hear, understand, and attempt to act out.

Have students write and illustrate their own fairy tale. Let them alter real ones (i.e., a male Cinderella) or combine two ("Sleeping Beauty and the Beast") or do their own entirely. On the day they are due, bring in milk and cookies, pillows, blankets, etc. and relive story time from Kindergarten days as they read each other their stories.

JOKES AND HUMOR

Because they are heavily influenced by cultural references and values, jokes are the most difficult things for students to read and understand. Comic strips are short and lack redundancy, but have the advantage of visuals to go with the story. Few of either will be funny to your second-language learners, but don't overlook trying them anyway. The occasional one that works will have enormous payoff in terms of interest and, as we saw in Chapter 1, that means that an awful lot of learning is taking place, which will "stick" better because of the humor.

SMALL-GROUP DISCUSSIONS ABOUT READING

Group discussions about reading combine the benefits of reading and practice speaking and listening (and sometimes writing), so here are some activities you may wish to use:

Beginning Classes	*Advanced Classes*
Correct errors in written or spoken statements.	Paraphrase/retell the story to each other.
Fill out a bio sheet for characters in the story.	Present a page/scene/chapter that the rest of the class hasn't read.
Answer either/or questions about the story.	Identify which character made a given statement, and in what circumstances.
Given a list of adjectives and characters' names, determine who the adjectives refer to.	Create a new title for the selection.
Line up incidents from the story in chronological order: these may be written on strips of paper or in numbered picture form. When done, retell the story to each other.	Personalize the story: "If I were in X's situation…"; "If I met X, I'd tell him…"; "I like/dislike X because…"
Complete a summary of the selection.	Substitute synonyms for underlined words in the selection.
Find recurring words and discuss why they are repeated.	Choose and justify a color to associate with each character.
Make graffiti using a list of key words from the selection.	Do TV or radio coverage of the story: either a newscast, or a talk show where the characters are interviewed.
Given an answer card (card with written answer) respond aloud when the teacher asks the question to which they hold the answer.	Conduct a trial of one character in the selection.
Bring in a picture that represents something in the selection, or something that relates to the selection. Share these and discuss them.	Given a movie review, decide if the writer liked the movie, and agree or disagree with the writer.
Collaborate to report on setting, plot, theme(s), literary devices, author's life, characters from the selection.	Make an ad for the selection read.

WRITING

Reading is, of course, closely associated with writing, so I will continue the above list of activities to do after reading, adding written activities, listed here in approximate order of how much creativity is required (from low to high):

- List as many facts as possible about the selection.
- Given three columns of vocabulary, combine one element from each column to make statements about the reading selection.

- Replace nonsense words inserted in the text with appropriate vocabulary, or delete extraneous words that have been inserted in the text.
- Give a paragraph written as one long word, separate it into component words, adding punctuation and accent marks as needed.
- Write a summary of the selection.
- Write a review/critique of the selection.
- Write a letter to a character in the reading selection.
- Change the story, adding class members as characters.
- Write an epitaph or obituary for the main characters.
- Create a dialogue that could have taken place in the reading selection.
- Create a new ending for the story.
- Create a sequel for the selection.
- Write a review of the selection.

The easiest way to encourage writing is to make it short and personal. I like to make the writing portion of each test require students to write about themselves. I also include an extra credit question about the student, or the student's opinion, on a topic of my choice. Topics might include an old question from a previous unit as review, an attitude survey, something about current events, or even something on a topic in the new unit we are about to begin, which would test their ability to guess meanings based on context.

RIDDLES

Riddles and verbal puzzles especially interest students. Find a source of riddles in the target language (try the Internet), or translate stories for your students to read. Give them the beginning of the story, and have them write an ending for it. Then show them the ending in the original document. Or give them the whole story, and have them figure out and write out a solution. Have advanced students write riddles for the lower-level classes on a large piece of butcher paper on the wall. Riddles can be spelling-based ones, such as "My first letter is in 'book' but not in 'look.'..." They can be ancient ones such as "In the morning, I walk on four feet; at noon on two, and in the evening on three—what am I?" (The answer is a man: as a baby, he crawls; as an adult, he walks; and as an older person, he walks with a cane.) They can be modern ones such as "I walked into the living room and Romeo and Juliet lay dead on the carpet. I didn't call the police, and no one will be charged with murder, yet they did not kill themselves. What happened?" (Romeo and Juliet are goldfish and something knocked over their bowl.) Students love these, and they may be used as sponges for early finishers, as extra credit assignments, or as group reading/discussion/writing exercises.

NEWS WRITING

Students find it easy to read news articles, and writing them is good practice, too. Have your class write a weekly or monthly column for the school paper or the local paper. They could report on national, local, or school events, write puzzles or riddles, poems, or stories. They love to see their names in print, and it is great public relations for your program. Interviews with students, staff, or community members are of high interest to both those writing and those reading them, and your students will undoubtedly be asked to read the articles to friends or family who are not taking your language classes. In fact, why not have them publish their own paper, especially as an end-of-the-year project. First-year students, sophomores, and juniors could tell of travel or work plans, and seniors can "will" their belongings, lockers, or bits of wisdom to their younger colleagues. Upper-level classes can report on the fun things they did, and give advice to lower-level students (again, these activities provide good possibilities to recruit students into upper-level classes). If your school has daily televised announcements, write something short for selected students to do live, once a week (telejournalism practice).

STORY WRITING

Short stories, because they are generally not illustrated and often have little dialogue, should probably be reserved for more advanced classes. Anecdotes are the easiest to begin with: a typical day's activities, a hobby or collection, a real or imagined meeting with someone famous, an accident or illness they had, their best/worst birthday or holiday. For writing fiction, put students in groups for more success. I like groups of three: a secretary, a dictionary researcher, and a leader. Before beginning, I strongly recommend also that you have the students help you prepare a rubric (see Chapter 6 on assessment) that spells out clearly what elements a good story should have, and how much of the grade each element should comprise. Then have the group brainstorm to develop a list of key vocabulary terms and get the bones of the story ready ahead of time (a good homework assignment). Students should also fill out and attach a checklist such as the one in Figure 2.8 before handing their story draft to another group for peer editing, using a response sheet such as the one in Figure 2.9. After receiving peer feedback and making necessary adjustments, the story is then submitted to the teacher. This process usually results in an interesting story with all the required elements, a draft that requires much less correction (for both the teacher and students), and a better grade for students, which builds confidence in their ability and results in higher satisfaction with the class.

As I wrote earlier, folk tales and fables are always rich in cultural traditions and may be studied on that basis alone. After reading several, develop a "formula" such as (1) an animal (2) with a personality flaw such as greed or gullibility (3) has an adventure in which (4) it is tricked by another animal and (5) his appearance is altered. Then, assign a similar story using that formula, or have them rewrite one they read with a human subject instead of the animal (maybe

FIGURE 2.8. COMPOSITION CHECKLIST

	Yes	*Sometimes*	*No*
Content			
♦ Do you provide the information requested?			
• Introduction			
• Body			
• Conclusion			
• Conflict			
• Conflict resolution			
Vocabulary			
♦ Do you use a variety of verbs and adjectives?			
♦ Did you check the spelling and gender of words you were unsure of ?			
Structures			
♦ Do your adjectives agree with the nouns they modified?			
♦ Do the verbs agree with their subjects?			
♦ Are the verbs used in the correct tenses?			
Miscellaneous			
♦ Did you use any English words in the story?			

even a classmate?), or have students update a story to the present (e.g., the tortoise gets run over while crossing a superhighway, or the hare takes steroids).

As a followup activity, read or perform one or more of the student products for the elementary or middle school students—this provides speaking practice, feedback, and it could recruit many more students for your foreign language program.

FIGURE 2.9. PEER EDITING SHEET

A. Exchange compositions. Read the composition through once and answer these questions:

1. What is the main idea of each paragraph ? List them below:

   paragraph 1 ______________________________

   paragraph 2 ______________________________

   paragraph 3 ______________________________

   Are there any paragraphs for which you have difficulty trying to decide what the main idea is? Mark them with a star above (not on the paper itself!).

2. What message or theme is in this writing? What words or phrases specifically show this theme (quote them below):

3. Is there something else not mentioned that would be useful or interesting to read about?

B. Now read the composition again and fill out the chart below:

Structure	*No Problems*	*One or More Errors*	*Examples*
a. adjectives			
b. articles			
c. verbs			
d. other concerns			

GAMES FOR LINGUISTIC INTELLIGENCE

Any games that encourage reading, writing, and speaking such as crosswords, word searches, word jumbles, and any sort of role-playing games use primarily the linguistic intelligence. Scrabble, Hangman, and Pictionary are good examples of commercial games that emphasize verbal and linguistic skills.

LOGICAL-MATHEMATICAL INTELLIGENCE

Students with strong logical and mathematical abilities are able to detect patterns, reason deductively, and think logically. It also can be stated as the ability to calculate, quantify, and consider hypotheses. This "scientific reasoning" is most often associated with sciences or mathematics, but may be quite effective when applied to a foreign language, as well.

STORY PROBLEMS

Performing calculations is a basic skill that can be and is practiced briefly in most foreign language classrooms when teaching numbers. Teachers or students take turns calling out numbers to be added, and so on. Vary this a bit by converting them into simulation-style activities: The T-shirt costs 100 pesos/francs/marks/yen, and you give the salesperson a 200 pesos/francs/marks/yen bill. How much change do you get? Have students take turns ordering from a menu, adding the costs, paying, and calculating change. Do a metric measurements unit: their height, shoe size, and many other measurements will be metric in most of the countries that they could visit.

Story problems are another good way to practice numbers and vocabulary: Paco has one cousin and Maria has three; how many do both Paco and Maria have altogether? If Hans and Peter are going to Berlin and drive on the Autobahn at 100 miles an hour, how long will it take them to get to Trier? Have the class tell you what to add, subtract, and so on. Teach some basic algebra in the target language, or tricks such as how to see if a number is divisible by 3. (Add the integers, and see if the sum is divisible by 3. For example, give the number 1,083, show them that 1 + 0 + 8 + 3 = 12 and 1 + 2 = 3, so 1083 is divisible by 3.) Have students make up a number series such as 2,4,6,8,10 or 1,1,2,3,5,8 and see if their classmates can figure out the sequencing pattern. (Of course, the numbers are either said aloud or written as words rather than as numerals!)

Other story problems could be as complex as brainteasers: There are five students. Pierre is not afraid of anything alive, or the dark. Anne and Antoine live in the Alps and love it, and they also love stories about haunted houses. Marie likes things that go bump in the night. David likes to climb mountains at night. Use the following chart to indicate who is afraid of what:

	Spiders	Dark	Ghosts	Heights	Snakes
Pierre					
Anne					
Antoine					
Marie					
David					

(This also has students chart the results, so it is both a good logical-mathematical and a good visual intelligence task).

GRAPHS

Graphs appeal to right-brain students, as we saw in Chapter 1, and they also are perfect for students whose logical-mathematical intelligence is strongest. Whenever it is possible to use a graph or chart, for example, to show preferences in music or food, attitudes towards different issues, the rise and fall of intonation in a spoken sentence, verb endings from singular to plural, or whatever, use the visual method, and as early as possible in the lesson.

Students can also make graphs. Have them survey their classmates on various topics and show the results in graph form, with a verbal explanation of the graph. Topics for a survey can range from easy ones such as how many have a cat or a dog, or ate breakfast or made their bed on that day, or drive to school regularly, to the more complex opinion surveys on vacation likes and dislikes, thoughts about capital punishment, and so on.

DEDUCTION

There are three basic steps in this method, which was first used in scientific investigation:

- First, a set of data on the topic are created, either by the students or by the teacher;
- Second, these are grouped into categories based on similarities students observe; and
- Third, these categories are labeled, or named.

When students identify the similarities, they are using many higher-level thinking skills (interpreting, inferring, generalizing) which lead to a greater ability to manipulate the category and apply it to new situations, so this strategy is very often used to teach basic grammatical concepts. Without your having to teach the concept in English and without using grammatical terms, students will discover, like Sherlock Holmes, that the power of deduction will lead them to the truth. Students, for example, who are provided with sentences with all the adverbs underlined, can group them into categories such as location, time, or description, and then you could discuss, still using the sample sentences, where words that fit these categories are in a typical sentence (i.e., immediately after the verb) without having to use the word "adverb."

A couple of warnings: the more examples the better, and, even more important, the simpler the better. Make sure the only element that varies is the concept that you are presenting. Use the concepts in sentences, so the students learn to handle them in context. Another application might be to present students with sets of irregular verbs and have students discover the patterns for forming them, using deduction (sometimes called concept development), and then apply it to new verbs.

Let's try some deduction, using French adjectives:

Masculine	*Feminine*
africain	africaine
japonais	japonaise
chinois	chinoise
allemand	allemande
belge	belge

Now try to formulate a rule to explain how to change from the masculine to the feminine form. Got one? Look at some more:

Masculine	*Feminine*
russe	russe
danois	danoise
anglais	anglaise
espagnol	espagnole
canadien	canadienne

Look at your rule again. Does anything about it need changing? Now, try to make feminine forms for the following:

Masculine	*Feminine*
siamois	
francais	
américain	
australien	

At this point, I would check the answers, asking volunteers to state the rule, refining it to everyone's liking, and having them verbalize their discovery process: what did you first notice, and then what, and so on. This last step is *very* important for retention of the concept they have discovered, so don't skip it. Deduction has cut the time I need to teach some units practically in half, with much fewer practice activities needed, because they found it out for themselves instead of my just telling them. Even though a lot of time was spent in the discovering, their ownership of the concept is much more permanent.

Most research shows this method to be the most effective when done in a whole-class setting, as the more input there is, the better, but I find that Steps One and Two are good pair or team activities, with a Roam Around the Room and then a time for revising categories before the class unites to list these categories and make our final discoveries about the concept. One small variation is to have the students create their own data file, perhaps by looking at a page in a text and making a list of what they see/read. For example, in French, by making a list of fruits, they might discover that all fruits listed are feminine in gender, and end in "e," a useful generalization to learn.

SYLLOGISMS

Syllogisms are another form of deductive reasoning. Students must use/devise them to apply the rules of grammar to new words. A syllogism is a logical argument with two premises and a conclusion. A categorical syllogism helps fit items into a category: for example, "All feminine words end in 'a.' This word ends in 'a.' Therefore, this word is feminine," is a syllogism. Statements such as "*aller*'s past tense form will be *allé*, because it ends in 'er'" is actually the result of a syllogism: All "er" verbs change to "é"; *aller* ends in "er," therefore *aller* changes to a*llé*.

The other types of syllogisms seem to be easier to use for cultural items. A hypothetical syllogism has at least one hypothetical ("if") portion. Example: If a city is in Germany, it has a Rathaus. If Bonn is in Germany, it has a Rathaus. Bonn is in Germany, so it has a Rathaus. A disjunctive syllogism has at least one either/or statement: Either soccer or baseball is the most popular sport in the world. Soccer has the most TV viewers, therefore soccer is the most popular.

For visually oriented students, draw the syllogisms on an overhead, with a big circle for the main category, and a smaller circle for the subset within that category. This will fix the syllogisms more firmly in students' minds.

INDUCTION

Induction is something I use to introduce new material, replacing the traditional lecture method. Prior to beginning the activity, the teacher selects the concept to introduce, and also chooses and organizes the examples that contain characteristics of this concept. At least 20 pairs are needed, especially for more complex concepts. Few texts provide such lists, so it will involve a bit of work and thought. This method of reasoning works well for introducing concepts such as masculine/feminine/neuter endings, teaching students to identify a particular style of art or that of a particular artist, or learning how to form a new verb tense.

In Phase One of the activity, in class the teacher lists several examples, either on the board, on an overhead, or on a handout. The examples are labeled as positive (good/ yes) examples of the concept or attribute, or as negative (bad/no) examples. The teacher asks the students to contrast the positive examples with the negative (to themselves, not out loud), and to take notes on those differences. (This would be a good sponge activity.) If he or she wants, the teacher could underline portions of the example in order to call attention to the important portion to examine. Then the teacher adds a few more examples, asking students to make a hypothesis about what the difference is between the positive and negative ones. Then, a few more examples are given, to test the hypothesis and refine it. Then, introduce a new step: present unlabeled examples and ask students to guess (still working on their own, and not out loud), using their hypothesis, if they are positive or negative. (Students love this approach: it is challenging, yet like a game.)

Phase Two begins when it looks like most of the students have a workable hypothesis. (Use body language to identify this: nodding heads, smiles, etc., or use signaling—cards, a tap on the desk, and so forth—for feedback on who has a good idea/hypothesis.) Pair the students and have them share hypotheses with their partner. Test these new, combined/synthesized hypotheses with a few more unlabeled examples, and then ask groups to share their methods with the class. At this time, the teacher confirms the correct hypotheses, refining how they are stated if necessary, and supplies the name of the concept (i.e., "This is called the future tense, and you have correctly identified how it is different.").

Now, have the student pairs (or combine two pairs to form a team, perhaps using a round robin) generate their own examples of this concept, or assign this as homework.

Phase Three is to check these new examples for accuracy, and to have students describe what thoughts went through their minds as they attempted to identify the concept: What did they concentrate on first, what did they reject; how did they modify their hypothesis based on additional examples? This is very important to voice, either to the entire class, or within their groups, because it more firmly fixes the concept by reviewing the steps they went through to find it. This is also an excellent review tool or evaluation tool if you want to check to see if some material you covered previously has been mastered: By giving good and bad examples of the concept, you will determine the students' depth of knowledge by how quickly they catch on, and also reinforce their understanding of this concept.

VENN DIAGRAMS

A Venn diagram is a visual representation of the relationships between two objects or concepts. It consists of two interlocking shapes, usually circles. In the circle on the left are written characteristics of only one object or concept, in the circle on the right are those applying to only the second, and where the two circles overlap are written concepts that apply to both. This quickly and easily (and visually) identifies similarities and differences; the differences are the "critical attributes" which will help the students identify and store these in their memory. Figure 2.10 is a typical Venn diagram, which helps students organize the facts about two things; they compare and contrast them by filling in the diagram with items generated during thought or conversation about the assigned topic. For example, a student might be asked to compare and contrast table manners, homes, clothing, foods, or anything cultural from a foreign country with the U.S. equivalent. One circle would represent the foreign country, and the other the United States. If the student thinks of an item that only the foreign country has, it goes in that circle; if only the United States has it, it goes in that circle, but if both have it, it goes in the center. After visually organizing his or her thoughts, the student is ready to speak or write about the topic. As a paired activity, two students would converse about a topic, listing things they don't agree about in their own personal circle and things they both like or dislike in the center. Again, their opinions are organized and ready to talk or write about at the end of the activity. The Venn diagram is a big help to students whose linguistic intelligence skills are not very good. It also becomes a good product for assessment purposes, or even to post on the bulletin board if the class is still getting to know one another.

FIGURE 2.10. VENN DIAGRAM

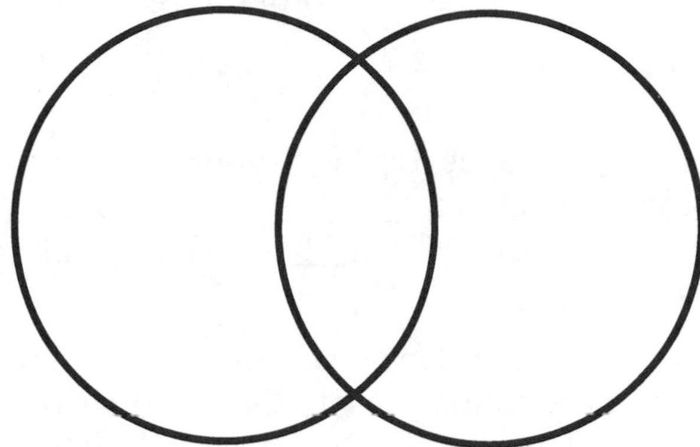

ANALOGIES

Analogies enable students to see how things they have learned connect to new learning and new contexts. After learning a topic, use an analogy to examine the similarities and differences between one system and another:

- How is Japanese food like ours? How is it different?
- Compare and contrast Napoleon and Hitler.
- With what the United State has learned about environmental issues, what advice can we give to Mexico?

To make it easier for logical-mathematical students to see the analogy, have them use a Venn diagram or some other form of visual representation (see the descriptions in Visual-Spatial Intelligence).

PATTERNING AND SEQUENCING ACTIVITIES

Discerning relationships and connections between objects or facts is the final facet of logical-mathematical learning:

- Assign students to bring an object to class that they don't usually bring, or provide each student with an object you have randomly gathered, and put them into groups. Have each group organize their objects by any method they wish, and then "show and tell" their collection of objects and method of organization. Concepts such as shape, color, size or use are a few of the ways to categorize objects.
- Do any project that involves step-by-step directions: Build something simple, cook, do origami or some other activity where steps clearly must occur in a certain order.

- "Postcards"—Students will use their prior knowledge to fill in missing elements on a "postcard" in which words have been wholly or partially blotted out by "rain," in order to reconstruct the message. An example:

  Dear Paul,

  I am very h_____y to be coming to your c_____y next week. I can't wait to meet your _________ and say _________ to them. My plane arrives at n_____ o'clock. Will you meet me at the ________?

  Obviously, some of these blanks have more than one correct answer. "C______y" could be country or city. Others, such as "h____y" could be "hungry" or "happy"(or other words) but from the context, "happy" seems to be best. Filling in blanks using clues and context is a logical skill.

- Have students assemble a puzzle, using only the target language, preferably a puzzle with a scene of a country or a building studied in class. When it is completed, talk about the picture.
- Have students list objects based on common characteristics rather than categories. For example, they could list anything that is triangular, or shiny, soft, curved and so on. For "soft" they could list a kitten, a sock, a marshmallow, lips, sand, and anything else they can think of. Have them illustrate their list (to involve visual intelligence), and label the pictures in the target language and share the results.
- Use pattern blocks or task cards to teach or learn things. A pattern card is one that is cut down the center in an irregular pattern, much like a puzzle piece:

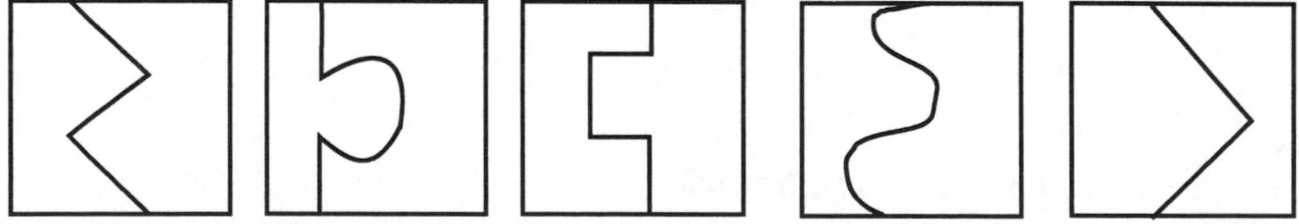

  Each card has only one other card that is its match. Use these cards to pair a verb with its subject, a question and its answer, a numeral and its number (written as a word), a word in Spanish with its translation in English, a country with its capital, or any other obvious pairs. This is also a good way to pair students before a partner activity; have each take one and find their partner.

GAMES FOR LOGICAL-MATHEMATICAL INTELLIGENCE

Any sort of game that involves calculations or logic would be appropriate. Calculation games would include card games such as Mille Bornes, or board games such as Monopoly. Logic games would include Clue, Battleship, Stratego, chess or checkers. Finally, puzzles are the best application possible for logical-mathematical intelligence.

VISUAL-SPATIAL INTELLIGENCE

Even though the name refers to the sense of sight, blind children also have visual-spatial intelligence. This is the ability to visualize, manipulate, and create mental images in order to solve problems. People with visual-spatial intelligence think in three-dimensional ways, and are able to recreate, transform, or modify these thoughts and perceptions and to navigate and both produce and decode graphic information.

DISPLAY AREAS

One of the easiest and most commonly used ways to appeal to visual-spatial learners is to have a classroom display area with information (photos, articles, posters, projects) posted that can be handled, read, and so on. However, it is very important that this be changed regularly *and* that students be encouraged to check it by:

- Scavenger hunts whose answers are/were on display
- Posting high-interest items such as classmates' work
- Extra credit questions on tests based on displayed material

A wonderful source for posters which contain information worthy of a scavenger hunt is The Old Poster Peddler (see Chapter 7 for the address). He offers posters in many languages—art, movies, elementary classroom vocabulary posters (e.g., Farm Animals), and up-to-date road and metro maps, most under $5.

ROTATING SEATING

Another easy step to take is to change students' seating fairly often. A move from the back to the front, or right to left, will change a student's perspective on the items displayed in the classroom. Visual-spatial–oriented students will benefit from the change in perspective, and it will give everyone a change of pace to have new neighbors.

NONVERBAL COMMUNICATION

Any use of nonverbal communication techniques or activities appeals to, and practices, visual-spatial intelligence skills.

- Have students perform actions (e.g., walk or dance) the way someone happy would do it, then have them try doing the same action if one were sad, bored, excited, and so on.
- Have them show you nonverbally how a character in a story feels, or a person of a particular nationality, an animal, a food, a piece of furniture, or whatever else you are studying.
- Have students mime activities while classmates guess what they are acting out. If you are doing this like a game, prepare two lists of words, expressions, or sentences to be acted out. Teams should take turns. Keep track of how much total time the teams take to guess the items; the lowest total time wins.
- You can also give nonverbal signals. For example, have a signal to call for students to be quiet and listen, or a praise signal (such as Carol Burnett's earlobe tug).
- If possible, teach some typical gestures used when speaking the target language, such as the French shoulder shrug, or Italian gesture of disbelief, the European method of counting where raising the index finger indicates you want two of something, not one, and so on.

IMAGE MANIPULATION

Image manipulation is a great help to those with visual-spatial skills. Writing items on different colors of cards or paper or with different colors of ink, such as highlighting sections of an activity or notes, provides strong visual cues, as any college student knows. For example, when the vocabulary involves a lot of nouns, put feminine words in pink, masculine words in blue, and neuter words in yellow. I guarantee you will hear students say something such as, "No, that's a pink word!" Make action verbs green, and linking verbs red. Varying the sizes of letters in a word to emphasize unpronounced letters or commonly misspelled portions helps fix the correct spelling in a visual-spatial learner's mind (examples in English: recEive, Aisle, cloTHes).

Dellawanna Bard, of the FL-TEACH list (see Resources section at the end of the book), gave me this idea: Have students think of some sort of dress, look, or behavior that just screams "masculine!" or "feminine!" (for neuter, think of drab clothing and color). Then, every time you learn a noun, picture it wearing/doing that thing. The example she gave was a butterfly, which to most people is a very feminine thing; but in German is masculine. So, picture a butterfly, badly in need of a shave, walking around in boxer shorts, smoking a cigar, or whatever your masculine stereotype is. Perhaps the feminine stereotype is a pink tutu, so picture an apple in a pink tutu. Then, picture all the masculine words at a party, or all the feminine ones doing a Rockettes-style number, such as the hippos in *Fantasia*. This sort of active-imagination visualization should be quite successful for the visually oriented students in your classes.

Another image manipulation activity is the old standard party game I call Word Search. I give my students a fairly long word, and have them compete to see who can make the most shorter words using only the letters found in the base word.

A form of image manipulation that teachers should use is to be very aware of how items are listed on handouts, chalkboard, and so on. If the items are of equal importance, they should be listed *horizontally*; items which are of varying importance should be written *vertically*, with the most important at the top.

VISUAL ARTS

Any sort of visual arts are the most common and most necessary aspect of visual-spatial intelligence to incorporate into a lesson plan, and what many students will remember and enjoy most. However, doing a craft must be done in the target language, and students working on the craft should be encouraged to converse *only* in that language, or else the craft should be done as homework instead of wasting class time on an activity done in English! My students usually remember vividly vocabulary (paper, scissors, glue) that we used when doing a craft in class. A well-designed craft activity can be a perfect way to provide input, imitation, assimilation, and invention as students work to meet their needs in the activity. Visual arts would include all of the following, and more:

- Draw yourself, a map, a house plan (fully furnished), your favorite meal, etc.
- Create a calendar, using student artwork.
- Create a slide show (or PowerPoint presentation) and narrate it.
- Start with a supplied shape such as a triangle, and create something.
- Design T-shirts for the pétanque or foreign language club, or for Foreign Language Week.
- Illustrate proverbs.
- Translate, or invent, sayings for bumper stickers
- Make posters to recruit foreign language students, advertise a fictional product or restaurant, or show mastery of a concept.
- Construct dioramas of volcanoes, marketplaces, or typical shops, starting with an old shoebox.
- Also using shoeboxes, make mini cultural floats to take through the halls/ classrooms or cafeteria during Foreign Language Week.
- Make edible maps of countries being studied, using pudding, peanut butter, candies, marshmallow, etc.
- Sculpt your feelings, or typical people from a certain region of the globe that speaks your language.
- Make mosaics out of scraps of torn paper, beans, rice, beads, and so on. For a Latin class, use mythology as the subject for the mosaic.

- Draw murals for inside or outside the classroom: life-sized outlines of students, with body parts or clothing labeled, graffiti walls of words from the target language that we also use in English, a typical city scene from Madrid/Paris/Munich/Kyoto/Roma, a backdrop of a news studio for "broadcasts" of the news.
- Sew or paint quilt squares or tiles with items that represent bits of cultural information.
- Make puppets of famous people and take turns guessing who they are and/or having them perform.
- Draw storyboards or scrolls and read them to each other.
- Make felt banners with phrases or cultural items on them for the classroom.
- Map out a complex and interesting scavenger hunt for each other.
- Cut and paste collages on themes or ideas of interest/being studied. Use foreign language magazines as the resource for the collage, if possible.
- Use clay, paint, storyboards, or felt-tip markers to express a feeling or emotion (hungry, sad, sleepy).
- Make block prints of vocabulary, cities, or symbols using old inner tubes, blocks of wood, and an ink pad. Cut the design from the tube, glue it to the block, and stamp away!
- Sew simple traditional clothing items: a Basque apron, a Roman toga, a bib attachment to turn shorts into Lederhosen.
- Make cultural artworks such as: God's eyes (*Ojos de Dio*), piñatas, origami, sculptures, *Scherenschnitte* (paper cutting), Mardi Gras masks (or for *Dia de los Muertes*, or *Fasching*), sculpt santons (traditional Christmas dolls for a French manger scene), make a Chinese character chop and prints, models of Roman temples, Gothic cathedrals or Renaissance castles, or devices such as a guillotine.
- Write rebus stories in which pictures replace words, and read them to each other.

PICTORIAL REPRESENTATION

Visual-spatial learners need to see *everything* represented visually, and visuals such as flow charts, mindmaps, and concept maps help them organize and make sense of information. Concept mapping comes in many forms, with many names:

Mindmapping or mindscaping	Webbing	Visual brainstorming
Graphic organizing	Bubbling	Topic mapping
Semantic mapping	Clustering	Flow charts

Story mapping Chalk talk Venn diagram
Hierarchy

Many of the above names are synonymous. They are all ways to visually represent and organize the content of a story, a discussion, or students' own thoughts on an issue.

To use this method for vocabulary, I like to use my whiteboards (see Chapter 3 for more about those). I have my students write the topic in the center, such as "My Favorite Animals" and then draw pictures of their favorite animals in a circle around the topic, with lines attaching the drawings to the center. Then they should label this spider-like design. After you check them for accuracy, erase the labels, redistribute them to different people, and have them identify and label the animals as drawn. The same method could be used for a story: students could, as a group, list the key elements of a story they either read, or heard the teacher read aloud. After putting the title of the story in the center, for each element they name, they draw a picture, labeling it.

STORY MAP

A story map is a more advanced way to represent the content of a story. It looks a bit more like a family tree. The title goes at the top, and the themes or key elements are below it. Below each element are examples or evidence of that element. Pictures may be used if desired, but usually words are used—quotations from the story, brief descriptions of the plot, and so on. The visual aspect of this is that each branch is a main point, with the supporting information visibly attached to it. Seeing these connections more firmly fixes the information in the brain. See Figure 2.11 for a visual representation of this method. This method works very well for grammar also. I use it to list when to use the various past tenses, especially the imperfect. We use it for the various uses of the subjunctive, also.

FLOW CHARTS

Flow charts or chain maps are used for activities or ideas that must occur in a certain order. Pictures are drawn and the order they are to be read or looked at is clearly marked by numbering the pictures or drawing arrows from one to the next. We use these a lot when we are doing a food unit and cooking. Get an illustrated recipe and cut apart the pictures. Have students reassemble the pictures in the correct order. Then prepare the recipe! You will find the students make a lot fewer mistakes, and accomplish the task in less time. It also doubles as a logical activity. This works equally well for simple construction projects (we build simple things using Lego blocks to practice the prepositions of location), or sewing projects.

FIGURE 2.11. STORY MAPPING

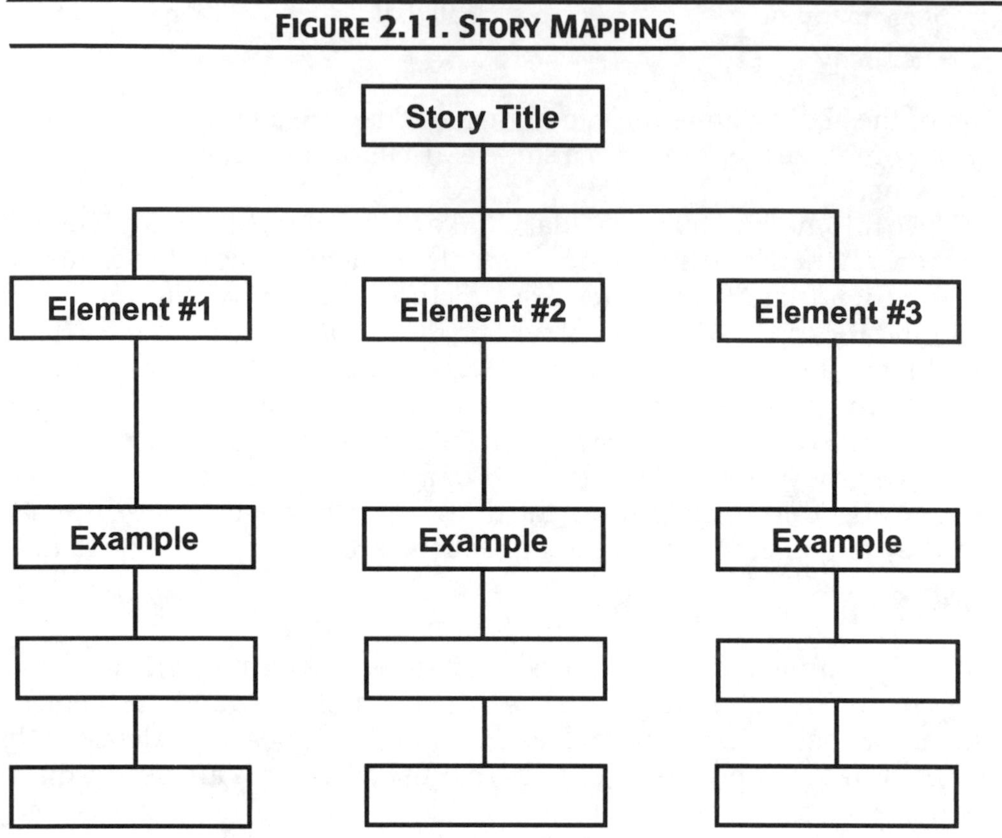

HIERARCHY

A hierarchy is used to show relationships between objects. The most important item goes on top, with the subordinate portions below. A family tree is a good example of this type of visual representation, and similar cultural items are what are best suited to this type of chart. A hierarchy would be good for showing the relative levels of the eight different forms of "you" used by the Japanese (for example, one is used between equals, another from a superior to subordinate, from a subordinate to a superior, and so on). Structures such as the feudal system or the food pyramid are routinely drawn using the hierarchy system.

LINE-UPS

A continuum scale is one that lists items based on where they fit between two extremes. These are great for practicing vocabulary. Give your students cards with the names of sports and have the students line up according to where their sport fits in the following situations: most violent to least violent, most difficult to least difficult, outdoor to indoor, cold weather to hot weather, requiring special gear to requiring none, or team to individual. Of course, you require them to discuss who belongs where in the target language, even if they sound like Tarzan: "Me, more!" And if you want to complicate matters a bit, at the end of each line-up have them hand their card to the person to their left or right.

Line-up sentences are also great to do. Give students cards, each with a word on it. Put colored dots on the back of the cards, and first have them locate other students with the same color. Then, have them line up to make an intelligible grammatical sentence. Have the groups take turns reading each other's sentences and translating them. Have people holding nouns come to you and exchange their noun cards for pronouns. Point out where an adverb goes in the sentence. This makes students very aware of sentence structure.

Line-ups have also proven quite valuable when doing a unit on history. Students often have difficulty placing events in the proper order: which came first, second, and so on. I give students cards with the names of events, people, and ideas. First, I have the events find their people (e.g., the Battle of Hastings finds William the Conqueror and Harold of England) and then they line up. Then the "ideas" find their people (e.g., "patriotism" finds Joan of Arc). Then each person steps forward and says who they are and a little about themselves, hands me their card, and is seated. This is great review right before a test, and it takes just a couple of minutes. Last year I also got a big piece of butcher paper and drew a huge time line on it. As we studied history, the students recorded the events on the time line, and were encouraged to add events they studied in other classes. They added mathematicians and scientific advances they learned about, when pieces of music (e.g., Handel's *Messiah*) were published, a bit of American history and literature, and several of their own birthdays (claiming they'd be famous some day). It was a high-interest display for the classroom, as students would check to see if anything new had been added.

OTHER PICTORIALS

Venn diagrams (discussed under Logical-Mathematical Intelligence; see Figure 2.10, p. 57) are also good for visual-spatial learners. They help students relate new material to familiar material as they write characteristics of each into a circle, but characteristics they both share into the space where the circles overlap. I use Venn diagrams to compare verb tenses and to compare stress pronouns with subject pronouns, but mostly I use them with literature, such as when I have them compare the Little Prince to Jesus, which makes the many similarities between the two not only visible, but memorable.

The final chart I often use is called a K-W-L. Before we begin a new chapter, video, or unit, we do an inventory of what we already know (K is for Know) about the topic. Then we think about what we want to know (W is for Want to Know), writing questions we want to have answered. Each day, for closure, we examine this chart, adding anything we learned to the L portion (L is for Learned), until all the questions have answers.

GAMES FOR VISUAL-SPATIAL INTELLIGENCE

Games for this intelligence include board games such as Scrabble, Monopoly, Clue/Cluedo, Bingo/Lotería (especially picture bingos such as Lingo, available from the UNICEF catalog, and others found in many teacher supply catalogs), Twister, Pictionary, and charades. Almost all card games use this intelligence, especially ones of the Go Fish type where students' cards show clock faces or other pictures that represent vocabulary words.

MUSICAL INTELLIGENCE

This intelligence is defined as the ability to recognize and compose musical pitches, tones, and rhythms. Deaf students would be handicapped in this area, but still able to master rhythm. Every foreign language teacher knows how important pitch, tone and rhythm are to languages.

Willis and Mason (1994) discuss the use of popular music in the target language as a tool in language instruction. They argue that not only are songs more relevant to the students' experiences than textbook material, but that songs, in addition to providing authentic use of the target language, also are a good source of exposure to the target language culture. Songs can serve as a culturally relevant listening activity in areas of the country where access to any other sort of target language media is limited or nonexistent.

LISTENING TO MUSIC

Bring in a tape or CD of music to class. Play a song several times, interrupting it frequently to say the words loudly and clearly, explaining the meaning. Then encourage the students to sing along. The best sorts of songs for this would be those that are highly repetitive, and those that can be acted out (such as *Sur le Pont d'Avignon*, the Hokey Pokey, the Chicken Dance, and others) or those that have special steps, such as the Macarena. Songs with an interesting message will also be favorites of your students.

Another way to get students to listen and appreciate is to do one of the following:

- Have them keep a tally of how many times they hear a phrase you tell them to listen for.
- Give each student a card with a word from the song. If they hear their word, they should stand up.
- Have students listen for a particular verb tense and signal when they hear it.
- Give students the song lyrics, which have been cut into strips of one line each, and have them figure out what order they think they are in. Then listen to the song, and let them see how close they were.
- Give each student half the lines to the song and one piece of paper. Each takes turns reading their line to the other, who writes it down.
- Have students create a cover for the song. It should include the title, singer's name, and at least three items representing themes/ideas/ things mentioned in the song. This is good as it involves several

other intelligences and creativity, and you end up with a visual you can display to jog their memories.

Good music to use for the above activities is popular music in the target language. Spanish music is fairly easy to find: music by Selena, Gloria Estefan, Enrique Iglesias, Magneto, Ruben Blades, and many others may be purchased via the Internet or in many music stores. For French, try to find some Patricia Kaas, Celine Dion, Patrick Bruel, Francis Cabrel or Jean-Jacques Goldman. German teachers tell me the following are good: Rolf Zuckowski (over 10 CD's, including *Ich hab' einen Walkman* and *Es Macht Spass* that are good even for first-year classes) and Die Prinzen.

MUSIC AS MOTIVATION

Use music as background while students are writing. Warning: teenagers especially are very close-minded about music, so for this purpose, don't use "their" music or let them provide the music. Instead, play classical music, or music of the folk/ethnic variety in the target language, preferably some that is unknown to the students. The object is to play something that will *not* distract them from the task at hand or encourage them to sing along, comment on whether they like it or not, and so on. It is to serve as a sort of subliminal motivator. For example, music with a fast beat will speed completion of an assignment. Music sung in the rhythms of the target language will help jog memories for vocabulary. Mood music such as Debussy's *Clair de Lune* influences the setting and characters of the story they are writing, or the content of the poem. Others, such as Saint-Saens' *Danse Macabre* may be used to jumpstart creative writing; it is a musical representation of the dead, witches, and so forth rising and riding about the night, only to fall back asleep at the rooster's call announcing dawn. Tell this to the students, and let their imagination run wild as they listen.

Music can also provide a topic for conversation. Music with a message about the environment, human rights, or love can be used to introduce a discussion of those topics. You can also bring in examples of several different styles. Play a little of each type, and have students identify the style: pop, reggae, folk, and so on. Talk with them about the possible use, audience, popularity, and so on of each type.

Music, used correctly, will help focus students' attention and relax them or invigorate them (for example, after something very lively, or a fire drill or some other interruption, soothe them with soft, slow music). It can also provide transitions: some teachers use certain music to signal when a regular activity begins or ends, and playing that music tells the students to close their books and get into their groups, or whatever. Music will definitely jumpstart creativity.

SONGS THAT TEACH CURRICULUM

Sometimes we are lucky, and a good, traditional song exists for teaching material. For example, *Alouette* is good for teaching body parts, as you sing about plucking feathers off various parts of a bird. *Il était une bergère* is good for introducing the passé simple. Two of Selena's songs, *No Me Queda Mas* and *Si Una Vez* mix the present, preterite, and imperfect, and are perfect for a verb unit. Other songs can be translated; I use *Head, Shoulders, Knees and Toes* in my French classes when we study body parts.

The best songs for teaching are the simplest. Take material from a chapter, especially more difficult things, and put it to familiar childhood tunes such as *Twinkle, Twinkle, Little Star,* or *Jingle Bells, Kumbaya, Yankee Doodle, She'll be Comin' Round the Mountain, When the Saints Come Marching In,* or some more modern ones, such as *We Will Rock You* or *The Addams Family,* among many others. I have some wonderful vocabulary songs created in this way (my current favorite is the days of the week to the Flintstones theme) and grammar songs that I have gotten from other teachers. Some of my favorite verb songs are in Chapter 5. Here is a sample song, involving the possessive adjectives, sung to the tune of *Jingle Bells:*

> Mon ma mes,
> Ton ta tes,
> Son sa ses, la la!
> Notre, nos
> Votre, vos
> Leur et Leurs, c'est ça!

I also like to involve my students in making up their own songs; not only are they proud of making up a song (or a rap) but they have learned the material it covers, "accidentally." We have "verb operas" when students are challenged to make songs that conjugate difficult verbs.

If you are not feeling creative, the *Sing, Dance, and Eat Tacos/Quiche* tapes have lots of songs set to nursery rhymes. I also have a CD by Etienne (Stephen Langlois, a very creative Canadian who writes songs to teach French grammar and vocabulary). Many companies have books of songs: The National Textbook Company has a book called *Cantando* that was recommended to me. There is also a Scholastic Books collection of nursery rhymes and songs in both Spanish and English called *Arroz con Leche* that comes with a cassette.

DANCE

Dance belongs in musical intelligence because of its reliance on rhythm. There are many dances you can teach your classes, and dancing to a song makes you appreciate music even more. Is there a flamenco society in your area? They may sponsor classes, or at least come to your class to demonstrate the castanets and steps for you. Get a video (Audio-Forum has one on how to play castanets!) of folk dances from a teacher catalog, or get something silly such as the German dance from the movie *National Lampoon's European Vacation.* Check out ballroom dancing opportunities: the cha-cha, rhumba, tango, mambo, and merengue are fairly easy to learn. Many of the calls in square dancing are in French: "Allemande left" (a German dance step), "dos à dos" (back to back), and so on, and many of the steps are in traditional French dances.

CHORAL READINGS

Choral readings are included under this intelligence because, in order to read together, pause together, and so on, students must really learn the rhythm and tones of the language—where to accent syllables, what sounds the vowels make, and many other aspects of the sound of the language. They do not necessarily have to know what the poem they are reading is about, but they must feel the beat, rhymes, and mood in order to read it well. For this reason, it can be a wonderful change of pace activity in the beginning classroom and in an advanced class.

MAKING MUSICAL INSTRUMENTS

Are any of your students musically talented? Have them bring in the guitar, get them a piano, or whatever. For the rest, why not make them the rhythm section? Making simple rhythm instruments is the easiest, and involves the kinesthetic intelligence as well. Easy instruments kids love to make are rainsticks and maracas. To make a rainstick, take a cardboard tube (mailing tubes are more durable) and nails that are almost as long as the tube is wide (but not quite). Nail them right next to each other in a spiral pattern down the tube. Cover one end of the tube with masking tape, tissue paper or papier-mâché (don't use anything slick) and pour in some dry rice, lentils, popcorn, or really small pebbles. Cover the other end, paint and decorate the outside. When you tip the stick, it makes a sound like raindrops on leaves.

For small maracas, use a paper plate, decorate on one side. Cut it in half, folding each half in half and putting some dry popcorn kernels inside. Staple or tape it shut, attaching a piece of dowel or a craft stick as a handle, and you have two small, triangle-shaped maracas that are cheap to make. For larger ones, use a plastic bottle partially filled with dry rice or popcorn. Use duct tape or package strapping tape to firmly tape a wood dowel in the mouth of the bottle. Wrap with paper (crepe, construction, tissue), decorate, and use. Another way to make maracas is to cover old light bulbs with papier-mâché, break the bulb (that's what rattles inside), then paint and decorate.

BODILY KINESTHETIC INTELLIGENCE

This intelligence challenges the commonly held belief that mental and physical activity are unrelated. Kinesthetically talented people use their mental abilities to coordinate their bodily movements and to manipulate objects. Recent research has found that physical activity enhances memory to a large extent; the mind-body connection definitely exists!

LEARNING ENVIRONMENT

How your classroom is set up physically is very important for kinesthetic reasons. Kinesthetic learners must have movement. An easy way to provide this is to organize the classroom into areas designated for seatwork, performances (skits), crafts, computer or language lab work, and conversations, and having a clearly defined entry, library, and storage place. One teacher even wrote me that she has an area marked off by masking tape on the floor where students leave book bags and other items, making it easier and faster to move and not trip over things.

This can be done visually by putting up different colors of paper, marking areas of the room floor with tape in different colors, or strategic placement of desks, file cabinets, and so on. The purpose of these areas is to have students move about the classroom during the course of a day's lesson. Unfortunately, many of us have large enrollments and full classrooms, but by rearranging seating for different activities, it is still possible to provide for movement. For lecture and class discussion, a "fishbone" formation is good: short rows, facing each other, around a wide central aisle. For conversations or group work, set up "pods" of three to five chairs pushed together into one large unit.

Drama

To make any topic a kinesthetic activity, turn it into a play. Write a script and make costumes. Choreograph a poem, dance to one of the grammar songs, memorize and lip-synch a tape (music or conversation). Have a puppet show version of the dialogue in the chapter. The more senses you can involve (sight, sound, hearing, touch) the more they will remember the material.

Simulations

Simulations are probably what foreign language classes have always done best: How you make students see that the vocabulary and behaviors you are teaching them are really useful. Most kids know that movies are not real life, so videos have some, but not significant, impact on their ability to perceive that grammar or vocabulary is relevant. But put them in a situation where they must actually perform, using the language, in a lifelike "reality" situation, and they suddenly see the relevance of what they have been learning and get feedback on how well they have mastered these communications skills.

In short, simulations are the "meat" of foreign language teaching. A good simulation has several different parts. When choosing a simulation, a teacher makes several decisions, based on time available, what classroom resources are needed (and finances), how to assign teams (small groups of no more than five are best, says the research; I prefer even smaller ones), and, especially, how to distribute the high-status roles in a manner the students will perceive as fair. The teacher must also decide if this activity will be graded, and if so, how this will be done. Of course, a simulation usually follows extensive preparation by the students (learning vocabulary and practicing skits and conversational skills), and preparation of the students by the teacher, by explaining the goal or goals and the rules of the simulation, and assigning the students to teams, modeling the correct behavior, and giving the students a small practice session before beginning the actual simulation.

Some good, easy, short simulations are:

Ask directions	Buy tickets	Shop for food, clothing, toiletries, etc.
Make a phone call	Bargain for a taxi	Make a complaint at a restaurant or a hotel

A good example is the simulation that my students do after they practice vocabulary and culture. I have my students check into my "hotel." As they enter my classroom, singly or in small groups, they ask for a room, specify the type of bed and bathroom facilities they want, ask the price, whether or not breakfast is included, and any other information they need. I hand them a room key, and they fill out a form such as those used in most hotels, with passport number and other relevant information, which they return to the desk, picking up a sheet with vocabulary about a standard hotel room, and which, at the bottom, tells them that there is a problem with their room, and they must complain to the desk clerk. My check sheet for this activity looks like this:

CHECK-IN	Began conversation	Yes	No
	Answered questions	Yes	No
	Asked price	Yes	No
	Asked about breakfast	Yes	No
	Said thank you	Yes	No
FORM	Turned in to clerk	Yes	No
	Filled out correctly	Yes	No
COMPLAINT	Registered	Yes	No
	Understandable	Yes	No
	Polite	Yes	No

Each *Yes* is worth one point.

A good, longer simulation has two characteristics: it is like real life, and it involves an ongoing process, or series of necessary behaviors. In a game called El Mercado/Le Marché/Das Kaufhaus, students go shopping. First they study vocabulary on clothing, which is sold at the market, and the tradition of bargaining that is in the text and videos ("too expensive," "3 for 10 pesos/pesetas/francs/marks"), if possible. Then the students are divided into teams. Some are the store owners, and their goal is to sell as many items for as much money as possible. Other teams are shoppers, who want to buy clothing "outfits" (what good is a shirt if it doesn't go with anything else?) for as little as possible. Stores are given identical sets of cards with clothing items pictured and money for making change. Shoppers are given money to spend. After a brief planning period when stores set prices and shoppers plan strategy, the teacher must explain a few more rules. As I have done this simulation over the years, the rules get longer: I now add "No armed robbery" and "No shoplifting" to my usual "No English" rule (smile), and also explain the scoring system.

After handling any questions, the stores open and shopping begins. During this time, the teacher has two roles: that of referee, to see that rules are followed, and that of coach, to give advice in a supportive way, while still allowing the students to make mistakes. Because most stores close for a noon break, or a siesta, a closing bell is rung after about 20 minutes, and shoppers finish their current buying and everyone regroups. The teacher can use this time to highlight common errors observed, the stores to mark down prices, and the shoppers to lay out their outfits and see what is still needed. Then shopping begins again. When time is called, the exercise is over, scoring is done, and the winning stores and shoppers are rewarded.

Then comes the most important portion of a simulation: debriefing. How closely did this exercise resemble the real world? What difficulties did shoppers encounter, and what solutions did they find? What cultural differences did they observe? What would they do differently next time? Students need time to analyze what happened, compare it to their previous experiences, and appraise their performance, planning how to redesign it for future simulations, or, hopefully, during a real trip to that country.

Grading a simulation is up to the teacher. It could be a simple participation grade: 4 points for participating fully in the target language; 3 points if the student used English; 2 points if the student had to be encouraged to participate; 1 point if the student broke rules, based on the teacher's observations while circulating. The activity could culminate in a written exercise that could be collected, or you could have a check sheet similar to the one for the hotel activity. My classes enjoy three longer units I wrote: a Murder Mystery, an Action Adventure, and a Soap Opera, which all are extensive simulations combined with verb tense review, and dictionary-using lessons, suitable for any language.

There are many, many different ways to use simulation. Wish you could find a guest speaker, but don't have one? Simulate one: Have students write questions they would like to ask a guest speaker, and then research the answers. For example, have students prepare questions for a German/French/Spanish exchange student, and then, using encyclopedias, letters to embassies, or the Internet, try to find answers. I have a video called *Speak French and Double Your World,* purchased from the AATF, that interviews people who use French in their jobs here in the United States. Before the video, I have students write questions for a businessperson about how French is used, and then I show the video. As the people are interviewed, the students find answers to their questions. Afterward, we research any unanswered questions on the Internet, by posting e-mail questions to various lists, and waiting for answers.

Simulations *do not* have to have a lot of props, and a good simulation need not even involve a lot of preparation, because in real-life situations, the outcome of a conversation or situation will depend on the other person's reactions and responses. It is this unknown factor that is both a little scary and a little exciting for the students. Simulations can be simply setting up conversational situations. I have several of these I like to do primarily with upper-level classes. One is called Elaborating. In it, students are not allowed to simply answer yes or no to yes/no questions. For example, if asked if they live in town, they may reply yes, but then they must volunteer more: how long they have lived there, or what color their house is, or what street they live on. Then they must turn the question around on the interviewer: Do you live in town? Do you like living in town? I usually provide question cards for this type of activity, based on whatever topic we are studying: where to shop, driving cars, studies, or whatever.

Another variation on Elaborating is Multiple Responses, where students are asked to provide a variety of responses. In *la aduana* (customs), to the inspector's statement "*Su pasaporte, por favor,*" give as many appropriate responses as possible: (it is fun to play this in teams) "*Como no,*" "*Claro,*" "*Aqui tiene Ud. mi pasaporte,*" "*Un minuto, por favor. Esta en mi maleta.*" Translations: "Why not?" "Of course." "Here's my passport." "Just a minute please. It's in my suitcase." See how creative your students can get!

Another variation is called Reactions. After reading or hearing a description of a situation, students are asked to play the roles of different people and react to the event. For example:

> Ein junger Arzt, der eben aus dem Krankhaus gekommen ist, lauft uber die enge Strasse, die mit den vielen Wagen des Hauptverkehrszeit verstopft ist, ein unvorsichtiges Benehmen. (A young doctor has just left the hospital, running across a narrow street that is full of rush-hour traffic, very careless behavior.)

Roles to assign for this would be accompanied by a suggestion as to what type of reaction is desired: *ein Politzist/Frage* (a policeman/ask a question, such as "What do you think you are doing, young man?"). The policeman could also exclaim, or could question another person. Other roles would include such people as *ein Kind zu seiner Mutter/Frage, Bemerkung* (child to his/her mother/question or observation), the child's mother/reply, a bus driver/exclamation (*Ausruf*), the doctor's wife, a pedestrian, an elderly woman to the child/negative question, a merchant at the door to his shop, and so on.

Elizabeth D. Morie, in her chapter in *Teaching in the Block* (Canady & Rettig, 1996, pp. 155–160), lists these advantages to using simulations:

- Student interest and enthusiasm "for the content, the teacher, greater motivation for learning in general."
- Better attitudinal changes. Students are more empathetic and tolerant. Increased peer and student-teacher interaction. A more relaxed, open classroom.
- Skills enhancement: improved coping and decision-making, bargaining, and persuasive skills.
- Factual learning. Simulations make knowledge more relevant and understandable, leading to more transfer and long-term retention of material.

- Variety and change of pace, because the activity's outcome is unpredictable, and because simulations are not done as often. It is an opportunity for movement, also.
- Responsive environment. Students get immediate feedback, and know how well they are doing.
- Safety. A perception that it is okay to make errors, and keep going.

MANIPULATIVES

Even if full-body movement isn't always possible, involve students physically through manipulatives, things they can do with their hands. The "signal" sponge listed in Chapter 1 is designed specifically for kinesthetic learners. Manipulatives can be as simple as using different colored pencils to write a sentence (black for nouns, red for verbs, blue for other) or vocabulary (one color for each gender). TPR (Total Physical Response) activities are good, too: Give commands to the students to put their paper on their head, stack different colored blocks. The clocks with movable hands that many of us use when teaching time-telling are typical manipulatives. Have students assemble things: Lego structures, an origami bird. Here is a list of manipulative activities:

- Bring in dolls or stuffed animals that can be dressed, introduced to each other, placed in various regions of a map marked on the floor with tape, seated in various rooms of a "house" drawn on butcher paper.
- Using toy cars and a large map or a model of a city you have built, have students take turns driving the cars according to their partner's instructions. This provides practice learning places on a map and practice with prepositions and command forms of verbs. Even more fun is to have someone bring in a remote-controlled toy car to drive. The student could drive the car, describing what he or she is doing, or asking for advice such as whether to turn left or right.
- Use play money to shop or purchase food during a simulation. Make change.
- Teach students a magic trick in the target language, and assign them to teach it to a friend, parent, or sibling as homework.
- Living Mannequin: arrange students in various positions, and have them guess what vocabulary word they are.
- Get a book of string games such as Cat's Cradle and Jacob's Ladder and you will be able to see easily who is listening and following directions.
- Have students bring in a toy or hobby and demonstrate it, or pick a skill they'd like to teach the class.

- Eating a meal—how forks and knives are held, how to get food (serve yourself or ask people to pass it), how to use spices and sauces—is different from country to country. Set up typical table settings, and have students eat a meal according to the etiquette of another country (especially fun when it involves chopsticks or eating with your hands).

GAMES

Table games are the least physical, but anything using dice or cards will appeal to a kinesthetic learner. Board races also are good for students who need movement.

Have scavenger hunts (inside or outside the classroom). Play kinesthetically oriented games such as Simon Says, Mother May I?, Charades, or Twister. Draw or use masking tape to outline a hopscotch path on the floor with vocabulary words or verbs in each square, and have students define or conjugate the word they land on. Do calisthenics in the target language (practices body parts, commands, numbers, and adverbial expressions). Tai chi is good for both learning about Japanese or Chinese culture and for its kinesthetic value.

Mark off the floor into squares that have letters and numbers and then tell yourself to walk, hop, run, crawl, skip, jump, walk backwards, walk on your knees, and so on, to a particular square. Ask students to volunteer to participate when they feel comfortable. When you get a larger number of volunteers, put them in teams and see which team can follow more of your orders correctly. The next day, repeat, but direct students toward classroom objects such as the desk, chair, door, flag, wastebasket, pencil sharpener, and other locations.

Although it is technically not a game, palm reading is an entertaining activity that generates a high level of student interest. It also practices the future tense, and students can observe and comment on the similarities and differences between their "fortunes" and those of classmates. Books on palm reading are available at many libraries, or you can just pretend and make up a fortune.

Outdoors, demonstrate (in the target language) and then have them practice skipping rope to rhymes used in another country. Play a game of softball, soccer, or pétanque (boules, bocci) using only the target language (practice appropriate things to say first, of course). Arrange for contests of strength, speed, or agility, and have students encourage each other, measure the results and record and compare the performances in the target language. Begin an exercise program, and have students keep track of their progress and report on it.

COOKING

Once again, cooking is best done in the target language. I try to have metric measuring cups and recipes with photos. If possible, I have a local chef demonstrate how to make an omelet or a crepe; if not, I demonstrate in the target language (and a lot of nonverbal communication). Then, I turn the kids loose, and we make and eat the food. Here are some good recipes:

- Quesadillas: Start with prepared flour or corn tortillas (one per student or serving). Put slices of cheese on half, fold the top over, and heat until the cheese melts. Enjoy with salsa, beans, and other traditional accompaniments.
- Flour tortillas are also an easy dessert: Cut into strips, deep fry briefly (they will puff up), and sprinkle with cinnamon sugar.
- Sangria: a traditional fruit beverage (Spanish)

  1 12-oz. can frozen grape juice concentrate
  1 12-oz. can frozen pink lemonade
  1 2-liter (or 2 quarts) ginger ale
  orange, apple, banana slices

  Mix the first 3 ingredients in a large pitcher. Pour into cups filled with ice. Put an orange slice in each (apples and bananas for those who want them or hate oranges.) Serves 25.
- Crepes: (French pancakes)

  3 eggs
  1½ c. milk
  3 c. flour
  2 Tbsp. sugar

  Mix the above at least six hours before preparing crepes. Heat a small empty frying pan until it is quite hot (a drop of water will dance or sizzle). If the pan is not nonstick, oil it lightly. Take about ⅓ cup (or a bit less) of batter, and pour it all at once into the pan, quickly tilting the pan to spread the batter as thinly as possible. When the crepe is cooked on one side, check it to make sure it is loose, and flip it into the air to turn it (it's a lot easier than it looks). When done, place on a plate, fill with honey, cinnamon sugar, jam, or Nutella (chocolate spread), or melt in a little Swiss cheese, or cheese and ham. Other, less traditional fillings that could be used are canned pie filling or pudding. Roll up and eat with your fingers. Makes 8 to 10 crepes.

  We have the traditional crepe race afterward: make two "racing crepes" (thicker than usual) and have volunteers run from one point to another, flipping the crepes as they run.
- Kartoffelpuffer (German potato pancakes):

  2 large potatoes, grated (approx. 2½ cups)
  Water with lemon juice
  1 boiled potato, mashed
  2 Tbsp. milk
  1 egg, beaten
  2 tsp. salt

fat for frying (about 2 sticks margarine or butter)

Put the grated potatoes in the water, then drain, squeezing out any liquid. Add the rest of the ingredients, and drop batter for three or four pancakes at a time into the fat. Brown on both sides and serve with applesauce or sour cream. Makes enough for 3 or 4 people for a meal; more for students to just have a taste.

There are many, many other ethnic foods to fix; I just listed some very easy and inexpensive ones above as examples. Churros y chocolate, quiche lorraine et croque-monsieur, Apfelstrudel und Sauerkraut—the list of possibilities is endless.

My French club, outside regular school hours, baked, assembled and decorated a gingerbread replica of a French Renaissance castle, and entered it in the local gingerbread house contest. For several years, we have won a prize and spent the money for a video, cassette, or party that the students want. For many of my students, it is the first time they have ever done anything this creative, and we use our French, study architecture, and get to eat all the leftover candy!

FIELD TRIPS

Field trips are traditionally a kinesthetic experience, and if you have a museum, ethnic restaurant, a traveling theater company in performance, or other worthwhile site to visit, or feel that a change of scenery would inspire your students' creativity, by all means give your students that opportunity. I would, however, venture that most field trips would be best done outside regular school hours; interested students could still attend, and class time could usually be used more productively.

INTERPERSONAL INTELLIGENCE

The ability to communicate one's feelings to others and to understand their feelings and intentions is highly valued in our society today. Anything interactive will use this intelligence, which relies upon all the other intelligences. To improve or strengthen this intelligence, teach your students relational skills: Give students opportunities to practice listening, encouraging others, and reaching consensus. The real goal is for students to learn to feel comfortable about personal abilities and characteristics, and acknowledge and respect the opinions, ideas, values and characteristics of others.

COMMUNICATION AND EMPATHY

The first word in the definition of this intelligence is "communicate." Communication is both verbal and nonverbal. Begin with the nonverbal form:

- Have students use body language to express various emotions. Remind them to use gestures and sounds (but no words). Practice using body language to express encouragement and support for others. Point out, over the next few days or weeks, when students exhibit this body language, or ask the whole class to remember and show you this when they are inattentive.

- Practice people-watching. Show a video with the sound off. Evaluate the dress, gestures, and facial expressions of the characters in the video, and speculate about what they are thinking, feeling, and saying. Then watch it again with the sound on to check for accuracy.

To foster verbal communication, have students draw something related to the unit you're working on in the text as homework: a person's face, a plate of food, a fully clothed person, a room in a house, a town map. The next day, pair two of them back to back, and have Student A draw while Student B describes the drawing he or she did for the homework assignment. Neither can look at the other's paper, and no gestures or other nonverbal communication forms are allowed. Student A is allowed to ask any questions (in the target language, of course). When they are done, have them compare drawings, and discuss. Feedback is important.

INTERPERSONAL COMMUNICATION PROJECTS

Have students survey their classmates to find things they have or do that are unique (at least, for that particular class). For example, they might be the only ones who collect baseball cards, or have no siblings. They could also look for opposites to tell about: My dog is black and Henry has a white cat.

A standard project for interpersonal communication is some sort of "me project." This may take any form. Some teachers have students make a coat of arms, divided into four sections. One section is for family, one for hobbies and interests, one for the future, and one for school and studies. A student would then draw or paste pictures in each section that represent things in his or her life. To present this, he or she would show the pictures and explain their meaning (in the target language, of course).

A similar project would be a collage of pictures and words that have meaning to the student. This would be presented to a partner, who should ask questions about the items in the collage and comment on items he or she likes or dislikes.

An interesting variation that I read about is the "me portrait" in which a face is drawn with doors built into it: the forehead, eyelids, nose, and mouth lift up to reveal pictures beneath them. These are usually posted in the classroom and students are asked to walk around, looking beneath the doors. Then, the class holds a discussion about what was interesting, unusual, common, and so on.

I generally give my students several options of what sort of project they would like to do to help us know them better, but all projects must include:

- Some sort of audiovisual aid;
- A one- or two-page summary of who they are (in the target language for students beyond the first year); and
- An oral presentation that explains the project.

Another variation, that I do the second day of school with my advanced classes, is to tell students to bring in three items that represent them. They show and tell these (we use Inside-Outside Circle for this) to their classmates.

LISTENING INTERPERSONALLY

Verbal communication also means good listening skills. Have one student explain a typical day/a frightening or exciting experience/their last Christmas or birthday/a vacation taken as a child (or a similar topic). The listener should:

- Ask questions. Make a rule that after making the initial statement, the initial speaker must wait for a question from the listener before speaking again. The speaker may, however, volunteer more information than the listener requests.
- Make appropriate comments (See Figure 2.5, p. 36).
- Paraphrase to check for understanding, every other time the partner speaks.

Here's an example:

A: I went to Florida last summer.

B: What part? (Question)

A: My grandma lives in Miami. (Answer plus additional information)

B: Do you go to Miami often? (Paraphrase and question)

A: Yeah, it's very warm there even in winter. (Answer plus additional information)

B: I'll bet. Do you go to the beach? (Appropriate comment and question)

A: Every day. I get pretty tan. I like to body surf, too.

B: I can see the tan. Are you good at body surfing? (Paraphrase, comment and question)

EMPATHIZING

Interpersonal learners sense the perspective of others: mood, motivation, and intentions. In addition to the activity in which students watch a video with the sound off and guess at character's feelings and motives, you could also have students look at a situation from someone else's point of view:

On Saturday night, what were the following people doing?
1. Your mother 2. Your Spanish teacher 3. The bus driver

The student could also be asked to look at him or herself through the eyes of others:

On Saturday night, what would the following people say you were doing?

1. Your mother 2. Your Spanish teacher 3. The bus driver

Answers would be something such as: 1. My mother would say, "She's cleaning her room." 2. My teacher would say, "She's studying for the quiz Monday." 3. The bus driver would say, "She's watching a movie."

COLLABORATIVE LEARNING/COOPERATIVE LEARNING

There have been hundreds of textbooks written on cooperative learning activities. One of my favorites is by Spenser Kagan (see References), and I have a chapter on such activities in my book *Teaching Foreign Languages in the Block*. Cooperative learning is when students work together to maximize their own and each other's learning. Students are often more willing to share their personal feelings in a small-group setting than when they must answer before the whole class. Learning is done as a group, with individual accountability. Since 1898, over 700 studies have shown that cooperative learning offers these benefits:

- Higher achievement and greater productivity,
- Better and more supportive relationships, both among students and with the instructor, and greater self-esteem and better social skills on the part of the students.

Robert E. Slavin (1991) also found the following benefits: a greater liking for classmates, more acceptance for mainstreamed students, a development of attitudes such as fondness for school, peer models who favor doing well academically, feelings of individual control over one's fate, and expressions of altruism. These findings were true for high-, medium- and low-ability students. There are basically three different types of cooperative learning: formal (the group stays together until a project is done), informal (extremely short-term activities such as checking with a partner), and base group (a long-term group whose goal is to provide peer support for each other and to be accountable in the long term for grades and participation/performance).

Each student in the group must have one (or two) roles assigned to him or her. The checker is the role every group must have. Rosensline and Stevens (1986) found that checking frequently for comprehension was significantly correlated with higher levels of student learning and achievement. The checker makes sure everyone knows whatever the essential learning is, because, to be successful, the group must have group goals (filling out the worksheet, etc.) but individual responsibility: each person must know everything.

Cooperative learning strategies include: Think/Pair/Share, Pairs/Check, Pairs/ Read, Pairs/Listen, Pair/Drill, Get the Picture, Graffiti, Inside-Outside Circle, Jigsaw, Round Robin, Four Corners, Send-a-Problem, Team Test, and many others, most of which are found in this book and my previous book.

Perhaps, for interpersonal learning, students in a small cooperative group tell something about themselves that others don't know. After the group has learned each other's secrets, one person from the group picks a secret, tells it to the class, and the class guesses whose secret it is. Have the class vote whose was the most surprising, unusual, or interesting.

FOUR CORNERS

Four Corners is what it sounds like: the corners of the room are labeled and students go to the corner they prefer. As a regular activity, it is a good practice for conversation about vocabulary: I might, for example, label each corner something such as "fruits, vegetables, meat, dessert" and have students go to their favorite, and name as many foods as they can in that category, or each tell their favorite. If I want something written, I have the people in the corner record their list on the wall, each group in a different color, and then the groups rotate and compete to see which group can add the most words to the lists of other groups. Other topics could be: what students did over the weekend, living situations (one parent, two, adopted, etc.), vacations taken to various places, favorite teams or sports. For more advanced classes, corners could represent characters from a novel or from history, professions, types of cars, or even variations of one statement such as "The future is...bright, scary, what we make it, and so on." Again, discussion in the target language would take place.

For interpersonal purposes, the last variation mentioned would be good, as the students would be discussing feelings. An even simpler and very effective use of Four Corners, however, is in team-building (and a valuable lesson about stereotypes). Have students, without staring or pointing or talking, choose someone else in the room that they feel they have little in common with. Then run them through five or six sets of "corners" such as pets they'd like to have, types of movies they like, and so on. Students will find some surprises each time they move, and that they have more in common with the student they picked at the beginning of the activity than they thought.

DETERMINING VALUES OF THE CLASS

Why not let your students have a say in the rules for the class. Ask them to think of at least five rules that the class should have, for example, "We will have fun/be creative/respectful of others" and so on. Use Think/Pair/Share to list the suggestions on the board, combining or condensing and discussing them as needed. Have the class vote on their four favorites, and then have them rank these four in order of importance. This is good on several levels. You and they will be communicating expectations for the class. Students will feel the rules are theirs, rather than imposed upon them. They will also understand the rules better, and be more likely to follow them.

You may also want to discuss more controversial things, issues on which there will be many opinions: early versus late marriage, large versus small families, dress codes, public display of affection, legalized gambling, year-round school, politics, current events. List the issues on the board in the target language as students express them. Do a Line-Up. Have them write an essay or do a drawing to show their viewpoint.

Have the students also share their hopes and fantasies. Choose a particular one, such as the perfect house, the perfect job, the perfect trip, the perfect day, the perfect date, the perfect mate, "what would you do if you were given a million dollars," or "how would you spend the last day of your life." Have the students write down their ideas and then share them. Make comments on how the fantasy might fit the student's personality.

ROLE-PLAYING FROM DIVERSE OR GLOBAL PERSPECTIVES

I like to check out the diversity within each class with this activity: Find out how many students do things in different ways. Examples are: when they brush their teeth, where they study, what they do when they have a headache, what injuries or operations they have had, types of watches or footwear or vehicles owned, what their favorite clothes are. (See Four Corners for more possibilities.) Point out the diversity you find, and ask them to imagine what the answers would be in a country where the target language is spoken.

Barnga is an interesting card game that can be purchased. In it, students are divided into groups and provided with a set of rules. In complete silence, the students read the rules, and begin playing the game. After several rounds, one student (with the lowest score) will rotate to another group, and begin to play with them, still in total silence. However, this new group does not have the same set of rules, and the new student will experience the "culture shock" of not understanding the rules, still without speaking, and the group will experience his frustration and puzzlement. These rotations continue until you judge that frustration has built up, some students are quitting, and so on, and then you debrief the class about what happened. In the discussion you should reach some truths about cultural differences and how to deal with them.

Another way to present cultural differences is to give students articles to read about current events, articles from other countries that have a different perspective. Viewpoints vary widely right now about the Euro (new European currency), the role of the United States in settling international disputes, and many other topics. Reading how other nationalities feel about us and our country gives a different perspective on events.

WORKING WITH AN ADULT

Students need to also work with adults and with their peers. Here are some things you could ask your students to do with an adult (and have the adult sign a paper as proof that it was done):

- Read a story to the adult. Talk about what it means.
- Teach an adult something you learned in class.
- Cook an ethnic food together, and rate the new dish.
- When current events are taking place in a country that speaks the target language, sit down and locate the country on a map. Talk about what is happening. Compare your points of view.

- Document a typical day in the life of the adult. Find out what he or she does, and how they feel about it.

VOLUNTEERING / SERVICE PROJECTS

Arrange for students to participate in several volunteer service projects during the year. Possibilities are things such as tutoring Spanish or other language speakers in English through the local Literacy Coalition or raising a house with Habitat for Humanity. Outside the local area, have a bake sale or project to raise money for a humanitarian organization such as Doctors Without Borders/ Médecins sans Frontières (provides medical care in war-torn areas internationally), Oxfam (Nobel Prize–winning group that feeds the hungry worldwide), UNICEF, the Make-A-Wish Foundation, or other similar groups which, since they are international, could also provide you with classroom materials in the language you teach. My students make Christmas cards for shut-ins in Quebec (I send them to a church to distribute for me), and I started a chapter of Amnesty International at my school. Amnesty International is a Nobel Prize-winning human rights movement, and we write monthly letters on behalf of people being tortured, imprisoned, or discriminated against. You can even ask to be given cases that involve only teens, or only in countries that speak the language you teach (and have students write in that language). We also, as part of our final exam, write about which projects we enjoyed most, and why.

INTRAPERSONAL INTELLIGENCE

The seventh intelligence is the ability to understand one's own feelings and motivations, and to use this self-perception to plan and direct one's own life. The teacher must provide an environment where the student feels free to express him or herself. If things are told to you in confidence, do not bring them up before the class. As in one of my favorite books, *Up the Down Staircase,* let students choose an alias at the beginning in order to feel free to express himself or herself (only the teacher will know who is who).

SELF-ESTEEM

Self-esteem is often based upon self-knowledge. Have students answer a "deep" question each day, keeping the answers in a journal. In the journal, they could write, paint, draw, feelings, ideas, insights, and important events. Questions help them get started; you might want to pick a question and require they all answer it, or simply provide one in case they are in need of inspiration for that week's writing. Questions could be:

- Who is your hero/heroine?
- If you had three wishes, what would they be?
- What is one of your fears?
- If you could change anything about yourself, what would it be?
- What is your life motto?

- When I am in school/at a dance/at home, I am…
- Ideal parents are…
- Teachers seldom are…
- Agree or disagree: Sports are very important.

They could also make lists: "Things I think are beautiful," "Things I want to finish," "Things I want to buy," "Things to do in my free time," for example.

In their journal, they should also keep a "mood graph" of their high and low points each day or week, noting the external events that contributed to these different moods. Have students, with a partner, explore personal perceptions of themselves: Have them talk about "Who I think I am," "Who you think I am," "Who you think you are," "Who I think you are," and so on. Then, in the journal, have them reflect on how their self-perception differs from the partner's perception of them.

Have students write a character sketch of themselves, using their fictitious name to protect their identity, since these will be shared with the rest of the class. They should use as many senses as possible to describe themselves, and describe their behaviors and why they do them, significant people in their lives, their own hopes and dreams for the future, and the impact they have on other students. Choose some to read and discuss in small groups, put them in a scrapbook for students who finish assignments early to read, or just post them in the display area for a high-interest bulletin board.

Have students write, draw, or compose a song or poem about an event that changed their lives and what they learned from that experience. Have students time-travel into the far future, and view themselves as they are now from that distant perspective (an old person looking back at his or her youth). Have them write a future newspaper article about their achievement(s).

COMPLIMENT CIRCLES

Teach students to get and give compliments gracefully. Have students write their name on a paper and pass the papers around the room. Have everyone write something they like about a person on the paper. Collect them long enough to make sure everyone took this assignment seriously, and hand them out. I have had students tell me that this changed their whole life; perhaps someone wrote that they had a nice smile, so they made an effort to smile more, and people were nicer to them, and good things happened to them. A variation on this is to sit in a circle and give compliments face to face, but I find teenagers aren't too comfortable with this. Once I taped papers on students' backs and they wrote compliments or suggestions on each other's papers (again, I read the papers before I removed them for the students to see).

PEER SUPPORT

Choose a partner for each student and occasionally give them time to meet. Their goal is to make a list of each other's strengths, and then plan how to use those strengths to achieve future goals. Each time they meet, they would report on their progress toward their goal(s). I usually have them set a goal for my class, a goal to accomplish before they graduate, and one other goal of their choice. Having a peer to report to, one who expects effort and progress from them, is a great motivator. Having a list of goals, with a written record of progress, is great for a student's self esteem.

METACOGNITION

Another form of self-knowledge is to know how you learn best (see p. 16, Metamemory Techniques). We all have seen that some people learn slowly, remember inaccurately, and seem lost and clumsy when faced with tasks requiring creativity or evaluation. A good learner will think and plan first, and self-correct. He or she also has more "tools" with which to learn. The deliberate teaching of cognitive strategies that are successful has not been done very much in the public schools. Teachers must often teach students how to take responsibility for their own learning first. Many students believe that it is the teacher's responsibility to make them learn. Use these six steps:

1. Provide explicit instruction in what the task is, what the objectives are, and how to assess progress or completion. For example, set time limits and clear expectations about how much should have been accomplished during that time.
2. Provide opportunities for the class to work cooperatively.
3. Provide explicit instruction on how strategies may be transferred, and provide practice. Suggest various strategies they might use.
4. Help students link newly acquired knowledge to previously learned knowledge. Remind them of rules previously learned.
5. Hold a discussion after the task to talk about what was learned, and how, problems they ran into, and what strategies worked well to solve them, and how to avoid such problems in the future.
6. Model metacognitive behavior, using techniques such as thinking out loud during problem solving, explaining the process of deciding how to attack a problem or issue, doing some explicit self-monitoring for comprehension, checking the final answer, etc.

Students should be taught to plan how to study, select a strategy, self-monitor, self-question (e.g., "Is this all I need to do?" or "What does that mean?"), self-evaluate, and predict the answer. Cooperative learning will help them learn how to do this, as other students voice their thought processes.

Memory Model is a good strategy to use, one that few students know.

MEMORY MODEL

This method is good for learning new material as a group, but Memory Model is better for memorizing data such as names (both from novels and geography) and vocabulary lists. Memory Model is a form of mnemonics also called

Link-Word that attempts to make it easier for students to recall words by drawing from their own personal experience to form word associations. In Step One, the students select the terms they must know: by reading and then underlining or listing unfamiliar words, by choosing the key points in a story or speech they wish to memorize, or by looking at a list the teacher has given them.

In Step Two, students link the unfamiliar material to something they know, using several methods. To make the image memorable, the new idea must be sensual (using the senses such as taste, smell, etc.), or motion-oriented, perhaps very colorful, or very exaggerated in size. In short, the link should be as creative and as humorous, outrageous, absurd, or downright silly as possible. Even if they are a bit off-color, let the students use whatever works. In Step Two, therefore, the students, in teams, will look at the vocabulary list and try to make as many crazy connections as possible. My students have come up with things such as, for haricots verts (green beans), the idea of "green haircuts," a translation of one word, and a look-alike for the other.

Step Three: make it concrete. Draw a picture of this idea, making it visual, auditory, and as exaggerated as possible. My students took the above connection and drew a picture of a punk with a bright green Mohawk, ring in nose, tattoos, etc.

Step Four is to practice the words, using the visuals with their associations, until they become familiar. *Warning:* No matter how silly, the students will only remember these associations well if they are the ones who thought of them. Giving them a good one from last year's group will not be remembered as well as one they themselves have created.

With Memory Model, you can present more vocabulary more often, with greater retention. Your students will experience more success, and will add this to their selection of strategies to use when studying.

ASSIGNMENT PLANNING AND REFLECTING

Encourage students to keep an agenda and list their assignments in it. Many foreign language teachers also require students to keep a notebook of things learned, written, and so on. These will be discussed in more detail later in the book. Again, this strategy leads to self-awareness, which is intrapersonal intelligence.

EDUCATE FOR HUMAN VALUES

Help your students learn human values such as altruism, honesty, compassion, mercy, loyalty, courage, justice, enthusiasm, tolerance, helpfulness. Service projects will help fulfill some of these. Reading examples of these values (e.g., the George Washington cherry tree story) will reinforce these values. Watch videos/movies such as *Au revoir les enfants* or *Schindler's List*. By seeing examples of these qualities modeled for them by people they admire, they will learn them, and enhance their self-esteem by adhering to them.

NATURALIST INTELLIGENCE

The recent addition of this intelligence by Gardner reflects, I think, a sort of global perspective together with the modern concern for the environment, yet undoubtedly our caveman ancestors also were keenly aware of their surroundings and changes in their environment. It is this awareness that forms naturalist intelligence. A student with strong naturalist intelligence will observe and remember patterns and things from nature easily; this student loves animals, camping, hiking, and being outdoors. They have keen sensory skills—sight, smell, sound, taste and touch, and this is probably the best way to appeal to them.

Because they so easily learn characteristics, names, categorizations, and data about objects or species found in the natural world, try some of these activities:

- Do an expanded unit on animals beyond the vocabulary for the usual cat, dog, and bird. Learn the specialized vocabulary for animals: paw, claw, wing, beak, snout, hoof, mane, tail, nest, burrow, and so on. Have each student pick an animal, and do a report on it, including these items:
  - A full-body illustration, with body parts labeled.
  - A map showing where this animal may be found.
  - A description of the animal's habits: food, home, babies, life span.
  - A poem about the world, from the animal's point of view.
  - For the upper-level classes, do an environmental unit, maybe even as an interdisciplinary unit with the biology or environmental studies class, plus a writing/composition class. A unit on endangered species could also involve a current events or even a government or history class (foreign policy, etc.) Most upper-level texts have a unit on the rain forest or recycling. If yours does not, go on the Internet, where there are many resources. The books *Perspectivas* and *Juntos* (Spanish) and *Discovering French Rouge* are examples of texts that devote an entire chapter to these issues.
- Take students various places around the building, and have them list things they see, smell, touch, taste, and hear at each spot. When you get to the classroom, have them list their words on separate pieces of butcher paper, and then group the students to make a poem or a poster about each place. Places could include: the parking lot, the football field, the outdoor eating area, the school's greenhouse (if there is one), and for contrast, the boiler room, the kitchen or home economics room, or backstage in the auditorium. Make it a French/Spanish/German/Italian-only excursion!

- Take a short field trip to a nature preserve, forest, meadow, river, or park nearby. Have students do their choice of labeled drawings, poems, stories, an article for the "travel" section of a newspaper, a postcard or letter to a friend, or even just make a list of things for a potential scavenger hunt in that area, in the target language.
- Get a live pet for the classroom: a fish, gerbil, or just a plant. Have students take turns caring for it, have a contest to name it, make up stories about its many adventures "in the wild," make a video about it and its habits, get a book in the target language about it (or write your own). Keep a diary from the pet's perspective of what goes on in the classroom.
- Have students create collections, scrapbooks, logs, or journals about natural objects—written observations, drawings, pictures and photos, or specimens.
- Join an environmental group that is active in an area that speaks the target language and can send you brochures, posters, or pamphlets in that language (or offer to make some for them). Sometimes you can even find materials in unusual places: for example, the Cracker Barrel restaurants had a coloring book on the rain forest animals.
- Have students write to companies that have locations in various countries, asking them about their environmental policies. They may also have posters or literature to send, but just getting a reply is thrilling to students.
- Subscribe to a magazine that features nature: an example in Spanish is *Geomundo,* a *National Geographic*–type magazine with articles on cultural, environmental, and scientific issues. So is *Americas,* published by the Organization of American States (OAS).
- Watch a video or movie in the target language about nature or environmental issues in areas such as South America, central Africa, or other places that speak the target language. Fellow language teachers recommend movies such as *Medicine Man,* filmed in Mexico, in which Sean Connery plays a scientist who fights to save the rain forest, or the series *La Catrina,* in which the use of harmful pesticides is a theme.
- Music is a big motivator. Use a song such as Mana's *Donde jugaran los ninos* (*Where will the children play?*) or Cabrel's song about the inhumanity of bullfights to begin a discussion about naturalist issues.
- On the Internet, there is currently an environmental studies discussion list called ENVST-L which could give you some further leads. Use a search program to locate it. There is also a Canadian Web site on recycling, and several other places to help you organize a unit of

study, listed in Chapter 7 of this book. And don't forget to look for newspaper articles on the newspaper Web sites, too.

- Take advantage of volunteer opportunities: Adopt a section of highway, recycle cans, clean up a park, plant trees or flowers somewhere in town, paint signs or picnic table, or even decorate bags for the local grocery to use on a Save the Earth or Support the Humane Society day. Some states, such as Maryland, require students to volunteer a number of hours for community service.

The next few chapters provide various examples that include the eight intelligences and right- and left-brain activities applied to specific classroom situations.

3

REVITALIZING THE BASICS

We all know that students need a break from listen-drill-write monotony. Even crossword puzzles, word searches, board races, Pictionary, and hangman get old fast. This chapter provides some alternatives that will help your students practice the basic groups of vocabulary that are taught in any language. Of course, the new national standards mandate throw in a lot more communicative activities, so the majority of these exercises emphasize speaking and reacting to spoken language. Try a few; your students will love you for these!

GREETINGS

- For several days after teaching greetings, have students greet their teachers in French. Each day, you will have arranged with a colleague to be a "Mystery Educator" who will put a note in your mailbox with the name of the first student who greeted them (or give that person a candy bar, or some sort of reward). Post that student's name. This is also a great excuse to teach the other teachers in the building how to reply back, in your language, and is good public relations for your area.
- On Day One, once students have chosen a name, make name tags to wear for a few days. Have students sit in a circle, and snap their fingers twice (or clap their hands), slap their desk top twice, and then,

as they snap or clap twice again, say their new name, and then the name of another. Snap, snap, slap, slap, snap-Marie, snap-Pierre! The student just named waits through the first four beats, and then replies with his name, and the name of another classmate. Snap, snap, slap, slap, snap-Pierre, snap-Marc! This is fast paced, an easy to way for everyone to learn the names of classmates, and also a pronunciation drill that they don't even realize is practice because it's so much fun! I play along with the class, as I need to learn names, too.

- Props are great: Students who don't wish to greet each other face-to-face seem quite willing to do so when both are provided with a toy telephone and are seated back to back, or with a partition separating them. Having puppets or other toys greet each other are another way to get around the shyest student's reserve.
- An authentic Spanish game to get to know each other: Sit or stand in a circle with one person in the center. They point at or approach a classmate, and say, "I know you, (name), but I am better friends with (another name)." Immediately, all three people, the two named and the one who made the statement, get out of their seats/places, and change places. Because there are only two spots, the person remaining starts the game anew.
- Tape other faculty members who are not part of the foreign language department giving a greeting in the target language, and have the students guess who is speaking.

Numbers

ONE

THREE

FIVE

- Present the numbers from 0 to 10 using the TPR (Total Physical Response) method. Show them your fist, saying in the target language: This is zero. Extend your thumb, saying: This is one. Extend your thumb and index finger, saying: This is two. Then ask the students to show you zero, one, and two. Then give them the same numbers in random order. When that goes well, add in the numbers three, four, and five and practice those numbers in order; first those three, and then from zero, and finally once again in random order. Then add the numbers six, seven, and eight, and so on until you have covered the numbers to either 10 or 12, depending on the text (in some texts, the next unit is telling time, and so they present the numbers to 12).

- Now, what else is there to do but play Bingo/Lotería? Try these:
  - This is *very* important to do, and very well worth doing. *Never* have students just count from 1 to 10 (or whatever number). Make them do it backward. Doing it backward shows that they can connect the sound of the word with its meaning. Anyone can learn a string of meaningless sounds in order one way, but to reverse the order requires knowing what those sounds mean, as well as where each word begins and ends.
  - Play Flute (French), Chihuahua (Spanish): Have students count, but when they hit a specified number (e.g., 3, 7, or 9) or a multiple of that number, they call out "Flute" instead of the number. When they get to 30 (if the number is 3), they would say, "Flute et un, Flute-deux" and so on.
  - Knock loudly on your desk, having students count silently. When you stop, they shout the number in the target language. Then have students take turns doing the knocking.
  - Sing the numbers to the tune of *Ten Little Indians:*

    Uno, dos, tres amigos
    Cuatro, cinco, seis amigos
    Siete, ocho, nueve amigos
    Diez amigos son.
    (Eins, zwei, drei Freunden… Un, deux, trois camarades…)

  - Play Slapjack. Put students in groups of no more than four or five and have them push their desks together to form a playing surface. Give each group a deck of cards.
  - Also using decks of cards, remove all the face cards, and have each team lay out the cards face up so that everyone can see them. Call out a number, and have the team assemble cards that add up to that number. Make everyone on the team responsible for making sure that each member knows how to say each number; stronger students seem to enjoy helping the not-so-strong ones. Call on one person in each team to name the numbers. As he or she says them, write them on the board, and add them up. This is a good way to practice the bigger numbers.
  - Have a lottery, with students picking their own numbers. Call out or draw the winning numbers each day, just like on television. Give the winner some object or privilege.
  - It is very important to have students use numbers in a communicative way. Each day, give students a short form to fill out on

which they must ask five classmates their name and one of the following: their telephone number, their address, their shoe size (use international sizes, usually written on most athletic shoes), their height (use metric measurements, and have them measure themselves on a "growth chart" you have drawn on the wall or on the board), their lucky number, their father / mother / grandmother's age, and so on. They write the classmate's name and answer down, and when the form is full, they sit down. Specify that no one may give more than five answers, so that everyone gets asked five times, too.

- Play connect the dots, but with a twist. Randomly number the dots of a basic connect the dots picture. Then, you call out the numbers in the order they should be connected: for instance, 15, 3, 49, 22, and so on. This exercise requires better listening skills, and because the numbers are random, it requires a more thorough knowledge than the standard way of playing connect the dots.
- Worksheets for practice (speed practice, if you prefer):
  - Three columns of numbers written out in the target language, with missing numbers to fill in.

Example:	one	______	three
	______	five	six
	seven	eight	_____

    Of course, I would mix the numbers up more.
  - Greater than/less than tables. Two columns of numbers, written out in the target language (not as numerals), and have students mark a greater than/less than symbol in between.

Example:	dos	_____	cuatro
	zwanzig	_____	sieben
	onze	_____	quatorze

  - Pair students, giving each a worksheet, either worksheet A or worksheet B. Each worksheet has half the items in the classroom listed: desks, pencil sharpeners, globes, televisions, doors, blackboards, boys, girls, students, etc. Each student takes turns asking the other, in the target language, how many there are in the room and writes down the partner's answer.
- Have a brave person stand, back to the chalkboard. Write a number on the board, and have him or her guess the number in the target language, with the class shouting "Higher!" or "Lower!" Write down the time, and challenge others to beat that time.

- Play penny toss: Write the numbers on a large paper or on posterboard. Have students toss a coin (peseta, franc, Mark, etc.) onto the paper, calling out the number it lands on. To practice larger numbers, play this game in teams, with each team keeping track of its score by adding together the numbers their members call out.
- Hand out M&M candies or something similar, such as Skittles. Have the students report how many they have, and then recount in sets according to colors. They can also subtract (by eating, announcing the number they will eat) and then report the new total.
- For a more advanced class that is reviewing the numbers, have them draw "phone numbers." Have half as many numbers as there are students in the class, but have each number on two strips of paper. "Dial" a number, and have the two students with that number come to the front of the room and either have a short conversation (review of other skills from earlier years) or compete to answer a question.

TELLING TIME

- ♦ I purchased a set of clocks for classroom use in practicing time, but have had a lot more success asking students to make their own clocks. Give each a paper or styrofoam plate and a brass brad that will poke through the plate and then split, folding each half flat on the back to hold the hands on, while allowing them to turn. As homework, have them make their own clock. If you wish, have a contest to see whose is the fanciest, most expensive looking, and so on. Then, say a time to the class. While you are adjusting your clock to that time, or getting ready to reveal the drawing on the overhead, the students are setting their clocks. Somehow this is much more motivating when they have made their own clocks.
- ♦ The above activity easily converts to a bulletin board: Give each student a different time of the day and a paper on which they illustrate what they usually do at that time of the day on a weekend or a

vacation (otherwise, you will have many pictures of school). Then post the picture next to the clock, adjusted to the correct time. Having the clocks on a bulletin board also means they are available the next day: As the students enter the classroom, they retrieve their clocks.

- Use a bell, or borrow a triangle from the band. Strike it a number of times. Ask what time the "clock" just struck. The student who gets the answer first gets to strike the next time. This is especially great in the grade school and middle school levels.
- Another activity that works well with young students or with an older group that is kinetically oriented is to ask the students to be human clocks. Have them stand and, with their arms, show the time.
- Photocopy TV schedule pages from countries that speak the target language. (Many newspapers are now on the Internet and you may easily get the schedule for the same day you do this activity, if you wish it to be current.) Not only will students enjoy seeing the 24-hour time system in use, they will enjoy seeing American shows listed, and guessing at the movies. After a few minutes, ask selected students what they want to watch, and what time it is on, or what they would most like to see at 8 o'clock.
- A related activity would be to copy the movie theater listings from a major city. Again, ask what they want to see, where it is showing and at what time, how much it costs, who is in it, how they will get there, who they will go with, and anything else you can think of.
- Develop a set of cards for playing Go Fish. Half the cards should be pictures of clock faces displaying various times, and the other half of the cards should be the clock times, written out in the target language. Each student is dealt from four to six cards to begin, with the remainder in the center of the desks (pushed together to form a table) as the draw pile. Student A asks, in the target language, "B, do you have eight o'clock?" If B has this card, he hands it to A, who lays the pair out for the others to see, and A asks a question of B or any other student in the group. If B answers no, A must draw a card, and his turn is over, and B asks a question. The game is over when all the cards are matched, and the winner is the person with the most matches.
- There is a traditional French game that is played outdoors, something like this: One person is the wolf (*le loup*) and the others are the sheep (*moutons*). The *moutons* line up in a straight line, facing the wolf. (It is easiest to play this somewhere that has lines—a soccer or football practice field, for example.) One sheep will ask the wolf, "Mister Wolf, what time is it?" and the wolf answers with a clock

time of his or her choice. Then another person will ask the wolf what time it is, and get a different answer, until the wolf answers that it is noon (*"Il est midi."*). At that time, the *moutons* try to run past *le loup* to a given spot and line up again. Any student that the wolf is able to tag is now a wolf, and the game begins again, with several wolves and fewer sheep, until only one sheep is left. This would be easy to modify for any language.

ALPHABET

A B C X Y Z

Once you have introduced the alphabet, and sing the Alphabet Song, what else is there to do?

- Give each student a small cup half full of *Alphabits* cereal. With a partner, each will hold up a piece of cereal, say the letter in the target language, and when the partner okays the pronunciation, he or she may eat it.
- Sing the alphabet not to the standard tune, but to the theme song from the game show *Jeopardy*—and then sing the alphabet backwards, to the same tune.
- Call out the initials of celebrities, and have the students guess who the celebrity is. Each day, read a few of the following acronyms. See what student can identify it, and call out the long form (e.g., ESP = extrasensory perception)

NFL	ESPN	CBS	AWOL
USA	MTV	VIP	NBA
ASAP	NAFTA	NCAA	FBI
OPEC	UFO	UPS	CIA
RSVP	UNICEF	your school initials	

  Try some language-specific ones, too. For example:

  French: *OVNI Objet Volant Non-Identifié = UFO*
  SIDA = AIDS
  ONU = UN

- Have a spelling bee, but a nontraditional one. Pass out big cards with the letters of the alphabet. Call out a word, in English or in the target language, and have the students spell the word by standing, shouting their letter and holding up the card for the class to see—or have them run to the front of the room and quickly line up.

- A good followup, using the same cards, is to have each student take a piece of tape, and have them post the letters somewhere in the classroom. Anywhere, even on a fellow student! Then, ask them, first, to point at the various letters, which are, of course, not in order. ("Donde esta /Où est/Wo ist ______?") Then add more detailed questions, giving choices: "Where is the letter X? On the window or on the door?" or "What letter is on the window? S or Z?" As the students become more familiar with the locations in the target language (incidentally, this is a great way to introduce or practice classroom items at the same time), change to a yes/no format, with students giving the location if they answer no: "Is S on the door?" "No, on the window." You may be surprised, the following day, to see students turn to the spot where the letter had been the previous day, when you practice using one of the other activities in this section.
- Using the same cards again, sing either alphabet song, but students must stand up with their card held high when their letter is sung. Even high school seniors seem to like this.
- This one is well suited for the energy level and cooperativeness of grade school (FLES) or middle school students, I think: Put the students in groups, move the desks and chairs out of the way, and, as you call out letters of the alphabet, have the students actually make that letter with their bodies, either standing up or lying on the floor. Reward the fastest.
- Begin spelling the name of a student in the class. When a student recognizes his or her name, the student raises his or her hand and completes spelling the rest of his or her name.
- An old game my family used to play on long car trips works well here: Have one student say a word in the target language; the next student must say a word that begins with the last letter of the preceding word (in French, ban words ending in "x").
- Play Hangman in small groups. For extra culture, give them the names of famous people of Spanish/Mexican/French/German/Japanese/Italian origin or descent, well-known places, or products from the target countries.
- Play Wheel of Fortune with the topics listed for Hangman.
- A variation I found called "Schreibmaschine" (Typewriter) involved assigning each student in a team or row a certain number of letters of the alphabet. When another team (or the teacher, or a student on the team drawing a slip of paper from a dish) calls out a word, the team

must immediately spell it, each student contributing his or her letter when it is needed, but staccato (with no breaks) just like a typewriter: "bleiben." "b-l-e-i-b-e -n" "Richtig, nächste Gruppe!"

- Because many letters, especially the vowels, have the same name as the sound they make, there are more activities in the Pronunciation section of this chapter for your use.
- Make an Abécédaire (French for ABC book), an illustrated book that lists something for each letter in the alphabet: A is for Alligateur, B is for Bacon, and so on. (This is good dictionary use practice, also.) If you are working on verbs at the same time, why not tell them to use verbs instead of the traditional nouns, or adjectives/nationalities/foods, depending on the unit?
- Have each student write out his or her name and address. Pair each student with another. Tell them they have to phone in their name and address to (country that speaks target language) in order to receive a free gift, but they only have enough money for a 90-second telephone call. Have them give their name, spell it, and then their address, spelling it also, to their partner. Stop them after 90 seconds, and have them compare the information their partner wrote with the correct address and spelling. Repeat with the partner dictating.
- Prepare a letter, gearing the difficulty and subject matter to the level of the class. Fill the letter with names, places, and so on, which will need to be spelled. Have one student as the boss, and the other as the secretary. (I usually make the student who is a weaker speller the secretary.) The boss dictates the letter, spelling any words the secretary asks to be spelled. Give the original to the secretary, and have her tell the "boss" what went wrong where, if there are errors.
- Buy several sets of magnetic letters for preschoolers, which should stick to most chalkboards. Put each set in a box on the ledge, and divide the class into teams, one for each set of the letters. Send one person from each team to the board. Define a vocabulary word, and the first student to find the letters and correctly spell the word gets a point for their team. Let the team coach the speller in the target language, but they cannot yell or stand up, or they are disqualified (this keeps things more manageable.)
- Learn ASL (American Sign Language) from a book in the library. As you say the letter, sign it also. This is a little "extra" for students who pick up on it: Visual learners will associate the sign with the letter. Hearing-impaired students will definitely love this.

FAMILY

What do you do after everyone has drawn a family tree?

- The first day of class, my students begin a "Me Book" by stapling together several pieces of paper. On the front page, they leave space for a photo and write their name and their French/Spanish/German name they have chosen. As they learn more vocabulary, they add to it their nationality, hair color and other descriptive terms, likes and dislikes. When we hit the unit on family members, they add their entire family to the book, one page for each family member. They may bring in actual photos or cut photos from magazines in the classroom—many kids' mothers seem to bear a strong resemblance to Cindy Crawford—and then describe their family in the same way they have described themselves. Throughout the first level, we add to the book, and it becomes both a graded portion of their final exam and part of their student portfolio. It is also something their classmates like to read during free time and is a good show-and-tell item for parent conferences.
- Give each student a different description of a person, asking each to draw that person (we often use whiteboards for this). Using their picture, they will then try to locate other members of their person's family. The descriptions they are given have carefully chosen characteristics (e.g., long curly dark hair, or a dimple on the chin, or ears that are long and large) that will help them locate the other family members by looking at other students' drawings. The descriptions will also help establish who is the father, mother, brother and sister. They then make up a story about their family (last name, where they live, etc.) and then introduce themselves to the class.

CALENDAR

- With very little difficulty, the days of the week can be sung to the theme song from *The Flintstones* in Spanish, French, and German. Try it!
- Show pictures, and have students name the month and the season. For example, a fir tree covered with snow and colored lights would be December, winter; a firecracker would be July, summer.
- Make dominoes: Cut colored paper into pieces of equal size. Draw a line down the center. Each one should have the name of a day of the week in English on one half and the name of a day of the week in the target language on the other (note: not usually the same day, but combinations such as Dienstag/Friday, lundi/Sunday, and viernes/Tuesday). Divide the students in teams, giving each a set of dominoes, with each student drawing four or five pieces to begin. Students should match the word in the target language with its English equivalent, moving in a straight line or to the side, until all pieces are used up. This could also be done for the months.
- Make a crossword, but with no clues. Fill in one month to begin, and have students fill in the others based on the length of the word in the target language, the letter "clues" that filling in other months have given them, and so on. I usually give this activity as homework.
- Pair students, giving them an envelope with the months written on little strips of paper. At your signal, they will open their envelope and see which pair can put them in order fastest. As a variation on this, the envelope could contain seasons and holidays to match, or months and typical activities for each.
- Pair students, giving them an envelope with the months (or days) cut up into "tiles" as for Scrabble. Call out, in English, a month (or day) and see who can assemble it, spelled correctly, the fastest. Let them call out the next one.
- In Four Corners, the teacher "labels," either orally or literally, the four corners of the room with the four seasons, and instructs the students to get up and move to their preferred corner, where they will

discuss activities to do during that season or weather that is typical during that time, food to eat, and so on.

- Make story calendars: Run off a calendar page for each one for the current month. Have the students cut each square so that it opens like a door in an Advent calendar, and then paste it to a blank sheet of paper. Under each door, have them write a sentence in the target language. Sentences could describe what they will do on that day, or they could make up a completely different story for each week, while keeping each very short and simple: On Sunday Juan got a bike, on Monday he rode it, on Tuesday he crashed, on Wednesday he was in the hospital, and so on. Then have them show their calendar to others in the class, having the partner name a date, and having the student open the door to the date named, so both are still practicing the vocabulary.

WEATHER

- Duplicate the weather pictures from your text (especially important, so students recognize them on the test). Make Bingo-style cards with the weather pictures on them, a different picture in each portion. Make several different variations of these cards. Beneath these, list how to say "Put," "square" and other words they will need for this activity. Also make blank Bingo grids, and envelopes with the weather pictures in them. Pair students, giving one a filled-out Bingo grid, and the other one a blank grid and an envelope. Student A will describe his grid to Student B, in the target language, until Student B has the same illustration. This is great for practicing prepositions: "Put 'it is snowing' to the right of 'it is sunny.'"
- SPONGE activity: Using the pictures from the text, make a transparency and cut apart the different pictures. At the beginning of class, ask the students to look at the screen and name the weather expressions. When you are ready, turn the overhead off, remove several of the illustrations and rearrange them a bit, and then turn the overhead back on and ask which ones are missing.
- This activity requires some clothing: Get donations from students, relatives, or go to garage sales or resale shops. Divide the clothing

into piles that have the same items in each pile. Divide the students into as many teams as there are piles, and have them number from one to four. Say a weather expression and a number, and the designated student must run to the team's clothing pile and select items appropriate to wear for that type of weather and put them on. The first team whose delegate is correctly dressed and who sits back down with the team gets a point.

- Have students take turns giving weather reports each day, using props. Don't tell them when their turn will come; draw names daily, so every day when they enter, they will check what the day, date, weather, and so on is. Have them begin with a greeting and their name, just like a weather reporter, and then report the date and weather. If you want, also have them give one item of news, such as "Today I am playing basketball" or "Today is Juan's birthday."
- Give students the weather map from the newspaper. Describe the weather and have the students write down what city you described.
- Have students in groups draw a five-day weather forecast, with a different type of weather depicted for each day, represented by a large symbol on the poster. Each day would also be labeled in the target language. Have students present their weather forecast, with the poster as a backdrop, and videotape.

NATIONALITIES

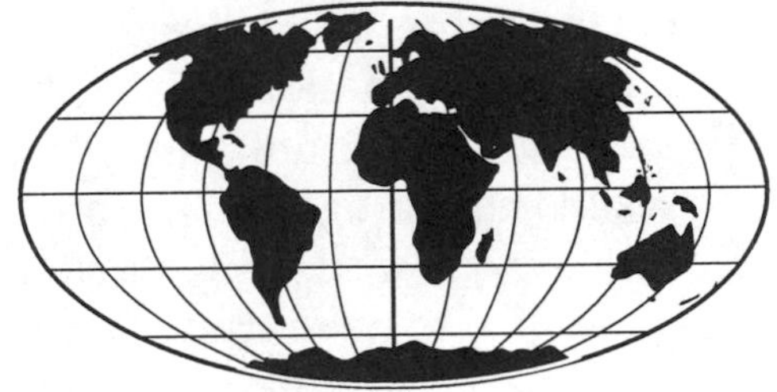

We all know how difficult it is to teach nationalities, due to students' generally poor backgrounds in geography. I wish I had a nickel for every kid who, when presented with the sentence, "Hilda is from Bonn. Hilda is_________," in which he is expected to fill in the nationality, looks at me and assures me he doesn't know of any city on this planet named Bonn. I have no real assistance for the geography problem, but here are some fun activities to add to your repertoire when practicing nationalities:

- Have each student select a different famous person, and then introduce themselves to the class. For instance: "Hello, my name is ________. I am from (city) and I am (nationality)."

- This is a great motivator for all ages, and especially for shy students. Give each a stuffed animal. For their animal, they make up a name, address, and nationality (plus any other information you would like them to practice.) Then, have them circulate freely in the room, introducing their "friend" to each other's "friends." Even the shyest kid will talk, because it's not about himself or herself.
- Another variation on the above activity is to make paper bag puppets. Buy inexpensive brown paper lunch bags and have students, either in class or as homework, decorate them with a face, arms, and whatever else they wish. I would suggest writing a good rubric for this activity (see the chapter on assessments.) Maybe you'd even like to have a beauty contest for the puppets, or prizes for most creative, prettiest, ugliest, and so on. Once each student has a puppet, have the class proceed as stated above: Invent a name, and so on. One advantage to these puppets is that they fold flat and may easily be stored, either in the classroom, or in the student's folder or book, for use during later chapters. For example, during the food unit, the puppet may be brought out once again to talk about food he or she likes and hates.
- My students really like this game, which provides for purposeful student movement and vocabulary practice: I call it Exchange Students. Each student quickly draws a strip of paper from a bowl. On the strip of paper is the name of a city. Give the students a few seconds, if needed, to find out what country that city is in, and then they stand and, in the target language, try to locate people of the same nationality. Please note the word "nationality." I make sure that each student has a *different* city, so that they must use the nationalities rather than the cities. This encourages a little bit more geographical knowledge, too, as I have overheard students saying, "I never knew (city) was in (country)!" I like to have students from the same country link arms as young people do in many countries, and have some sort of reward for the most numerous nationality (which is determined by the luck of the draw, as I always have more slips of paper than I do students.)
- I call this game Suitcases. I put the students in teams, swear them to secrecy, and give each team a nationality. They have overnight to identify (or to draw pictures of) some items that are typical for that nationality. For instance, for the nationality "English" students may produce Big Ben, a tea bag, a British flag, or other stereotypical items. Then, the next day, they show the contents of their suitcase, one at a time, to the other teams, with points for the first team to identify the nationality the suitcase contains, in the target language, of course. For even more vocabulary learning, have the students

name the items as they produce them from the suitcase in the target language. It's great TPR, as the item is displayed as the word is pronounced, and many kids will easily acquire new vocabulary well before it is introduced in the text.

- A similar activity is to play "You Don't Say" with nationalities. Give students cards with a nationality written at the top, and a list of places, people, and items that are typical. They read these clues one at a time, trying to get their partner(s) to say the nationality.

FOOD AND DRINK

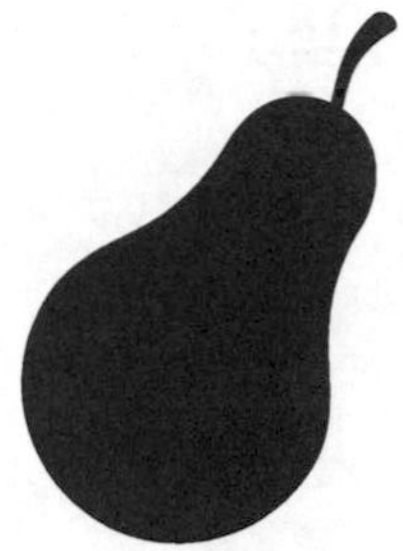

Tasting and cooking ethnic foods is a popular activity, and well worth the class time (see Chapter 2 for some recipes) but there are other authentic things to do that are just as educational.

- Have a Market Day. Have students sign up to bring a vegetable and a fruit or other food item (rice, yogurt, hard-boiled eggs, etc.) Make sure there are no duplicates. Give them a date to have these items in class (make it several days ahead to give them time to shop, but warn them not to wait until the night before.) They also need to have the name of the food and its cost on a card (changed to the equivalent in money from a country that speaks your foreign language), as well as a shopping bag or basket. On the appointed day, divide students into Shoppers and Sellers, and have them walk about and purchase food, either singly or in teams. When the activity is over, each must show the class what they have bought (in the target language, of course) and the vendors compare profits. Things such as grapes and berries may be tasted by all, and everyone takes home a purchase, with instructions to teach parents or siblings how to say it in the target language.
- Give students a quiet writing activity to practice this vocabulary (or as a game or a quiz or a journal entry.) Give them one point for each correct answer, and minus one for inappropriate ones. Try some of the following writing prompts:

- You run a sandwich shop. List the choices of sandwich fillings for your customers.
- Write out a shopping list for making a really fancy fruit salad.
- You are a chef. List what you might use for making an omelet.
- You are choosing a dessert at a restaurant. What choices do you have?
- I'm thirsty, and it's summer. What advice could you offer me?
- Doctors say a balanced diet has five servings of fruits and vegetables each day. List three days' worth, with no repeats.

However, I have had more success with more unusual writing prompts:

- Tell things you would never want to see/use in a sandwich.
- List all the people in your family, and a food and beverage each one hates.
- Make out the strangest possible menu for a meal (e.g., roast beef in raspberry jam)
- Write drinks that athletes should probably never drink.
- List all the foods that a vegetarian would despise.
- Make up the most colorful meal possible.

For journal writing, more open questions encourage higher-level thinking:

- I saw Godzilla, and he was eating…
- Holiday meals are always memorable, because…
- I visited a (French/Spanish/German/Italian) restaurant, and saw…

♦ This activity requires either plastic (play) food, or cards with large pictures of food on them. I have cut some nice photos from food magazines over the years and laminated them on colored paper, and these work well. Have everyone sit in a circle. Explain the rules to the class: You are going to hand out several items of food, evenly spaced around the circle. The student with the picture will try to give it to the student next to him, but that student will refuse to take it, saying, "What is it?" or "What is that?" The first student must tell the second what that food is, in the target language. They must repeat this conversational exchange three times, before the second student is allowed to take it. He or she then tries to give the food item to the next person. To make it even more difficult, send some items to the left, and some to the right.

CLOTHING

- Buy a bag of clothespins, and write the name of an article of clothing on each. There are several activities that use these clothespins. One would be for students to move about, pinning the clothespin on someone who is wearing that article of clothing. Another would be to provide a clothesline with the pins already on it, and to have students look through a bag of old clothes, hanging each item up with the pin with that article's name on it. (Toddler clothes are smaller and perhaps easier to use for this.) If a lot of old clothes aren't in your budget or storage capability, have the students look through magazines, cutting out pictures of those articles of clothing and pinning the pictures to the clothesline.
- Have your students look at classmates and jot down what they are wearing, then take turns describing each other's clothing. First one to guess who is being described wins.
- Using what the students are wearing that day, have them stand, and tell them to exchange any clothing possible, including accessories. They must keep track of who has their stuff. After a few minutes (use your judgment on how on task they are), have them stop, and report orally or in written form where their items are: "Mark has my left shoe, Anne has my right shoe, Bob has my watch, Mike has my shirt." The oral version of reporting has a slightly interesting aspect, as the person they gave it to may have given it to another person: "Mark has my shoe," to which Mark would reply, "No, I don't have your shoe; I gave it to Paul," which is not only a wonderful conversational simulation but which also requires the use of a direct object pronoun.
- Have two or three volunteers stand in front of the class for 30 seconds or so, then go into the hall or somewhere else nearby, and change three things about what he or she is wearing: take off jewelry, pull sleeves up or down, exchange shirts, and so on. When they come back into class, have the class tell you what is different.

- Play Name It or Wear It. First, you need to go to garage sales, resale shops, Grandma's attic, or other places to find a variety of clothing in outrageous sizes (from tiny to huge) and colors, preferably in styles that have long been obsolete. To play, hold up an item and name a student. If the student cannot name the item in the target language, he or she must wear it. After you are finished, have a fashion show. Maybe even take Polaroids, or use the snapshot to make a PowerPoint presentation for review. Some kids miss on purpose, just so they can model.
- A variation on Name It or Wear It is to get three volunteers to pull items from the bag. Holding the item up, they ask a classmate (or teammate) to name both the item and its color. If the student can do this, the item goes into a discard pile, but if they can't, the volunteer has to put the item on, somehow. Then after all the clothes have been taken from the bag, as a review of items missed, the volunteer will undress, and the group will name them again. If playing this with teams, make sure each team's bag has similar items.
- If you have learned the names for body parts, add that to the game. Tell them to put the glove on their head, or the shoe on their hand. After a few minutes, let students give the commands. For a treat, let them give *you* the commands.
- Send the kids to the Internet to buy an outfit. Every language has on-line catalogs with full-color pictures, where the kids can "shop." See the Internet section of this book for a list of sites.
- Have students stage a fashion show, but have your students help you write the rubric for this activity. Let them decide how many times each should talk, if everyone has to model, and so on, and you will get a lot more cooperation. Also, give them the option of doing the show live, using PowerPoint or on videotape; shyer students will thank you. Each show, however, must have a theme: winter, sports clothes, hippie garb, retro fashions, or whatever. Letting students have a say in deciding what is done has wonderful results; they have a firm recollection of what is required and do better shows, and you get to give more As on the results.
- Have a magazine Scavenger Hunt for clothes. Give students a list in the target language of things such as a red shirt, a green dress, blue socks, purple shoes, or whatever, and turn them loose with a bunch of old magazines to hunt for them.
- Post several similar pictures cut from magazines. Tell the students that one of these people has just committed a crime. Describe the criminal for them, using as many negative statements as positive ones; for example, He is wearing a hat. The hat is not black. He is not

wearing a raincoat. He is wearing a brown jacket, etc.. Have them help you "catch" the criminal.

- Have a more advanced class make a page of fashion "do's and don'ts," illustrated from magazines. This practices the command form of verbs also (or the subjunctive).

COLORS

TPR is usually the best way to introduce colors. Take sheets of construction paper in various colors and introduce the colors two or three at a time. Circulate through the class, asking students within reach to "Touch the orange paper" or "Point to the blue paper." This is a very low anxiety activity. Then, get another set of papers in the same colors and shapes, but smaller, and introduce the words "big" and "little"; introduce adjective placement as well. Practice again for ten minutes or so, wandering about the room, and, for your visual learners, putting a vocabulary list you have prepared beforehand on the overhead or on the board. Then try one of these activities:

- Play Elimination. Have the entire class stand. Draw a paper from a bowl full of strips of paper with the colors written on them. Students who are wearing this color may remain standing and others must sit down. If some sort of reward or privilege is connected to this activity, I find that the students who are "out" stay involved in their desire to monitor the honesty of the students who are still playing. Continue until most of the students are seated, reward the remaining students, and start over, or go on to another activity. They will beg to play this again. Be sure you replace the strips already used; the luck of the draw determines the winners (or a taste for wildly colored clothing).
- A wilder variation of Elimination, which has no winners or losers, is to call out a color, and anyone wearing that color has to switch seats. To make it more interesting, remove one seat so one student will be left standing. Let him or her pick the next color. To practice clothing, name a color and an item, e.g., "white T-shirt."

- Play I Spy: Say, in the target language, "I see something that is (color)" and have students guess what it is: "El globo?" "No." "El mapa?" "No," and so on.
- Bring in fruits of different colors, and teach the names and color of the fruits as you cut them up. Give kids pieces, as they tell you what fruit and color they would like to eat.
- Buy a bag of multicolored balloons, enough for each student to have one. At your signal, have them blow up and tie off their balloon, telling what color it is. Then, they throw it into the air, and bat it from student to student, calling out the color before they touch it. This gets pretty noisy (expect a balloon or two to pop), but kids of all ages enjoy it.

BODY PARTS

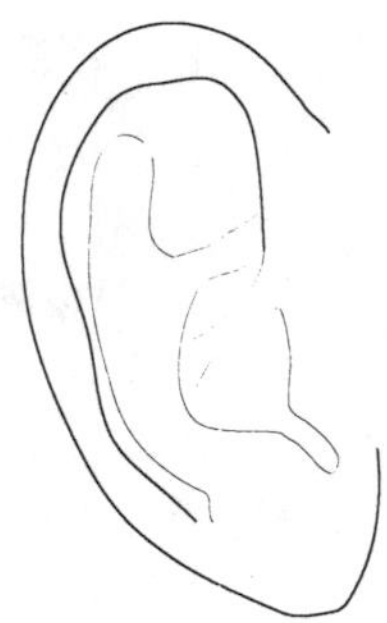
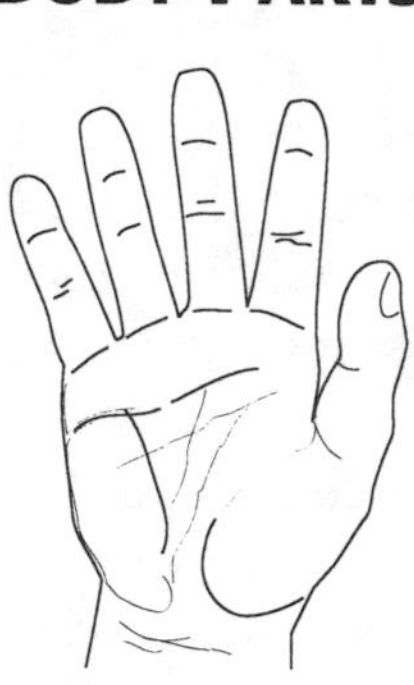
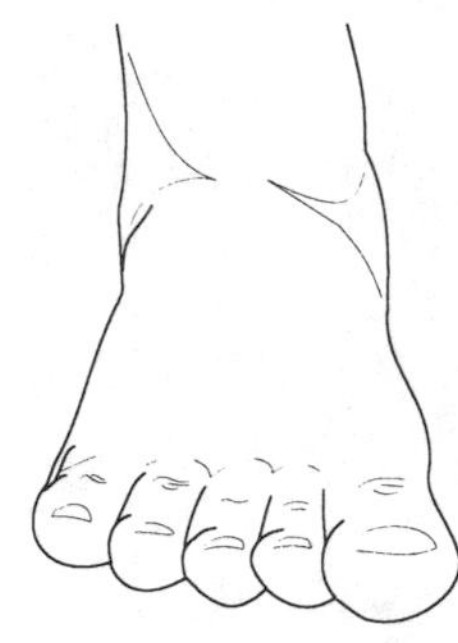

Besides Simon dice/ Simon dit/ Simon sagt:

- Take turns singing *Head and Shoulders, Knees and Toes* (to the tune of *There is a Tavern in the Town*):

  Head and shoulders, knees and toes, knees and toes (touch these parts as you sing),
  Head and shoulders, knees and toes, knees and toes,
  Eyes and ears, and mouth and nose,
  Head and shoulders, knees and toes.

  In French, the third line is rearranged so it rhymes: "Les yeux, le nez, la bouche et les oreilles." Sing this over and over, and faster each time. See who can sing it the fastest.
- Lead an exercise class. This will teach body parts as well as verbs, prepositions of location (up and down), and a review of the numbers. After this, it is fun to assign groups of students to make their own exercise videos, and then show one each day whenever the class needs a break from sitting (or at the beginning of the hour, especially first thing on a Monday when they are fairly lethargic). I even encourage them to use finger lifts, eyebrow raises, and other

silly things as a small part of the routine, because they practice the more obscure body parts.

- Have student volunteers go to the board. Give each a piece of chalk, blindfold them, and then have them draw a person. Have the other students in the class tell them what body part to draw. (They may also use adjectives: a big hand, a small nose.) The class is usually enthralled as they watch these masterpieces develop.
- Divide students into groups, giving each group a large piece of white posterboard or paper and markers. One of each group will lie down, and either you or a person in the group who the student trusts to do this will outline his or her body. Then, they color it and label body parts. Specify how many parts must be labeled.
- Using Post-It notes, have students write one body part on each piece, and then stick them onto the appropriate parts of a volunteer from their group. If he or she prefers, the volunteer may stick them onto him or herself. Give a certain number of participation points for this. Then, the volunteers go to another group, who removes and reads the papers aloud, checking the spelling and grammar of the other group. Points are given for finding errors, and points deducted from the group who made the errors.
- Make a collage "Frankenstein" of various pieces of people taken from different bodies, assembled, and labeled in the target language. This makes a high-interest bulletin board.
- Play Mannequin—Have a student volunteer to be the mannequin, and another who will pose him or her as you instruct: Bend the elbow, extend the finger, place one hand on the knee, and so on.
- If you are lucky enough to have a lot of old Mr. Potato Head pieces around, or can acquire them from friends and family, great! Otherwise, here is a substitute: using felt, cut out a head shape, ears, eyes, nose, mouth, and other face parts. Felt pieces usually cling together, especially if they are assembled on top of a desk or other flat surface. Using either set (the real ones, or the felt), have students assemble a person while you describe it. Or, have one student describe to a partner while the partner assembles it. Display a face with parts in unusual places, and have the students tell you where they should go.

PREPOSITIONS

- Hide the Pencil: Have a student volunteer give you a pencil or a pen. Send him or her from the room, and hide the object somewhere in the room. Have the student come back in and ask, "Where is the pencil/pen?" ("Wo ist...," "Où est...," "Donde esta...") The students answer using the prepositions: "behind Sam, far from the teacher, to the left of the clock" and so on. The clues may not repeat any prepositions; if one has been used, students must think of a clue using a different preposition. After five clues, if the student has not found his object, show him where it was, and let him or her select the next student volunteer. You can play, too.

- Give students a drawing of an empty classroom. Below it is a series of sentences telling what objects to draw, and where to draw them: "Put the book on the desk. Draw a map to the right of the window. Put a desk in front of the window." Use as many prepositions as possible. Have students compare drawings to see if they correctly followed directions.
- Try origami. Get a book on origami and tell the students how to make something. My two most popular shapes have been a bird that flaps its wings if you pull the tail, and a box that is flat when finished, but which you inflate by blowing into it. (We call it a balloon.)
- Get a map of Madrid/Paris/Berlin/Tokyo (any major city in the target language) and have students plot a route from a place you have predetermined to a major monument. If you have a laminated map, have them trade instructions and draw their route (following the instructions as written). Or, use a student volunteer and a copy of the map made into an overhead transparency. Have the volunteer(s) try to follow directions given by classmates.
- Tell students they must help a new exchange student at school. Giving each group a different class schedule, have them write directions from before school when the student gets off the bus, to each of his or her classes, and back to the bus at the end of the day. This also practices time expressions.
- Tape the directions from the preceding activity on a cassette and have students (using a walkman and headphones) follow a route through the school to a "treasure" (cookies?) you have hidden somewhere. I suggest not sending groups out all at once.

Activities that Work for Any Subject

Because we all know how to do board races, crossword puzzles, and word searches, here are some other ways to practice vocabulary and concepts covered in class.

Mobiles

Cut pictures out of any category: clothing, colors, food, family members, professions, animals, transportation, or whatever unit you wish. Paste them on cards, writing the word for the picture in the target language on the back of the card. Make an X-shaped hanger from dowels, pieces of coat hanger, plastic drinking straws or anything else rather stiff, and hang the items using thread, string, or yarn. Hang them from the ceiling, where they will catch the eye, and reinforce the vocabulary. Don't forget to take them down before the test, though.

HEAR AND CIRCLE

Write the vocabulary all over a paper, in both languages (English and target language). Pair students, giving each a different colored pen, pencil, marker or crayon. Call out the vocabulary: If you say it in English, they circle it in the target language. If you say it in the foreign language, they circle it in English. At the end, the student with the most correct circles wins.

HOT POTATO

Set a timer without telling the students how much time it was set for. Choose an item and hand it to a student. In order to pass it to someone else, the student must correctly answer a question. The student who is caught holding the item when the timer rings is the loser. To keep students on task, have everyone take notes or review their notes as the questions are asked. I suggest you place a time limit for answering questions, so that students don't spend a long time looking through their notes for the answer.

BLACK BOX OR POISON BOX

A variation on Hot Potato, with no timer. Give a student a box, telling him or her only that inside it is a slip of paper. Written on that paper is a task. If the student correctly answers a question, he or she may pass it to someone else. Once all your questions are used up, the person holding the box will open it, and perform the task. Examples of tasks: Go up to the blackboard and write your name, holding the chalk in your mouth, with your hands behind your back. Walk to the door and back like a duck, singing *Frère Jacques*. Sing or lip-synch a song in the target language for the class (or dance to a song).

ROUND THE WORLD

Prepare a series of questions or a list of vocabulary words. (You might even ask the students to submit these the day before the activity is scheduled or at the beginning of the hour as homework they turn in to you.) Give everyone a review sheet. Have one student either in the front or back of the room stand next to the person seated closest to him or her. Tell them you are going to ask a question, and whichever person says the answer first gets to move on to challenge the next person in the row, and so on around the room. Anyone who makes it all the way around the room wins.

TWISTER

Use the purchased party game mat, which works for colors, but can be converted, with words written on paper and taped to the circles, as practice for almost any vocabulary, as well as body parts and left and right.

CARAMBA!/FLUTE!/VERFLIXT!/DARN!

First, either type a list of the vocabulary words you wish to practice, leaving enough space between the words so they may be cut out, or print them on cards. (I use the Business Cards setting in my software, which spaces them for me.) Include one card with the word "Darn" in the target language for every four or five vocabulary words. Cut these apart, and place them in an envelope. You will need one set for every two teams of students. If you want, you can write the definition of the word on the back, or have the students do this.

To play, a student from Team A draws a word from the envelope, and Team B has five seconds to give the definition of the word (if the cards are double-sided, go with the side up as it is pulled from the envelope. If the side up is in English, they must give the Spanish/French/German/Latin/Japanese. If the target language side is up, then they give the English.) If Team B correctly translates the word, they keep it and then decide to either pass or continue. If they continue, Team A draws another word, and they continue to answer. Once a team decides to pass, the envelope changes hands, and the round is ended.

If Team B answers incorrectly, Team A has a chance to steal the word. If they successfully translate the word, they not only keep that word, they may take another from Team B's pile, and the envelope changes hands, with Team B reading the next word. If one team draws the word Darn from the envelope, the team they are reading to loses all the word cards it has accumulated during that round (it is important to keep cards from different rounds separate from each other), puts them back in the envelope, and the envelope changes hands. The Darn card makes the game unpredictable enough to keep one team from monopolizing the entire game.

A variation of this game that works for all levels is to ask the students to use the word in a sentence rather than provide a definition of the word. Using vocabulary in context is, after all, one of the main goals of the new National Standards.

CASINO

Have students take out a piece of scratch paper, making three columns labeled Bet, Answer, and Total. Then, have them number from 1 to 10 (or whatever number) down the side of the page. At the top, have them write 100 francs (pesetas, pesos, Marks, yen, etc.). Before you read the first question have them place a bet—any amount, but if they go broke, they lose their participation points for the activity (This way, they don't bet too wildly). After they have all written an amount, the first question is read, and they write down their answer in the answer column. Then, the teacher reveals the correct answer. If students answered correctly, they add the amount they bet to the original 100. If they answered incorrectly, they subtract that amount. This seems to get even the unenthusiastic students excited about reviewing vocabulary.

FORTUNE TELLERS OR COOTIE CATCHERS

If at all possible, give these directions in the target language:

1. Start with a perfect square of paper. Fold it in half, side to side, forming a rectangle. Unfold.
2. Fold it in half the other way. Unfold.
3. Fold it in half diagonally, forming a triangle. Unfold.
4. Fold in half diagonally the other way. Unfold. The paper will be very creased.
5. Fold each corner point into the center. Crease well.
6. Turn the paper over, so the folded parts are not visible. Again, fold each corner point into the center, and crease well.
7. Flip the paper back over. Slide the thumb and forefinger of each hand into the four open square flaps, bringing your finger tips inward to meet each other and voilà!

Now that you have the paper made, you must decorate them. As a child, we used these to tell fortunes: We would say a number, and then open and shut the device, alternately opening it keeping the top and bottom flaps together, and shutting it, then opening it again, keeping the left and right sides together, counting as we did so. On the inner flaps were numbers or nouns or adjectives, and when a choice was made among those visible, the flap was lifted to reveal a "fortune." Use your imagination: Write an adjective on the inner flap, with a profession below it—You will be a fast race car driver or a famous scientist. High school students get really creative with these. If you don't wish to use the future tense, have them "describe" objects: You have a green car or a mean dog.

PANCHO CAMANCHO/JEAN VALJEAN/WALTER DER ALTER

This game works for any vocabulary for which you have a picture card. Give each student a picture card, and have everyone stand or sit in a circle so everyone can see everyone else's card. Let's pretend the category is food. You start, by saying, "*Pancho Camancho come* (food that Student A is holding a picture of)." Student A would quickly reply that, no, Pancho Camancho is not eating (food A), he is eating (food that Student B is holding a picture of). Student B would continue by saying, no, Pancho Camancho is not eating Food B, but he is eating (another food). Of course, my French classes say, "*Jean Valjean mange.*" And German classes use Walter der Alter. This game works well for other things beside food. Action verbs are easy to teach using this: "Jean Valjean is skiing." "No, he's not skiing, he's swimming." And this is really helpful when you have to teach direct object pronouns (see Chapter 4).

JEOPARDY

Just like the game show. I have a posterboard on which I have drawn a 5x5 grid of large squares, and then laminated. Write questions on Post-It notes to ask the students to use the word in a sentence worth $20, $40, $60, $80 and $100, for up to five categories. Write the amount in large letters on one side of the posterboard. Divide the students into teams, and begin: One student (the one who got the highest grade on the last test, the one whose birthday is closest to today, or whatever) chooses a category and an amount. Remove the paper, read the question, and let the team that responds fastest answer the question. If they get it right, give them those points; I prefer using the chalkboard for keeping score. If they get it wrong, they lose that amount from their total, and another team gets a chance to answer. The team with the most points at the end wins.

$25,000 PYRAMID

Give students a category; they must describe to their partner things that belong to that category in order to get the partner to name the category. Or give the students a list of items, having them read them one by one as the partner guesses the category. A version of this, called Taboo, gives the student a list with the category and five words about it, none of which the student is allowed to use when describing the category. For example, the category is "dinner" and the student is unable to use the words *meal, plate, lunch, evening,* or *time* as clues to the category. This really encourages circumlocution.

FLYSWATTER

Write vocabulary words on a piece of butcher paper, on the chalkboard, or on a transparency projected on the screen. Send two students to the paper, giving each a flyswatter, plus a stern lecture on what will happen if they use the flyswatters on each other or the floor. Call out a word in English, and they compete to see who can locate and swat the word in the target language first. This also works great for irregular past participles (you call out the infinitive form), comparative words in Spanish, numbers, colors—anything that you could make flash cards for. To have more of the class participate, have more papers (and more flyswatters). The students don't even care about keeping points, they are having so much fun swatting (and learning).

HUMAN SWATTER

We use a sponge baseball bat that is very soft. Students sit in a circle, holding pictures they have drawn of vocabulary words. One student sits in the middle with the bat. To begin, a designated student in the circle would look at the pictures and say another student's vocabulary word. The student in the center would try to strike the picture (or desk of the student with the picture) with the bat *before* the student with the picture named says another person's vocabulary word. If the student in the center is able to do this, the student with that vocabulary picture must take the bat and the seat in the center. It is against the rules to swat humans, but it sometimes happens by accident; that's why the soft bat is important.

BATTLESHIP

Like the game, you start with a grid of squares. Students should have two grids: one for their own ships, and one for locating their partner's ships. Ten by ten would work well for numbers review, 15x15, or 20x20 work better for other subjects. Students draw in ships that cover two, three, four, or five spaces, horizontally or vertically (not diagonally). They should have four or five ships, if you are doing the 20x20 size. If you are doing topics other than just numbers, fill in the grids with vocabulary in categories, or don't fill in the grids: Instead, write numbers across the top and letters down the side (students would ask for space A-2, for example), or nouns at the top and adjectives down the side (students would have to make the adjective agree correctly to score a hit), or write verbs across the top, and subjects down the side (students would have to conjugate the verb correctly to score a hit). Student A would begin by requesting a square in the grid, and Student B would answer "Hit!" or "Miss!" Then it would be Student B's turn. If a student incorrectly answered a grid square, and that square involved a ship, that ship would then be unsinkable. To sink a ship, all two, three, four, or five questions have to be answered correctly. The first student in each pair to sink all his or her partner's ships would win, or the student sinking the most of his or her partner's ships would win.

SCAVENGER HUNT

Compete to see who can gather information the fastest. Make sure the list includes not only information to be found in the text, but things they may see posted in the classroom, look up in a dictionary, or ask you or a specified classmate (e.g., birthday, father's name, shoe size).

PICTURE GRID

Give students a paper with 10 squares. As homework, they must pick 10 vocabulary words and, for each, draw a picture. On the back of each picture, they must write the word. The next day, they cut these pictures apart, and arrange them on the desk. Their partner will then attempt to guess what vocabulary word each picture represents. If they are able to correctly guess and spell the word, they keep it. When one person's pictures are done, they trade roles. The one with the most pictures at the end wins. Afterward, reuse the pictures—have each student draw two, and create a sentence using them, and continue until they have written five sentences for you to look at as an assessment.

DICE GAME

Divide the students into pairs and give each pair some dice. The dice must have words taped over the numbers, or (this is easier) use a list of numbered words on the board or overhead to correspond to the numbers on the dice. For example, if the student throws two dice, getting a three and a two, they must make a sentence using word number 2 and word number 3 and dictate it to their partner, who writes it down. They take turns doing this until they have written ten to twelve sentences, which they hand in as an assessment. Putting the dice in small paper cups and having students throw them into shoebox lids saves a lot of chasing after dropped/wayward dice.

CONCENTRATION

Play this just like the old TV game. Approximately 20 to 30 numbered cards arranged in a square are chosen in pairs by designated students. If what is written on the back of the cards is the same, a match has been made, and the cards are removed, revealing part of a phrase written behind the playing surface (or a blank if that is a space between words in the phrase). If what is written on the back is different, the cards are turned face down, and a different student takes a turn. The student or team who correctly guesses the phrase written behind the cards first is the winner. As a vocabulary review, the numbered cards would, of course, have vocabulary words written on the back.

YOU BET YOUR LIFE

This is played like the Groucho Marx show. Pick a "secret word" from the chapter vocabulary, and write it on a card. Then have students talk, using the vocabulary list at the end of the chapter. The first to use the secret word wins.

A FINAL WORD ABOUT THESE GAMES

Some of these games take a lot of time to prepare the first time you do them. Either grin and bear it, telling yourself you'll have them for many years to come, or assign the students to make games as a graded project. They are just as creative as you are, and will undoubtedly come up with games that you and I would never have thought of that will be valued additions to your repertoire. Many of them will undoubtedly involve students kinesthetically, which at least half of the above do not do. Let your students come to your rescue. The more they do themselves, the more they learn (remember Glasser's research). You can always recycle their favorite games for other chapters by updating the questions.

USING WHITEBOARDS/MARKERBOARDS

Whiteboards are one of the most important discoveries I have made. They can be purchased from various supply companies, but a cheaper way to get a set is to go to a building supply store or lumberyard and purchase a sheet of showerboard—pressed fiberboard with a white, slippery coating on one side, usually used for bathroom walls. Have them cut the sheet for you into 20 to 24 (or more) pieces. If you tell them it is for your classroom, they may give you a break on the fee for cutting. The edges are not sharp at all.

Some people store their whiteboards on the rack under students' desks. Others punch holes in them and run a string through at least one hole, for hanging on the wall, or through two holes, for hanging around students' necks. I keep mine on an old teacart, along with the markers and erasers. Some teachers purchase dry-erase markers (or require the students to do so). There are also special markerboard markers that cost $4 or $5 each. In my room, we just use the darker-colored crayons. To wipe off the marks, many people use a bag of the unmatched socks they have collected over the years. These work well, but when I don't have enough socks I just cut up old flannel. Either way, it is quite easy to launder the whole bag occasionally. Crayon just melts right off the fabric and disappears. I also paint numbers on the back of my whiteboards for games we play, which are described in the next few paragraphs.

What are whiteboards for? Anything that can be done on paper can be done on a whiteboard, and somehow it feels more fun to do it. Here are some ways I use mine:

- Play Draw What I Say with body parts, clothing, and other vocabulary.
- Have students draw their favorite meal, and then hand the boards from person to person, having them "read" their board aloud.
- Have students draw a family member, listing some personality characteristics. Pass these around, having students compare this person to members of their own family. I usually make them write these comparisons on a separate sheet of paper.
- Ask students to draw something that represents them on the whiteboard. Have them share this with a partner. Collect the boards and line them up on the chalk rail, writing a number above each. Have students try to guess whose drawing each one is. (This is good at the beginning of the year, to get to know each other.)
- My students love to play Family Feud with whiteboards. I give them a category such as Dairy Products and 17 seconds to write (or any number that is not a multiple of 5). Then I call a number, and the student whose whiteboard has that number on it shares his or her answer. Anyone whose written response matches that answer gets a point (or a point for their team).
- Ask students to draw three items in a category: hobbies, clothing, weather, sports, foods. Then tell each student to take a card; each has two question words on it. Half the students stand up and move about the room to ask questions of the seated students about their drawing, using those question words. The seated students must respond. After a few minutes, have them hand their card to a seated student and return to their seats; repeat the activity.

- Add-ons. Have students all draw the same body part and label it, or write the same part of a sentence (e.g., a noun), or part of a meal, or one item in a room, then pass the whiteboard to the next student, who names/reads the first item and then adds another item. Continue until several students have contributed, and then pass the whiteboards around until each student gets his or her original whiteboard back. You can even write poems this way.
- Seat students in pairs, back to back. One student will quickly sketch a table with food on it/ a family member/a room in a house/a picnic with several different sports. Then, the student describes his or her drawing to his or her partner. When they are done, they compare drawings.
- Verb drills—call out a subject pronoun, verb, and tense. See who can conjugate the verb correctly, fastest; have them hold up their whiteboards. After a certain amount of time, hold up your whiteboard so they can check their answer.
- Start with one whiteboard per row of students, but everyone has a crayon or marker. Call out a verb and a tense. The first person writes the first person form (je/yo/ich), and passes it to the next person, who writes the second person form (tu/du), and passes it, continuing until all six forms are written. The first row that gets the whiteboard back up front for the teacher to check and that has all the forms written correctly wins.
- After assigning a translation, done individually, put students into groups, assigning each a sentence or two, and giving each group a whiteboard for each sentence they are assigned. They must share their translations, and agree on what to write on the whiteboard. When it is done, they put it on the chalk rail for the class to compare with their own translations.

PRONUNCIATION SKILLS

Too often we leave students to figure out the pronunciation rules of a language for themselves. I like to incorporate a short unit at the first-year level, starting on Day One, when students choose names. On that day, I teach that the letter "a" sounds like "ah" and "i" sounds like "ee." (The "i" rule would not be true for German, of course; perhaps German teachers would teach that a "w" sounds like a "v"and a "v" sounds like an "f.") We then read through the lists of names, pronouncing them, and notice that there are no exceptions to this rule. On Day Two, as the students enter, their first activity is to read the list of words on the board. These are words we use in English but which are from the target language (in my case, French) and which maintain the pronunciation rule taught the day before:

garage visa Adidas chalet fiancé

Spanish teachers might use:

patio adios taco piñata enchilada

We would then try practicing some other words that have a's and i's in them, but which are not used in English.

Every day I introduce two or three more sounds, and we practice pronouncing unfamiliar words with those sounds in them until the students know the pronunciation rules. I tell the students that they must be able to pronounce unfamiliar words if they want to ask about them: for example, ordering in a restaurant, asking for directions when lost, asking for a ticket to the movies at a multiplex. Then, over the next few days, I set up short classroom simulations where they need to do just that. Of course I, as the French person, don't understand them until they can correctly pronounce the word they need.

To forestall complaints that the foreign language is "funny" or "stupid," I like to share the essays by Richard Lederer (easy to find on the Internet) called *English is a Crazy Language I* and *English is a Crazy Language II,* as well as my own experiences teaching English in France as a foreign language.

- Give your students a copy of the Pledge of Allegiance in the target language (see Figure 3.1), but take out all the vowels. Say the Pledge for them, having them fill in the vowels. It is fun to see their faces light up as they begin to recognize what it is. When they are done, have them say it with you. Begin class with it at least once a week. Have them memorize it for extra credit. Follow this up with any poems, or other short sayings. Some private schools have students learn the Lord's Prayer. All can be found on the Internet.
- Teach pronunciations through songs. Find a song and play it for them. Then teach the words little by little. The ideal song is one that starts slow, and then gets fast. Students will be so proud of themselves when they learn to sing it. Then, and only then, show them the words in written form. They will immediately notice that some words are not spelled like they thought they would be, and will internalize some valuable pronunciation rules.
- The University of Maryland University College recently completed an excellent video on Spanish pronunciation called *Smile When You*

Say That. The tape is basically about shaping the mouth to Spanish sounds and listening for rythym. To find out more and about cost, write to Amy Addison at aaddison@nova.umuc.edu.

FIGURE 3.1. THE PLEDGE OF ALLEGIANCE

En Español:

Yo prometo la lealtad a la bandera de los Estados Unidos de America, y a la Republica que representa, una Nacion bajo Dios, indivisible, con libertad y justicia para todos.

Auf Deutsch:

Ich gelobe Treue auf die Fahne der Vereinigten Staaten von Amerika, auf die Republik, die eine Nation unter Gott ist, vereinigt durch Freiheit und Gerechtigkeit für alle.

En francais:

Je prête serment au drapeau des États-Unis d'Amérique et à la République qu'il représente, une nation sous Dieu, indivisible, avec de la liberté et de la justice pour tous.

In Latin:

Fidem meam obligo vexillo Civitatium Americae Foederatarum et Rei Publicae, pro qua stat, uni nationi, Deo ducente, non dividendae, cum libertate justitiaque omnibus.

DICTIONARY SKILLS

When I was in middle school, we would all get a dictionary, and the teacher would call out a word, and we would compete to see who could find it fastest, holding the book up in the air, open to be checked.

I have dictionary practice sessions. First, we go over standard abbreviations from the dictionary, for example, vt: transitive verb—I tell them just to know that v stands for verb. We also practice the abbreviations n., m. and masc., f. and fem., adj., pl., pret., and any others we will soon need.

FIGURE 3.2. DICTIONARY WORK

Translate each of the following sentences by looking up *not* the word in quotation marks, but another word that you could substitute in place of it (a synonym) and that would have the same meaning.

- I want to "get" a job.
- I need to "get" up earlier.
- I study to "get" ahead in school.
- My classmates "get" together after school.
- Tomorrow I "get" a new car.
- My brother said he would "get" me for that prank.
- My sister has the ability to "get" on my nerves.
- You need to "get" out your homework now.
- I "get" to go to a party tonight.
- We "get" into trouble sometimes.
- I'm going to "order" a pizza.
- I put my books in alphabetical "order."
- The teacher gave an "order" to line up.
- He "found" a wallet on the sidewalk.

The activity in Figure 3.2 teaches students to look for synonyms. This worksheet is usually followed by a writing assignment such as to tell me what they "got" for Christmas, or to list items they will "get" for their family.

The activity in Figure 3.2 leads us to another discussion: the fact that one word can have many meanings. We look up words such as "fork," which can be something you use to pitch hay or eat with (nouns), or an action that people do (verbs). We look up words such as "gun," whose listed translations will range from a cannon to a handgun, and learn how to double-check all words before we use them by not just looking in the English-to-French portion, but checking the one we decide to use in the French-to-English portion.

The next step is to learn how to take a verb and add "ing" and "ed" to it.

- Circle in pencil all incorrect word choices students have made using the dictionary, and mark with a "D" for Diction. Give them a second chance to get the right word before counting it wrong. Students who are forced to do this will be more careful in their future dictionary use, as it causes them extra work.
- Have students make unusual name tags. First, they write their name vertically. Then, they use the dictionary section of the text (or a

dictionary) to find an adjective that uses each letter, and add that. For example: Marc would write

*M*agnifique
*A*imable
A*R*tistique
*C*harmant

Your students will learn a lot of new vocabulary that day.

- Have your students start a "Dictionary" portion of their notebook, where they write words they had to look up, the sentence the words were found in, and an original sentence using the word. Writing them a second time, in context, and taking a little class time to review them (we often do this after a test, while slower students are still finishing) seems to be helpful. Require a certain number of words each grading period. This will also help you see words that many of them need to learn or review, providing useful feedback for future classes.

4

CELEBRATIONS

Celebrating holidays, birthdays, and other events according to the culture of the language you teach is one of the most enjoyable activities in the foreign language classroom, and often one the students remember best and comment on most. This chapter provides ideas and resources for organizing your own celebrations. I list these in the order they occur during the school year.

ACTIVITIES FOR ANY HOLIDAY

BINGO

Give the students an empty Bingo grid, have them fill in vocabulary typical for that holiday, and play Bingo (or paste pictures of typical holiday items in the grid for Picture Bingo). You can play for diagonals, four corners, a T shape, a full card, or whatever, just like at real bingo games.

POETRY

Have students write poems about the look or emotions of the holiday, or simply have them write a "listing poem" with the first letter of each line spelling out the name of the holiday, such as "Weinachten."

VOCABULARY WORD SEARCH OR CROSSWORD

Use vocabulary from the holiday.

MAD-LIBS

These are short stories (a ghost story, a description of how a holiday is celebrated, the history of a holiday tradition, and similar topics) in the target language with key words omitted and blanks inserted. Each blank has a description such as "plural noun," "verb in the future tense," "a boy's name," and so on. Have the students choose words for each blank, and then provide the story. The results can be hilarious! It also practices awareness of parts of speech, verb endings, and so on. See New Year's Day activities for an example of this.

VENN DIAGRAMS

Have students do Venn diagrams (see Figure 2.10, p. 57), which are two interlocking shapes, usually circles, but for Halloween it could be pumpkins, for Valentines it could be hearts, and so forth. Using these, have the students compare and contrast the American way of celebrating with the foreign way; customs both have in common go in the center area where the shapes overlap. This could be done in English or in the target language.

VIDEOTAPED SKITS

Have students videotape a skit of something that could take place on the holiday: a tradition, how to make a food, a song to sing, decorations, and so on. See Christmas for another skit idea.

INTERNET SEARCHES

See Chapter 7 for some important pointers on how to structure an Internet lesson. For every holiday, the Internet will yield many worthwhile sites, many of which have pictures. My students have decorated Halloween pumpkins on a Canadian site, looked at masks for Mardi Gras, and watched live parades for various holidays. Newspapers in the target language on the Internet will yield many articles for advanced classes to read and discuss.

If you're not sure what holidays your target countries celebrate, or want to look up some of the more obscure ones, try this Web site:

http://www.lonelyplanet.com

It lists all sorts of information on the countries of the world, including holidays they celebrate. Then, type the holiday into a search engine, and read up on it. French teachers will like Marie Ponterios's French civilization pages

http://www.cortland.edu/flteach/civ

(which has links to other holiday sites), or this one,

http://www.maison-de-la-france.com:8000/cgi-bin/festivals

(Fêtes en France).

HOLIDAYS

SEPTEMBER

September 5th is Dia de los Ninos Heros (Mexico), which is a day to read/learn about child heros, or tell about something brave each student did. Ask your librarian to help you find a book about a child hero.

September is also National Hispanic Month in the United States. Contact a local Hispanic group and see if they have someone who could come share the culture with a talk, slides, dance, food, or whatever.

Mexican Independence Day (Mexico) is also in September and is a good excuse to learn a bit about the history of Mexico. On the Internet, there's a great site that tells the story of Mexican independence in Spanish and that has lovely illustrations of Padre Hidalgo, Juan Diego, and so on:

http://www.mexicodesconocido.com.mx/hipertex/hidalgo1.htm

OCTOBER

Oktoberfest

In Germany, Oktoberfest is celebrated beginning at the end of September. This German festival typically features copious amounts of beer and Gemütlichkeit. Although the beverage won't be possible in a school situation, the songs, traditional dances, and clothing are possible.

- Use two squares of cloth and two strips of ribbon to fashion the traditional Lederhosen suspenders or the dirndl bib, and use safety pins to attach them to the clothing of students.
- Learn traditional songs such as *Du, du liegst mir im Herzen* or the *Schnitzelbank* song.
- Dance the Chicken Dance, a traditional German activity. The kids will love it!
- On a more serious note, this is also a good time to study Munich, via a movie, text, slides, or filmstrip.
- There are sure to be several Oktoberfest sites on the Internet, also, but be very sure to preview them before turning your class loose: see the cautions and hints in Chapter 7.

WORLD TEACHER DAY

Since 1994, October 5 has been the official World Teacher Day. Why not assign a teaching activity, or an activity that has students remember good teachers they have learned from?

COLUMBUS DAY

In the United States, the first Monday in October is celebrated as Columbus Day. Make cupcakes and decorate them with toothpick masts with paper sails attached, and the names of Columbus's ships; eat them, sell them as a fundraiser, or give them to the other teachers for some public relations for your subject area. Here are some Internet sites with information about the life of Columbus:

http://sunsite.unc.edu/expo/1492.exhibit/Intro.html

http://deil.lang.uiuc.edu/web.pages/holidays/Columbus.html

http://marauder.millersv.edu/~columbus/aod.html

http://www.cin.es/cafenet/etayo/def_Ing.htm

http://www.fordham.edu/halsall/source/columbus2.html

MAKE A DIFFERENCE DAY

October 24 is Make a Difference Day in the United States. This is an interesting possibility for community service–based projects. See Chapter 2 for some ideas about types of projects to do. A site about this day, in Spanish, on the Internet is

http://www.uasweekend.com/diffday/diffday_spanish.html

HALLOWEEN

October 30th is Halloween. Give students a list of Halloween vocabulary, which they look up and include in a "scary" rebus story (a story made up of pictures connected by words—for example, instead of writing the word pumpkin, they draw one). Then groups take turns reading these to each other.

Have upper-level students write or read scary stories. Have lower-level students draw monster faces. For French teachers, Canada's quebectel.com Web site has Halloween activities for French children (good for elementary level and up) that enable them to make pumpkins, read a scary story, print out a picture to color, etc. Halloween is spreading to France. Reports of costume parties and town-organized dances are becoming more and more common, and pumpkins and a few decorations are now sold in supermarkets. Several articles in English about this may be found on the Internet at:

http:///www.wfi.fr/metropole/spooks.html

or

http://www.paris.org/Ric/nov/01nov95.

For Spanish, why not teach the students some sayings involving Calabazas (pumpkins), such as: *Calabaza, calabaza, cada uno a su casa* or *Que te pasa, calabaza?/Nada nada, limonada*!

Translate one of the children's poems, such as *Three Little Pumpkins:*

> Three little pumpkins, sitting on a gate.
> The first one said, "Oh, my, it's getting late…"

Check the local library or see an elementary school teacher for some ideas. If they have actions that go with them, it's even better. Even my high school students like doing the *Eensy Weensy Spider* in French (not really Halloween, but spiders are scary!).

NOVEMBER

ALL SAINTS DAY (LA TOUSSAINT/DIE ALLERHEILIGEN)

November 1st, All Saints Day (La Toussaint/Die Allerheiligen), is usually a day for families to visit graves to weed and decorate the plots. They also get together and share fond memories of the departed. A variation for the classroom could be to each draw the name of a famous dead person, and "reminisce" about that person, what they did, and so on (see Dia de los Muertos below for similar activities). An interesting variation is for every student to research a famous person, and then write one fairly easy question about that person, and prepare a tombstone with the person's name, birth and death dates. The students will tape the tombstones to their desks and lay the questions beside them. Turn off all the lights, play some somber music by a French/German composer, and have the students do a Roam Around the Room, answering the questions about each person as best they can on a worksheet you have provided. Reward the student who gets the most answers correct. This is even more fun when done with the lights off, using flashlights, according to Betty Tacard (on FL-TEACH list), who does a similar project with her students.

DIA DE LOS MUERTOS

November 2nd is Dia de los muertos in Mexico. The Day of the Dead is one of the quintessential Mexican holidays, and many teachers enjoy celebrating it. Emphasize that in most countries, it is just a day to go to the cemetery and *limpiar las tumbas.* The Mexican celebration is not the universal Hispanic celebration, as charming as it is.

- For this holiday, there are several traditional foods: sugar skulls and skeletons, made of a sugar paste put into molds and decorated (you could use chocolate or Rice Krispies in the same molds—not as authentic, but easier); *pan de muertos,* or Dead Bread.

  Here is a recipe for sugar skulls:

  Ingredients for Dough:
  1 tablespoon powdered egg white (available at health food stores and supermarkets)
  ¼ cup water
  1½ teaspoons vanilla extract
  8 cups powdered sugar
  2 cups cornstarch

  Ingredients for Royal Icing:
  ½ teaspoon powdered egg white
  3 tablespoons water
  1½ cups powdered sugar
  3 drops red food coloring
  2 drops cinnamon extract
  3 drops blue food coloring
  2 drops peppermint extract

  Preparation:
  To prepare the dough, mix the powdered egg white and water together until foamy. Add the vanilla extract and pow-

dered sugar. With a spoon, and then by hand, mix until a firm dough forms. Dust a jelly roll pan with 1 cup cornstarch. Knead sugar dough in cornstarch for a few minutes until it becomes smooth and pliable. Roll the dough into a log shape. Wrap it in plastic and refrigerate it until chilled. I also pack some small plastic knives for cutting it in class. Cut into pieces about the size of a small fist. Use more cornstarch to prevent sticking, if needed. You can make a flat cookie-like version that looks like a skull, or mold around tennis ball-sized Styrofoam balls, available at any crafts store. Scoop out eye and nose areas with a blunt knife or a toothpick. Skulls traditionally have lots of big teeth, so draw them on with a toothpick. These are generally dry in one day, but allow two to be sure.

To prepare the royal icing, beat the powdered egg white and water together until foamy. Add the powdered sugar and beat until smooth. Divide the mixture into two small bowls. Add red food coloring and cinnamon extract to one and blue food coloring and peppermint extract to the other. Mix to blend the colors in each bowl. Fill two pastry bags with icing mixtures. Decorate the skulls with the icing. Allow objects to dry. Weather conditions affect drying times. Objects may take anywhere from several hours to 48 hours to fully dry. Makes about eight sugar skulls.

- Decorations usually include papier-mâché skulls and skeletons, marigolds (the traditional flower), and a traditional altar (*ofrenda*). The *ofrenda* must contain:
  - Picture of the famous person
  - Arch done in marigolds or tissue-paper flowers on a chickenwire frame (the scent of marigolds is supposed to help the souls of the dead find their way back to the living)
  - Sugar skulls (use recipe above, or substitute shaped Rice Krispies treats); These often have the names of friends written on them, and are traded like we trade Valentines
  - Pan de Muerto (a sweet, anise-flavored bread—for a recipe, lesson plans, and other activities, go to this Internet site:

    http://star.ucc.nau.edu/FLI/DDLM/Grade3.html
  - Glass of water (for the dead to drink)
  - Candles (to light the way back to the land of the living)
  - Tablecloth
  - Table with shelves (card tables with boxes on it will work, when covered with tablecloth)

- Fresh fruit, such as apples or oranges
- Nuts
- Items associated with the deceased or that the deceased would have liked

♦ Create your own cemetery. Have students select a famous dead Mexican or Spanish person, and create a self-standing *lapida* andi small *ofrenda* to place around it. The tombstone can be made from a shoebox, with biographical information written or painted on the bottom, and a stone or something placed behind it to help it stand upright. Have "DIP" (*descanse en paz*) on the top of each. Electric or battery-powered candles add a nice touch. Have a snack among the "graves," or have lunch there, like they do in Mexico, while students explain the items in the *ofrenda* or talk about their famous dead person.

♦ Make the *ofrenda* you would like to have made for your yourself; invent a future for yourself, and place items on the *ofrenda* that would be fitting for your future self.

♦ Crafts to do could include making papier-maché flowered skulls, tin art, tissue-paper flowers (marigolds), a clay censer (for incense). *Papel picado,* or paper cutting similar to three-dimensional snowflakes, is also a traditional craft:

  - Using 2–3 sheets of tissue paper (some use the same color, but they may use up to 3 different colors), line up the edges so they are fairly even and then staple together two bottom corners, which will eventually be cut off.
  - Do this separately for each piece of tissue paper used: Fold over the top edge about ½ to ¾ of an inch. Place a long piece of yarn inside the fold. The yarn should stick out of both ends by at least 3–4 inches. Tape or staple the fold to the back side of the project. (3 pieces of tissue = 3 folds + 3 pieces of yarn)
  - Using straight pins or tape, fasten the tissue paper (back side down) to a piece of cardboard.
  - Have students draw the design they want on another sheet of paper for practice and cut it out. This way the student will know if there are any problems with "holes" before using the tissue. Change the design as needed. Then copy it onto the tissue paper.
  - Using an X-acto knife, or scissors, cut out the design. Remove from cardboard, and cut off the bottom corners.
  - Tie pieces of yarn together to make the cutting three-dimensional, and string the cuttings up around the room.

An alternate way to cut out designs is to fold the tissue accordion-style 3–6 times (3–4 is best) and cut out the design.

- Face-painting is also a popular thing to do; skeleton faces are the most popular.
- Writing activities should include assignments to write *Calaveras* (poems) that take a light-hearted view of death. Write *Calaveras en Verso* about a celebrity or teacher at school. Illustrate them and then display them in the classroom. At the end of the unit, wear black (as though going to a funeral), or have a costume party, with the kids as famous historical Mexicans.

Some books and other resources:

Dia de muertos—dizfrazate y juega (ISBN #968-6135-81-2)
My Aunt Otilia's Spirits (ISBN#0-89239-029-8 (bilingual))
Dias de los muertos/Days of the Dead, a booklet by Associates in Multicultural Education, Chicago, IL, 1987
The film *Macario* and these Internet sites:

http://majorca.npr.org/programs/seasonings/MuertosPhotos.HTML (pictures and sounds)
http://fledweb.home.ml.org
http://www.northstar.k12.ak.us/schools/beh/srclasses/spanish/Muertos.html
http://www.niles-hs.k12.il.us/north/depts/forlan/sp/dead.html
http://www.forlang.utoledo.edu/bookmark/BookmarkSPN.html (see especially numbers 23, 16, 34, 49, and 50)
http://www.dayofthedead.com/
http://mexico.udg.mx/Tradiciones/Muertos/muertos.html

Independence Day in Panama

November 3rd is Independence Day in Panama. I have no activities to suggest, but it is an excellent opportunity to look at the history of that nation.

Celebration of Sainte Catherine

In France and Canada, November 24th is the celebration of Sainte Catherine, the patron saint of unmarried women. On this day, single females over the age of 24 make huge silly green and yellow hats, and wear them to advertise that they are "available." Some Web sites to check for more information on this unusual holiday are:

http://www.amba-ottawa.fr/presse/scolaire/fetes.htm
http://www.lodace.com/fete/c/caterine.htm
http://frenchcaculture.miningco.com/library/weekly/aa111797.htm

DECEMBER

ST. NICOLAS' DAY

December 6th is St. Nicolas' day in Germany and France.

- Have students put their shoes outside the room and ask one of the secretaries to put some candy in each shoe. While they are doing this, introduce Christmas carols as an activity, or decorate the classroom.
- A French tradition my students like is to pour a thin layer of lentils or wheat in a dish and water them. In a few days, they sprout. Traditionally, these young green plants are part of the holiday table, symbolizing the coming of life in the middle of the cold winter. My students get to water and watch them grow, and we even have a contest to see which class's planting gets the tallest.

CHRISTMAS

December 25th is Christmas in the various languages:

http://www.geocities.com/Paris/LeftBank/3852/christmas.html

Why not have students write a skit based on the *Twelve Days of Christmas* song? You could be very traditional, or do school-based items (12 thumbtacks, 11 rubber bands, 10 hall passes, 9 detentions, and so on). This could be done live, or as a video, a Power Point presentation, a storyboard, or some other visual presentation. These can really be fun.

- Noël

Traditional foods for Christmas are the cake called a Buche de Noel. There are several good recipes for this cake in the archives on FL-TEACH (see Chapter 7 under French sites).

On the Internet, check out:

http://mistral.culture.fr/culture/noel/franc/noel.htm
http://www.quebectel.com/noel/ (Noël in France and Canada from the Ministère de la Culture; traditions and their origins)
http://www.laprovence.com/noel.html (Noël en Provence; includes photos)
http://mscomm.infinit.net/ency-voy/france/france.htm (Alsace and Provence celebrations)
http://globegate.utm.edu/french/globegate_mirror/fetes.html (Francophone Holidays and Traditions at Globe-Gate)
http://www.yahoo.fr/Sujets_de_societe/Fetes_legales/Noel/ (fêtes légales)

- Navidad
  - Make *luminaria*. The *luminaria* is the last in a chain of fires that light the way during *posadas*. I have read that originally tree branches were laid out stacked into a triangle, like a little fence. In the center was a fire. These were placed along the path that Mary and Joseph would follow (the Posadas).
  - Reenact the Posadas. Group the students into "houses" and have them take turns visiting each other's homes, practicing greetings, exchanging holiday wishes, and so on.
  - Make piñatas (I prefer to assign this as homework for extra credit, or to do as a club activity outside the classroom) and have the Posadas group carry them. Then break them!
    - For Internet sites about Navidad check out:

      http://cda.mrs.umn.edu/~ummspan/continuemos/lesson8.html (A Navidad lesson with other good links)
      http://teachers.net/lessons/posts/246.html (Mexican Christmas unit)
      http://langlab.uta.edu/span/tecla/Tecla13.html (Spanish unit)
    - Christmas song lyrics:

      http://gs1.com/www.Marlborough/SpanishChristmas/Spanish_ Christmas.html
      http://www.osmond.net/chill/christmas/carols/non-american.htm
      http://www.cyberserv.co.za/users/~jako/silent/Spanish.htm ("Silent Night")
      http://www.angelfire.com/me/music17/carols.html
    - Explanation of Navidad from Guadalajara in Spanish:

      http://www.gdl.uag.mx/eventos/navidad/navidad.htm
    - Christmas menus with recipes:

      http://www.hispanet.com/cocina/navmenu.htm
    - Night of the Radishes links:

      http://www.keva.com/oaxaca/dic26-3.htm
      http://www.jamesroe.com/rural/rabanos.htm
      http://mexico-travel.com/fiestas/events/rabanos.html
- Weinachten

For German classes, have each student read a German story or fairy tale and rewrite it into a 1990s version, using a minimum of 15 German words and at least two illustrations in the story. Alternate reading and singing *O Tannenbaum* and *Stille Nacht* or *Glöckchen Kling* (*Jingle Bells*). Make lebkuchen or gingerbread to enjoy.

- Other Languages

  http://www.ylw.mmtr.or.jp/~johnkoji/hymn/xmas/index.html (Christmas Carols—midis and lyrics in Korean, Japanese, English, and some in German and Latin)

JANUARY

NEW YEAR'S DAY

January 1st is New Year's Day. Here are some activities for the new year.

- Have students draw a symbol to represent their lives in this new year. Some examples: an arrow for a change of direction, a plus sign, a heart, and so on. Give them about five minutes for this, and have them discuss and/or explain the symbols and why they chose them.
- Write resolutions. For my lower-level classes, we have fun doing this as a Mad Lib–type activity: I ask them for an adjective in their own gender, a number, an object, a family member, a place, something they own, etc. and then we plug those into "resolutions" such as these (written in the target language of course).
  - I am going to try to be more __________ (adjective).
  - I want to lose __________ kilos.
  - I am going to buy __________ (object) for my __________ (family member).
  - I am going to visit __________ (place).
  - I am going to paint my__________ (noun).

  For the class that knows the future tense, I replace "am going" with that tense.
- January is "enero" in Spanish. Have kids match definitions with words that end in "ero," such as numero, mesero, sombrero, llavero, and caballero.

THREE KINGS DAY (LA FETE DES ROIS)

In Mexico, on the night of January 5th, children leave a sober, self-critical note assessing whether or not they have been good during the year, and listing the gifts they would like in case they were good enough. Here's an Internet site where you can send letters to the Reyes Magos and read letters from around the Spanish-speaking world:

http://www.3reyesmagos.org/

This would be a wonderful reason for them to do a self-assessment such as the one in Figure 7.1 (p. 175) to examine how they are doing in your class. Traditional foods on January 6th are *rosca*, a round cake encrusted with dried fruit (there is a small plastic figure of the infant Jesus inside, and whoever gets it must give a party on February 2nd, Candelaria), tamales made of cornmeal, and atole, a thick hot chocolate drink made with cornstarch.

In France, January 6th is Three Kings Day (La fete des rois). Here is a recipe for the northern-style *galette,* or King's Cake, which is baked with a small *fève* (I use a bean wrapped in tin foil) in it. The person whose piece contains the *fève* is king or queen for the day, gets to wear a plastic crown, and grants permission to other students to do things such as go to the restroom. I usually give the king or queen choices about what we do on that day, also (but choices between X or Y, not just a "what do you want to do").

King's Cake Ingredients:

2¼ cup flour
1 pinch salt
⅔ stick butter or oleo
1½ teaspoon baking powder
1 cup sugar
2 eggs
1 tablespoon almond (or vanilla) extract

Preparation:

Mix all together until the consistency of thick paste or cookie dough. Form into a circular shape, about 2 fingers thick. Insert the *fève*. Cut top in a diamond pattern and brush with a little milk. Bake at 350°F for 20 minutes or until golden. Cool and serve. Serves 20 (small) pieces.

Louis XVI's Execution

On January 21st, France celebrates the execution of Louis XVI. Why not stage a reenactment of it? One year, as an interdisciplinary project with the shop classes, we researched, designed, and built a small guillotine. Now, on this day, I bring cheese sticks to school, along with decorating supplies (coconut, those small colored sprinkles used on cakes, etc.) Each student has a statement to read such as would have been said at the execution, and then decapitates (and eats) the cheese stick.

February

La Chandeleur (Candlemas)

February 2nd is La Chandeleur (Candlemas, in English). On this day, crepes are the traditional food. Chef Paul Bocuse has a site with his recipe for crepes and an explanation about the French customs on this holiday (for example, the pancake-flipping races) at this Internet site:

http://www.gsquare.or.jp/bocuse/index-e.html

A poem is said on this day (a tradition similar to Groundhog Day in the United States): "A la Chandeleur / L'hiver passe ou prend vigueur." People look out the window, and if the weather is good, spring is on its way; if it is bad, there are six more weeks of winter ahead.

YAH-YAH MATSURI

Yah-Yah Matsuri is a Japanese festival that is held in early February. Have students take turns yelling "Yah! Yah!" and looking fearsome, as is the custom. Make some fearsome masks, after studying typical Japanese noh masks.

ST. VALENTINE'S DAY

February 14th is celebrated as St. Valentine's Day in all countries. Some activities are:

- Get a bag of those candy hearts with sayings on them (Conversation Hearts). Have each student take one, and translate what it says. (I usually tell students to translate the meaning, rather than just word-for-word. For example, "Honey Bun" should not be translated by the word for honey plus the word for bun.) Have them write the translation on a paper heart, and post the hearts on the board, and make valentines. I let students take them home for their mother, and send the remainder of our valentines to a home for the elderly in Canada, where they are really appreciated.
- Another fun activity is the Venn diagram one, with a twist. I have students draw a name from each of two boxes: one has names of famous men, and the other, names of famous women. Using the target language, and a Venn diagram, students then list the characteristics of both, putting the ones they have in common in the center. On the back of the page, I have them write a short statement of whether this "couple" is a good match, and why.
- For upper-level students, give pink hearts to each student, and have them write to "Tante/Tia (choose a name in the target language)" who gives advice to the lovelorn. Give prizes for the most creative problems. Then give each heart to a student in a different class to answer, with prizes for the most interesting answers. Staple both together for a high-interest bulletin board. Students will love reading these.
- Give students a sheet of paper with the names of all the students in the class, triple-spaced. Have them write the nicest thing about that person—either a compliment or a description of that person's best qualities. Cut these apart, recopying them to correct the grammar if needed, and give each person their envelope on February 14.
- As students enter, they get a card with a name on it. They must walk around to find their "match": Beauty looks for the Beast, Donald Duck for Daisy, Bert for Ernie, Winnie the Pooh for Tigger, and so on.

When they find their mate, both report to the teacher for the name of a real historical couple in the target language to research and report on (Abelard and Heloise, Don Quixote and Dulcinea, Paris and Helen of Troy, Goethe and Schiller, etc.).

- Have students describe themselves, likes and dislikes, favorite activities to do on a date, etc. Also have them choose an alias. Then have the class (or another class) read these, and match them up as potential dates. Post these matched sets, and watch the students eagerly read them.
- I organize students into pairs and have my advanced French students go to this Web site:

  http://poesie.webnet.fr

  and select a love poem. On February 14, they present these poems to each other and vote on the best poems. The winners receive a chocolate heart.
- Listen to romantic music, such as *Eres Tu*, and have students compete to see who can make up the most romantic lyrics.

FASCHING/CARNAVAL

This is a one-week celebration in France, Germany, Mexico, and Spain that features costumes, parades, and merrymaking. There are some really good sites on the Internet where you can learn about masks, watch parades live, and read about the history and traditions. A good site called Le Carnaval de Nice is at:

http://www.nice-coteazur.org/francais/index.html

The last day of Carnaval is Mardi Gras: a Tuesday 40 days before Easter (usually late February).

- Make masks from paper plates. Give each student a paper plate, and let them begin in class, but assign the finished masks as homework. On Mardi Gras, give prizes for the funniest, most beautiful, most creative, and other categories.
- Have food; fried foods are traditional Mardi Gras foods. My classes make crepes, eat a few, and sell the rest at lunch time (we use the money we earn to fix a big several-course French meal later in the year as part of a food unit, researching recipes in French cookbooks, etc.). Eggs (hard-boiled and served like deviled eggs, or baked into a special bread) are also traditional.
- We watch a movie about Mardi Gras, and I give each student a doubloon or a string of Mardi Gras beads purchased from a mail-order catalog.

- Have a parade through the school: use old shoeboxes as "floats" and have students decorate them. Have floats illustrate aspects of the target culture, or choose a theme. Wear masks for the parade.

MARCH/APRIL

DR. SEUSS'S BIRTHDAY

March 2nd is Dr. Seuss's birthday. I either have my students spend some time reading little children's books in French that I have collected over the years, or take them to one of the elementary schools to read to the children.

FIRST DAY OF SPRING

March 21st is the first day of spring. Celebrate by taking the class outdoors for a scavenger hunt. Each group should have a list, a paper bag, a dictionary, and a watch. Give them about half an hour to find as many items as possible from a very specific list of things such as "three smooth stones," "a green leaf," and so on. Count out the items in French as you check them, and have a prize for the winners.

NATIONAL FOREIGN LANGUAGE WEEK

National Foreign Language Week is usually held in March. Some activities for the week are:

- Label the room in the target language, and as much of everything else in the school as possible. We put a sign on every room to identify the teacher and the subject(s) taught, in French. Make posters about famous people from your language, and post them around the school.
- Talk to the cafeteria employees in advance, and arrange a menu of foreign food for one day that week (tacos, quiche, sauerkraut and sausages, egg rolls).
- Have high school students prepare a play, skits, video, or craft to present at the middle school or grade school (or on the televised announcements at their own school).
- Put a treat in each teacher's mailbox with a note, or have students prepare some ethnic food to leave in the teacher lunchroom.
- Try to schedule a movie, musical performance, or speaker for interested students some time during that week.

EASTER

Easter is celebrated worldwide. Here are some Easter activities:

- On the Internet try this site:

  http://www.geocities.com/Paris/LeftBank/3852/easter.html

  for French and German activities and games using Easter vocabulary.
- Buy plastic eggs and have a treasure hunt through the school, with clues hidden in the eggs.
- Fill plastic eggs with vocabulary the students have been studying. Have them write a story using all those words in the story.
- Fill plastic eggs with pictures representing vocabulary, and have students write rebus stories, trade them, and read them aloud to each other. When they come to a picture, they say the word it represents (good vocabulary review).
- Have students write what they are going to do over Easter vacation, put it back in an egg, and then draw one to read, and guess who wrote it.
- Have students write a command and put it in an egg. Have each person draw an egg, and do what it says to do.
- Put a small object in each egg. Tell students it is not just an ordinary toothpick/paperclip/ribbon (whatever) but that it has special powers. Have them tell what it is, what it does, and how they will use it (future tense). Alternate idea to use past tense: tell students each object was used in a crime. Have them describe the crime orally, or write out the police report or newspaper article about the crime.
- Put a small object in each egg. Have students try to sell these objects to the class, convincing them that they really need that object. Have the class evaluate who does the best job.
- Print an egg shape on paper, and give each student one. Have them get in groups, assign the group a last name, and let them decide which family member each egg will be, and decorate it appropriately (e.g., Papa might have a mustache and golf club). Below the picture should be a short biography: name, age, likes, and dislikes. Display each family on the board, each in their own paper "basket."

EARTH DAY

April 20th, Earth Day, is celebrated internationally. Some Earth Day activities are:

- Plant something outdoors in the name of your foreign language club.
- Do an Internet search for articles about Earth Day.

- Read articles about pollution or environmental concerns in countries that speak the target language. Write letters to the leaders of these countries about these concerns.
- Make posters that say "Save the Earth" and similar slogans in the target language, and decorate the school.

GOLDEN WEEK

April 27 to May 6 is Golden Week in Japan. This is actually three holidays rolled into one. First, the Japanese celebrate Green Day (try some of the Earth Day activities from above). Then comes Constitution Day. For this, study/read parts of the Japanese constitution. Do a Venn diagram to compare the Japanese constitution to ours. Look at the history of Japan and the events that led to the writing of its constitution. The third holiday is Children's Day. If possible, invite grandparents to class. Have the children bring them tea, and have small gifts ready for the grandparents to give the children. Sing songs.

MAY

INTERNATIONAL LABOR DAY/LE PREMIER MAI

May 1st is International Labor Day (Le premier mai in France). Some activities for May 1st are:

- On this day, workers all over the world enjoy a day off and parade through the streets. This would be a good day for a minilesson on careers.
- Make Cootie Catchers (see Chapter 3) and put careers on the innermost portion, adjectives on the outside flaps. When students pick a number, they will be told their "future": "You will be a tall architect" or "You will be a thin boss."
- In France, it is traditional to offer a bouquet of *muguets* to those you love. Have students make a card for someone with a drawing of lilies of the valley on it.
- A maypole dance to welcome the spring is also traditional on this day.

MOTHERS' DAY

May 10th is Mothers' Day in Mexico. The holiday is celebrated the third Sunday in May in other countries. Make a card or a small gift for Mom. An *ojo de dio,* a paper flower, some *Scherenschnitte,* or similar projects are easy to do.

GRADUATION/END OF YEAR

- A final project could be a student yearbook: Each student gets a page to put poetry, stories, or whatever about him- or herself. Seniors are required to write a "will." Also have a page for foreign language club activities and pictures, and teams and activities the students are in. Photocopy and staple these, and hand them out on the last day. Have them sign each other's books (in the target language, of course).

- Have students write about themselves (in future tense): "Ten years from now, I will be...." Or stage a "class reunion" and have them pretend to be themselves, and talk about what they have been doing since high school.
- Put up baby pictures, and have students guess who it is. The owner of the picture can type three to five clues.
- Make a video or PowerPoint presentation that includes the highlights of the year and a short interview with each student (wishes for the class, or whatever they'd like immortalized).

MISCELLANEOUS CELEBRATIONS

QUINCEAÑERAS

Here is a Web site that has interviews with different women about their 15th birthday celebration, usually celebrated in Mexico with a large party and other traditions:

http://clnet.ucr.edu/research/folklore/quinceaneras/

SAINTS' DAYS

Use a Catholic calendar and have students choose a Saint's Day during the time they will be in your class. On that day, give them a card, have other students compliment the student whose day it is, let them lead a game or choose an activity for the class, or make some small fuss over the student, just as they would do in countries where the target language is spoken. (Be careful, though, not to be seen as promoting religion.)

5

GETTING OVER THE ROUGH SPOTS

We all have topics that we must teach, but that we dread yearly as the time approaches to begin teaching them. There's no coincidence that the majority of these situations involve verbs. In this chapter, I offer some ways that I and several colleagues have tried that have worked for us, and that could add some variety to the way you cover the same topics.

GENERAL VERB CONJUGATION ACTIVITIES

- Use the whiteboards described in Chapter 3. Just writing on whiteboards makes verb drills more "fun." Give students a subject, a verb, and a tense, and let them go.
- Use two dice, preferably different colors, and a stack of 3x5 cards with verbs written on them. A student draws a verb, and throws the dice. One die will decide which subject pronoun they use (put a chart on the board or overhead: a 1 means I/je/yo/ich, and so on) and the other is the tense (1 for present, 2 for command, 3 for preterite/passé) or, for first year, list 6 infinitives. If the student writes the verb correctly, he or she or the team gets a point.
- Inside-Outside Circle: Place students in two circles, with the inner circle facing outward and the outer circle facing inward, pairing students. Give the inner circle students cards with subject pronouns on them, and outer circle students cards with verbs written on them. Students look at each other's cards and say the correct form of the verb in the tense you are working on. You may wish to designate which students should say the verb, or have them work together to do this. Then, either have the students rotate to a new partner, or have them pass the cards to the left (or the right) to have a new situation to deal with.
- Play Beanbag. Take a soft beanbag or similar object (my colleague Cynthia Jones uses a beach ball). The person who begins says first

person singular form of a verb in a given tense, and tosses the bag/ball gently to another student, who gives the next form (second person singular). When all forms of that verb have been correctly stated, you may start over and speed up the throwing, or change to a different verb. Because students don't know who will get picked next, they are all on task, thinking of the next form.

- Put students in rows of five or six. Give the first student a paper. Say a verb. The first student writes the je/yo/ich form, passes it to the next who writes the tu/du form, and so on. It's a race. Rotate students each round, so they get to practice different forms.
- Play reverse hangman. Name it anything you want: I usually pick an animal, but sometimes we draw a car or a house, depending on what chapter vocabulary we are working on (I tell them what parts to draw). Send one person from each team to the front of the room. The first to correctly write a designated verb form (or correctly conjugate the verb completely in a specific tense) can draw a part of the animal or object. The first team with a complete picture wins.
- Have students write daily in a journal on a topic of your choice. If you are working on the preterit/passé tense, have them tell something they did, or didn't, do. If you are working on the imperfect tense, ask them about grade school or middle school habits, likes, or dislikes. If you are studying the future, talk about vacation plans, and for the subjunctive tense, provide the beginning of a sentence such as "It's important that…" and have them also tell a reason why.
- Crossword puzzles are great, because if the verb is spelled incorrectly, it won't fit on the puzzle grid (which provides immediate feedback). Make the clues sentences with blanks where the verb would go, and after doing the puzzle, translate the sentences so the verbs are used in context.
- Use that most powerful of all reinforcement tools: music. Find a song that uses the verb tense or grammatical construction you wish to feature, and have the students learn it. "Que Sera, Sera" is good for the Spanish or French classes to remember the future of "to be," for instance.
- This one is from Faye Conway of Henrico County Schools in Richmond, Virginia. Choose teams of five to six students. Write five to six verbs on the board in columns. Have an entire team go to the board; each team member stands under a verb. You call out a subject such as "tu" and everyone should write the tu form of the verb that they are standing under. Then everyone moves to the right with the student on the end moving to the position of the first verb on the board. You continue calling out subjects until you have covered however

many conjugations that you wish. When the team sits down you calculate how many correct verb conjugations you have, giving them a point for each one. The next team goes to the board and you proceed in the same fashion as explained above until all teams have had a chance at conjugating the verbs. Whichever team has the highest score wins. You must enforce the rule that the students may not change another student's answer. You should also limit the amount of time given to write to 10 to 15 seconds.

FUTURE TENSE

- Use Concept Attainment for this or any other verb tense: Challenge the students by telling them you'd like to see how smart they are. Write the verb tense on the board; use regular verbs only and compare or contrast them with a tense with similar endings (I use present when teaching the future). Do this until their body language tells you they have a theory about how this tense is formed. Then give them some irregular verbs to look at. Then give them four or five sample verbs, and have them tell you if each is or is not correctly written for the new tense. Then ask them, with a partner, to formulate a rule about how to form this tense. Test the theory with a few more examples on the board, and then debrief: Have them explain the thought process they went through to come up with the theory. This step is *very* important, as it will more firmly implant the verb form in their mind. Finally, ask them to generate a few examples, and check these for accuracy. This can halve the time it takes to cover a new verb tense. I recommend it highly.
- For irregular verb stems, try to make up mnemonics. A good one I remember from my studies of Spanish was a way to remember *decir* and *hacer:* think of Clint Eastwood and remove the "CE" (his initials) from these two infinitives to get the future stem: decir → dir and hacer → har, for "Dirty Harry," one of Clint's famous roles.
- For French, I dress as a gypsy, set up a small booth covered with starred fabric, and tell my students' "future" (read their palm), announcing that my name is Madame R.... They all remember that name, and that helps them remember that all future stems end in an "r." They also hear and write down their future (in the future tense, of course).
- See the description in Chapter 3 of Cootie Catchers, which are used for predicting the future. Your students will be speaking in the future tense quite willingly when they use these items.

REFLEXIVE VERBS

- Try the following Learning Stations activity:
  - Station 1: Have students cut out (from old magazines) a picture of a reflexive activity, paste it to their paper, and label it correctly.
  - Station 2: Using a tape recorder and headphones, have students listen to a tape containing 10 reflexive verbs in sentences. On their answer sheet, students must rewrite the verb they heard on the tape with the new subject indicated (either by you on the tape, or printed on the answer sheet with a blank next to it).
  - Station 3: Given a list of verbs and a subject, students have to write a short story using all the verbs.
  - Station 4: Students pair up, with each pair taking a set of flash cards. They take turns timing each other as they pair each verb up with the card with its translation on it (or, take turns quizzing each other using flash cards with English on one side and the target language on the other). They write the score and initial it on the answer sheet.
  - Station 5: Using a set of cards, play Go Fish, either collecting a verb in all its forms (five or six verb forms, depending on whether you use *vosotros* in Spanish), or matching a verb and a sentence, or a reflexive verb and an object (for instance, to brush teeth and toothpaste).
- Using a Polaroid or a digital camera that takes pictures onto a computer diskette, assign students to take pictures that illustrate various reflexive verbs. Make this into a PowerPoint presentation (see Chapter 7), or post the pictures, now numbered, around the room, and have students do a Roam Around the Room, writing down what activity they see in each picture, in the target language. This seems to work much better than using the pictures from the text, because they are all involved!

SUBJUNCTIVE

- One of my favorite subjunctive illustrations is to ask what the past tense of "I am " is. After eliciting "I was," we all sing the Oscar Mayer song *Oh, I wish I were an Oscar Mayer weiner*.... That also firmly fixes the use of the subjunctive with wishes and desires.
- A good mnemonic for this tense is UWEIRDO:

  U—uncertainty
  W—wishing, wanting
  E—emotion

I—inquiry/impersonal
R—request
D—doubt
O—order

Or the one devised by Theodore E. Rose at the University of Wisconsin-Madison for Spanish:

W—wishing, wanting
E—emotion
D—doubt
D—denial
I—in certain phrases (impersonal expressions)
N—necessity and need
G—grief or guilt

After introducing either one, go through the phrases that use subjunctive and list them next to the letter they belong with. Then practice writing sentences using them.

- Once students have learned the subjunctive, have them practice it using Inside-Outside Circle. Have them stand in two circles, with the inner circle facing outward, and the outer circle facing inward, pairing the students. Give the inner circle each a "story" to read, usually a Dear Abby–type one such as, "I asked two people to the dance, and they both accepted. What should I do?" The outer circle members each have a card with a phrase that requires the subjunctive, such as "It's necessary that…" which they must use when giving advice. You can either have the circles rotate after each exchange, providing new partners, or simply have them pass the cards to the next person (or the person to their left in the opposite circle). Figure 5.1 lists some of the situations I give for this activity.
- Use music to reinforce this verb tense. It is fairly easy to find songs using the subjunctive. (I like *C'est bon que tu sois là,* among others.) Provide students with one of the following:
  - The lyrics to the song, with the verbs removed. In the blanks, have them write the verb in the subjunctive.
  - The lyrics to the song, cut into strips. As they listen to the song, have them arrange the strips in the correct order.
  - The lyrics to the song, with verbs removed, and listed in a box above or to the side. Have them guess which ones go where, and then play the song to check.
- Have the student write a story, with a prize given for the one that correctly uses the most subjunctive verbs. Give the winning story to the class to read.

FIGURE 5.1. "DEAR ABBY" SITUATIONS FOR ADVICE IN THE SUBJUNCTIVE

A. I have invited two people to go to the dance, and they both accepted. What should I do?

B. I like to sing, and I want to become a superstar. What can I do?

C. I have a crush on a guy/girl, but I'm shy. What should I do?

D. My two best friends want to get married. What advice should I give them?

E. I want to get a better grade in (name of class). What could I try?

F. I had an accident in my dad's car. What should I do?

G. I had a big party at my house last weekend, and we broke a window.

H. I want to learn how to dance better.

I. I want to go to the concert, but I don't have any money right now.

J. I want to go to France. Do you have any advice for me?

Advice Cards:

1. It is important that....
2. It is doubtful that you...
3. I am happy/sad that....
4. I want you to...
5. It is possible that...
6. I'm surprised that...
7. I insist that...
8. I'd like you to...
9. It is necessary that you...
10. I prefer that you...
11. It's normal that...
12. It's essential that...

- Show a movie. My class recently watched *Manon des Sources* and found many subjunctive verbs in it. I kept a running list on the board as they watched, and then we read them, and said where each had occurred in the movie—a good review of both the film and the verbs.
- Give students a simple story that frequently uses the subjunctive tense. Have them replace several underlined verbs with more "colorful" verbs. This is a dictionary-using, vocabulary-building activity I like to do with my upper-level classes.
- Have students plan a trip to a place that speaks the target language, suggesting what to take, where to go, what to do, what to eat, what to see and so on.
- Play a version of Go Fish: Give students pictures of objects. Student One says, "I think you have the cat"(present tense), to which Student

Two either says, "Yes" and hands over the card, or replies, "I doubt that I have the cat" (if they don't have it) using the subjunctive. This practices verbs of doubt, as well as object pronouns.

- Have students write 10 sentences in the present tense: I play tennis, I eat pizza, and so on. Then on the overhead place 10 phrases that require the subjunctive: It's important that, I don't believe that, I wish that, I'm happy that, and so on, and have students rewrite the sentences in the subjunctive, beginning number one with phrase number one, and so on.

PRETERIT/PASSÉ COMPOSÉ

- Use the Concept Deduction method; post examples of the new tense, asking students to see if they can figure out how it is formed. Check understanding by asking them to write a few examples. They'll have it in minutes.
- For passé composé with être, I have a lot of luck using the song two colleagues in Fort Wayne, Indiana, gave me several years ago (sung to the tune of *Yankee Doodle*):

  allé, parti, sorti, venu, descendu, retourné, arrivé, resté, monté, tombé, entré, né et mort

  devenu! revenu! rentré! passé!

  This last line can be chanted like a rah! rah! cheer. I have also added gestures with each verb, which help students remember what the verb means as well. I let the students decide on the gestures, so they have some ownership of the activity; this has made a lot of difference in the speed with which they learn this concept.

IMPERFECT VERSUS PRETERIT/PASSÉ COMPOSÉ

- My favorite lesson, either to introduce or review, is one in which I provide a brief story in the past tense, with its sentences scrambled, and ask students to categorize them by sentence topic. After this is done (and yes, I often have teams that have categories called "miscellaneous"), we look at each sentence in a particular category, for example, "Moving around" and discover that, within that category, they are all in the same verb tense. Then I ask them to group the categories by verb tense, and rename the resulting categories: a wonderful way for them to discover that, in French, the passé composé tense is used for action, and the imparfait tense is used for descriptive passages. After we voice this generalization (I say, "Look at these two groups and make a general statement about each"), we evaluate our statement by trying it on a new story, *Le Petit Chaperon Rouge* (*Little Red Riding Hood*), predicting what tense each verb would be in if it were told in the past tense, and checking our answers afterward. Using Concept Development and letting them find out for themselves how these tenses work has cut the time I need to teach this unit practically in half, with much fewer practice activities needed because they found it out for themselves instead of my simply telling them. Even though a lot of time was spent in the discovering, their ownership of the concept was much more permanent and better understood by them.

- On a similar note, you could have the student write their own short stories, using elements the class decides on (e.g., a banana, a sports car, and a blue raincoat) to reinforce the rules on using these two verb tenses.
- Arrange an "incident." This can be done in a variety of ways. If you have an upper-level student that you can borrow for a few minutes, arrange for them to enter your classroom and do something outrageous. Scream at the student, throw something (or another action very out of character for you), escort them to the door, turn and, smiling, tell the students that they are reporters who must now write down what they have seen. Another variation is to get a colleague, staff member, or other adult (or two) to enter the room dressed as strangely as possible and act strangely. Leaving this up to colleagues, I have had two people chase each other through the room, shooting cap pistols, a person in medieval armor writing *Bonjour* in pink on my chalkboard, a princess who handed me a rose and gave me a kiss on the cheek, and other odd behaviors. Once again, the students use the imperfect for descriptive sentences, and preterit/passé composé for actions.

  A third variation that I have tried is to enlist class members. Give each a slip of paper with an action, and tell them to do this action continuously until you tell them to stop. Have one eat or drink something, another dance or sing, or other actions. Then, tell them to stop. The class will then need to realize that the class members' "ongoing" actions are in the imperfect, while your command to stop and sit down were in the preterit/passé composé.

  There is nothing like real-life experience to bring home how to use these two tenses.
- For another real-life experience, take a short field trip. We go "uptown" to the coffee shop and have coffee (un exprès, un café crème, etc.). When we get back to school, I ask the following questions: What time was the trip? What were you wearing? What was the

weather like? Who did you sit with? What emotions did you feel? and the students write down their answers, using complete sentences, in the target language. Then I ask: What did you order? Who did you talk to? What did (a student in the class's name) do? What time did we return? Who got back to the room last? Then we discuss how the first five used the imperfect as they were description, and the last five were actions that required the passé composé/preterit.

- Have students draw and tell a rebus story. Give them a list of the elements you want: day, time, weather, location and ongoing activity, what happened, and what happened after that (two actions). For each element, they draw a picture big enough for the class to see. Holding these pictures, they stand up and tell the class their story, each person in the group telling about the picture they are holding. If they looked up any new vocabulary in the dictionary, have them write it on the board before they begin, so the others can both see and hear the new words.
- Another strategy we have tried is to imagine the story as a video with the sound off. If the verb would be a visible movement on the screen, it would be in the preterit/passé composé, but descriptive details, although they are visible, would not involve movement. We often use the fairy tale *Goldilocks and the Three Bears* for this activity.
- Use music: Here's a song my French 3 class helped me write to remember the imperfect uses (to the tune of *Jingle Bells*, with a few extra syllables):

  Imparfait, "used to be,"
  "was/were + verb + ing"
  Habitual action in the past
  Or interrupted by another thing, oh!
  Date and time, looks and clothes,
  Weather and emotion,
  Circumstances of the main event
  Description, but never motion!

- Tell a funny or an interesting story. I tell my students real stories about silly things I have done (I am definitely not a very good athlete) or interesting things I have read about in the paper. If you don't want to do this, then translate one of the stories from the *Star* or another tabloid; students are usually highly interested in or entertained by these stories. As you tell the story, have the students signal what tense the verb they hear is in: for example, clap for imperfect, hit the desk for preterite. They usually notice that the imperfect is clustered mostly at the beginning of the story.

Object Pronouns

- My favorite tool for teaching these is a PowerPoint presentation I made in which the brightly colored nouns in sentences "fly" off-screen, and are replaced with the object pronouns of the same color, accompanied by a loud, silly noise of some sort. Students quickly learn the idea of replacement, and note the placement of the pronoun in the sentence. See Chapter 7 for more on PowerPoint presentations. This appeals to visual, spatial, and auditory learners.
- Make the majority of the students into living sentences. Give each a large (laminated?) piece of posterboard on which a portion of a sentence is written. They must unscramble these to form logical sentences. Once the sentences are formed, give pronouns to a handful of students you have reserved; they must find which student they replace and tap him or her on the shoulder, like cutting in during a dance. The sentence would then rearrange itself to accommodate the new pronoun.
- This idea comes from Jocelyn Raught at Cactus Shadows High School, Cave Creek, Arizona. It is for teaching Spanish, but is easily adapted to French and possibly other languages: Because students tend to attain language in chunks, this rhythmic approach can also help the students learn the difference between the direct and the indirect. The direct object is chanted in a two-syllable sequence to match "di-rect," while the indirect pronouns are presented later in a three-syllable sequence to match "in-di-rect." What the teacher says is in boldface and the dashes represent pauses.

  1. Tell the students to listen carefully and repeat these pronouns:

     me me—**me** me—**te** te—**te** te—**me te** me te—**me te** me te—

     Call on different students to repeat and then return to group repetition:

     me te me te—**lo** lo—**me te** me te—**lo** lo—**la** la—**me te** me te—**lo la** lo la—

     Put these two-syllable parts together, and repeat many times. Alternate individual with group repetition. Add:

     nos nos—**nos** nos—**os** os—**os** os—**nos os**— nos os—
     me te me te—**lo la** lo la—**nos os** nos os—

     Then say all together: **me te—lo la—nos os**

     Add: **los** los—**los** los—**las** las—**las** las—**los las** los las—

     Build up to: **me te—lo la—nos os—los las—**

2. While presenting the pronouns, add hand clapping, finger snapping, swaying, and so on. Make it sing-songy. It's almost a tongue twister.
3. Oral modeling: Again, do not explain anything. Tell them to listen carefully to model sentences as you replace the direct object with a direct object pronoun. Stress the direct object and pronoun so they may understand number, gender, and placement without explanation.

   Example: **Pablo tiene *el libro*.—Pablo *lo* tiene.**

   After about 5 examples, the quicker students will start to click; more students will begin to understand after 10 examples. Then, as you say the sentence, allow the class as a whole to replace the direct object with a pronoun. When they seem ready, call on them individually.
4. Then begin sentence list practice: Students see and do the pronoun replacement on their own. Have them underline the direct object in each of five examples, and check their work with each other. Then have them write the sentence replacement, and check again, turning in one corrected paper for the group.
5. Finally, play the Lo Tengo game: This is the biggest hit of all. Use sets of cards with classroom vocabulary or pictures. Put the students in groups and have them lay the cards out on the floor so everyone in the group can see them. When the teacher names one, the student that grabs it, holds it up and correctly says "Lo (la, las) tengo" ("I have it") gets to keep the card. If the student uses the wrong pronoun or grabs the wrong card, another can correct him or her, and take the card.

♦ For French teachers: To remember the order of pronouns in a sentence, try the following song sung to the tune of *La Cucaracha* (hold *le* for 3 beats):

  me, te, se, nous, vous
  le, la, les
  lui, leur, y, en
  (repeat the above three lines)
  Les voilà

  Try putting pronouns to familiar tunes such as *Baa, Baa Black Sheep*, or *Jingle Bells*.

♦ Get 20 or so objects, with equal numbers that are masculine or feminine singular, or masculine or feminine plural (e.g., for feminine plural, rosas/ revistas/plumas/pelotas/llaves). Ask students individually if they want one of the objects: "Do you want the flower?" They must answer, "Yes, I want it" or "No, I don't want it," using the correct pronoun. If they don't use the correct pronoun, they don't get the object. Be sure to have some highly desirable objects such as stuffed animals, chocolate bars, or whatever you think the class would like.

- Using the same objects, have students work in pairs, asking each other if they like these objects, if they want them, or using commands such as "Give it to me."
- Have students bring in a show-and-tell object. They will want to see each other's objects. Have them trade objects: "What is that?" "It's a baseball card." "Give it to me!/May I have it?"(using the correct pronoun).
- Playing the card game Go Fish requires object pronouns: "Do you have *la robe?*" "No, I don't have it (pronoun used)." "Go fish." This uses pronouns in the command form.
- Use gifts to show the difference between direct and indirect objects: The present is the direct object and the recipient is the indirect object. Put cookies, candy, and "zonks" (a rubber band, a thumbtack, or some other less desirable object) in a small bag, and write a pronoun on each. Have them give each other gifts ("I give it to you") for two minutes, and then let them open them, and try to trade with each other for another minute or so.
- Don't forget the RID rule for pronoun order: RID stands for the order in which multiple pronouns appear in a Spanish sentence: Reflexive + Indirect + Direct + verb.

PARTNER ACTIVITIES

When using cooperative learning in the classroom, a lot of time can be wasted trying to find a partner, and often the same students end up working together over and over (and students usually choose others of the same ability level). To avoid all this, try one of the following pairing activities:

- Partner Clocks—suggested for lower-level classes

  Use several small clocks, or one large one (see Figure 5.2). Give students about five minutes to find partners (I call them *rendezvous* in French)—if using small clocks, find partners for every 12, 3, 6, and 9 o'clock. Students would write their partner's name next to that time on their clock. If using one big clock, find a partner for each hour. After this one-time choice, students have a variety of partners prearranged. All you have to do is call out one clock time, and they know who to go to. Have them leave these in the room in their folder, or tape them in their book, offer bonus points for not losing them, or have occasional candy rewards for everyone who has his or her clock on a given day.

FIGURE 5.2. MY PARTNER LIST

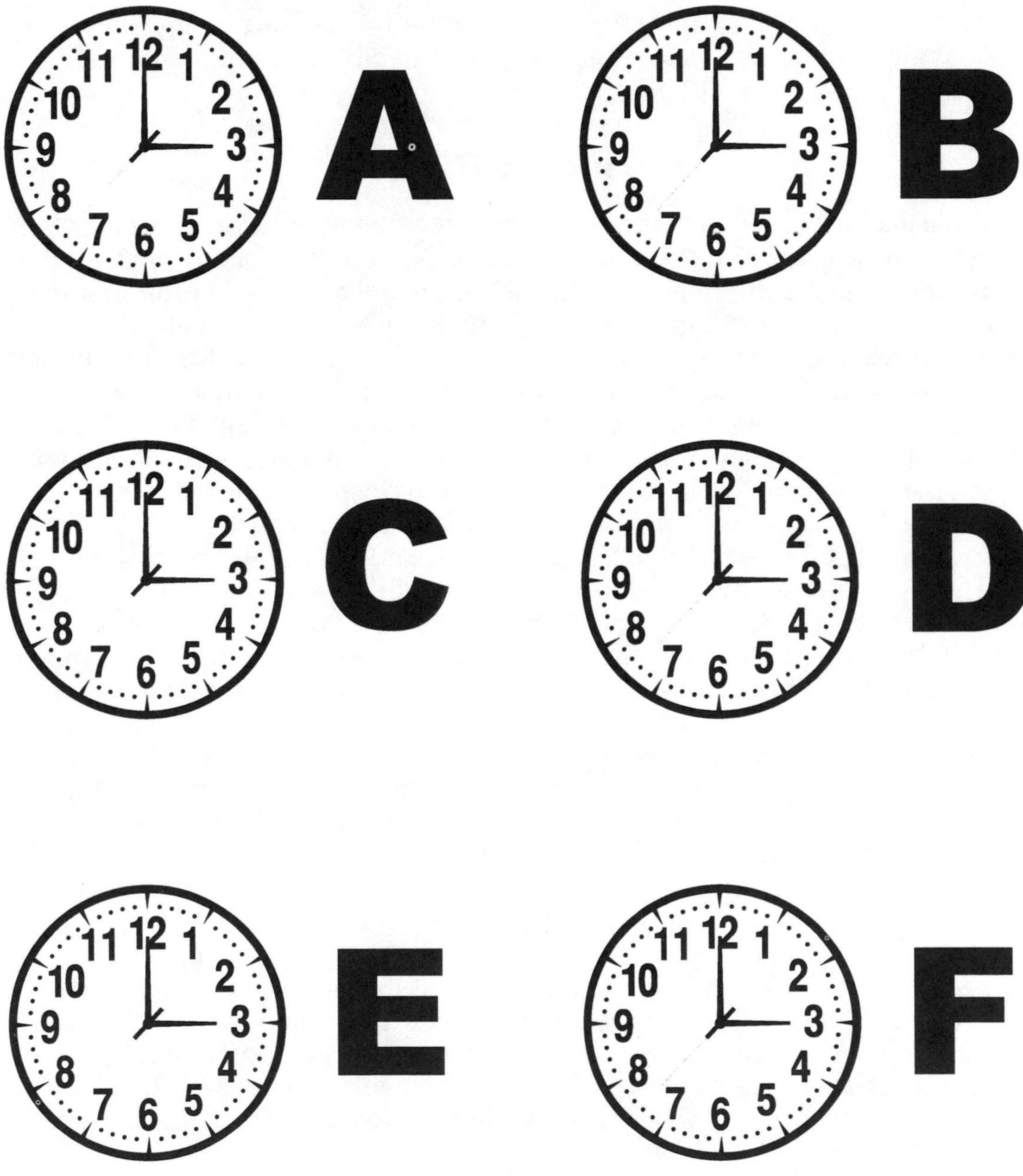

- Partner Maps—a good review for upper-level classes.

  Copy a map, either of a country or a city where your target language is spoken. Students again choose partners, writing each partner's name next to a different city (if a country map) or a monument or site if it's a city map. Then, all you have to do is say, "Madrid" or "Ringstrasse" and they know who their partner is. As a sponge (and review) have them go over all they can remember about that place as they move to sit with their partner.

PASSPORTS

A particularly good activity I have implemented in my classroom for over five years now is to issue every student a passport on the first day of class. For beginning students, fill in name, address, and telephone number the first day, and add to the passport (age, hair color, nationality, etc.) as that material is covered in class. For second-year students, this is a good review. Make sure that their passport includes several items not covered in first year, such as their class schedule, hobbies, or favorite food. Upper-level students will fill it in quickly as a review. Use a form that you have created or allow students to create their own.

On the second day of class, I pose as a customs inspector, and students must enter "France" (my classroom) and get an entry stamp. After that, I tell them that we are in France and must speak French and do as the French do. This clearly demonstrates my expectation that they will speak in the target language, as well as setting a classroom atmosphere of "another world."

Once the passport is filled out, it is still useful as a conversational tool in the classroom. Have students ask each other about the basics on the passport, and also additional topics, such as, "Where have you traveled? With whom? Where would you like to travel, and why?" Our passports are also used for simulations of real-life experiences such as checking into a hotel, getting a visa, picking up mail, paying for merchandise, cashing a check, seeking employment, and so on.

My passports also have five spaces on them, and serve as the student's hall pass (with permission from my principal.) After asking me (in the target language) if they may leave, and stating the purpose, they must stamp the passport as if they were leaving the country. A student without a passport may not leave, and each passport is worth five bonus points at the end of the semester if it is unstamped. Students therefore carefully evaluate how often they need to leave the classroom. I also make tardy students stamp their passport to enter.

Reggie Thomson uses a passport with his elementary (ages 8 to 12) classes in Japanese. He gave permission to list his Internet site where an eight-page document and full details can be found:

http://reggie.net/teaching/passport.htm

It is not only a passport, but the students also record daily participation points on them and keep records of grades received, and so forth.

HANDLING MAINSTREAMED/SPECIAL EDUCATION STUDENTS

With more and more states requiring a foreign language for all students regardless of ability level, we have to deal with more learning-challenged students. Repetition and memorization are very beneficial to all students, but are especially good for students who have difficulty learning. Use more gestures and hand signals, especially if the students are hearing impaired (see Chapter 1 and the research on how using gestures maximizes retention and retrieval of information). Here are some other basic things that are good for all students, but very necessary for students with Attention Deficit Disorder (ADD) and other learning-impaired students:

- Try to create a nonthreatening environment in which praise is given openly and criticism is done privately.
- Give a lot of oral grades, but make them low-anxiety ones by making them pass/fail, especially when practicing newly learned material. Also give "completion grades" for homework, as long as it is in the target language. This will foster a sense of accomplishment and encourage participation.
- Try to have as few distractions as possible. Cover windows in doors. Erase the blackboard completely before beginning a new topic.
- Encourage and reward good behavior. Make sure class rules about behavior expectations are expected are clear and enforced.
- Break tasks down into small pieces, with deadlines for each piece. Students at *any* ability level benefit from a more structured assignment. Don't give one big grade at the end, but rather make a series of partial grades.
- Use a variety of activities to appeal to the different senses and learning styles.
- Pair students to do cooperative activities when first practicing a new concept.
- Stand near students, make eye contact often, and be available for questions. Don't stand by the board or sit at your desk.

Here are some more specific strategies for these special students:

- Give them an extra text to take home.
- Talk to the special education teacher to make sure you completely understand what the student's special needs (and talents) are.
- Talk to the student. Ask the student how they study and what the student thinks works best to help him or her study. Watch the student work on a task to get a good idea of the student's learning style.

- If possible, vary the color of paper assignments are on. This serves as a sort of graphic organizer for the student, and helps the student organize notes as well.
- Give all directions both orally and in writing on the board or on an overhead transparency.
- Pair the student with another who takes really good notes, and give them time to interact.
- Help the student make flash cards. They need lots of extra drill and practice, and these really help. Again, if possible, make them different colors, i.e., red for masculine, purple for feminine, gray for neuter, and so on.
- Give the student a practice test the day before a test; make sure the student knows exactly what will be on the test.
- Give tests in several small parts on different days, or modify the test so the student makes choices rather than just fills in the blanks (two choices seems to work best.) Make the test open book, or allow the student to use a review sheet or list of endings, pronouns, and so on. If giving matching tests, group the matching part into sections of no more than five questions each, with lines in between. Make sure the student has extra (unlimited, if possible) time to take the test. It may be necessary to send the student to a quiet spot that is free of distractions to take the test, or even to have someone read the test to him or her.

Leading researchers in this field are Richard Sparks and Leonore Ganschow, so look for articles by them. For more information, check out The Foreign Language Teachers Guide to Learning Disorders Web site at:

http://www.fln.vcu.edu/ld/ld.html.

6

Instruction and Alternative Assessments in Literature

Teaching literature is a creative endeavor at any time, and accordingly it is probably easiest to try to implement an alternative assessment program in this area first. Later, when you have mastered the various types of assessment activities, extend them to grammar, communicative activities, and other classroom performances. Remember that the standard method of teaching literature—reading followed by worksheets or discussion—is best suited to the linguistic learners in your classroom. To reach *all* your students, you have to adapt this subject matter for visual/spatial, logical/mathematical, kinesthetic, auditory, and other learning styles. After all, because all students are a mixture of several learning styles, variety benefits everyone in your classroom. In Chapter 2, in the Linguistic section, I wrote about a four-step strategy for reading. In this chapter, I elaborate on this four-step strategy, with an emphasis on checking to see that learning has occurred (assessment).

Do a Prereading Assessment

If the reading is going to be difficult, such as an entire play or a book, I do more than just ask the student to do the activities described in Chapter 2. I give the student something similar to Figure 6.1 to fill out before, during, and after the reading. It assists the student, and gives me some feedback on adaptations I could make for the next group that does the same assignment. I have the students turn it in to me before beginning, and after completion of the reading, and give completion points for each section. I also discuss it briefly, suggesting resources they may not have thought of (especially Internet sites).

FIGURE 6.1. PLANNING AND EVALUATION FORM

Name ____

Before beginning:

Name and brief description of this assignment:

What I already know about this:

Questions I have about this:

Resources to use during this assignment

Activities that will make me successful:

Hand this sheet in to the teacher when the above portion is done.

During reading:
USE THE BACK OF THIS SHEET to write down words you find you have to look up frequently.

Reflections upon completion of this unit:

I learned I could:

I learned I need to:

I learned these facts and concepts:

I am now curious about:

I enjoyed most:

I enjoyed least:

STOP FREQUENTLY TO PROCESS MATERIAL

In Chapter 1, we saw that the results of recent research on how the brain works also show us that we must stop and use information often in order to transfer it to long-term memory. This must be done periodically during the reading process itself. Here are some activities you could use:

1. Draw a picture of the______scene, and explain it.
2. Describe an experience you have had that was like the experience of this character.

3. Discuss how this character is like or unlike someone you know.
4. Start a time line for one character, and chart the events in the book/story as they occur.
5. Make a graph of the character's emotions, with high points on the graph representing happiness, and low points on the graph representing sadness.
6. Explain what this character would like for Christmas, and why.
7. Write five questions you would like to ask this character.
8. If this character were alive now, how would he or she act?
9. Pick your favorite sentence you have read so far, and make a poster of it. Be ready to explain why you chose this sentence.
10. Start a list of new words that you learned as you read.
11. Start a list of words you have looked up more than once as you read.
12. What sort of music would the main character like, and why?
13. Draw what you think the main character looks like (including clothing).
14. Pretend you're a character from the story, and introduce the other characters to the class.
15. If you were directing a film of this story, who would you pick to play the lead characters, and why?

The above list is by no means complete, but there are elements there for artistic (9, 13, 15), musical (12), kinesthetic (1, 8), mathematical (4, 5), and other intelligences, and which cannot be done well by anyone who does not have a good understanding of the text. Several are also creative and fun enough that students would want to read the text in order to be able to produce the desired product or join in the discussion. The above assignments also ask students to apply what was read to their own knowledge and experience, making it likely that long-term storage of some of it will occur. And finally, these activities often involve Synthesis and Evaluation, the two highest steps in Bloom's taxonomy (see Figure 1.5, p. 15).

ASSESSMENT

ASSESS FREQUENTLY

Just as brief activities help students learn the material, so also do short, unannounced assessments test whether learning has occurred. Seventy to 90 percent of new learning is forgotten 9 to 18 hours after the initial learning, unless it is put into long-term storage in the brain (Sousa, 1995). Therefore, an assessment should be given within 24 hours of the reading (or any learning), and should test what you want the students to have retained. It should also be unannounced, so that you can be sure that students have stored the material in long-term storage, rather than cramming it into their working memory. Another advantage of a short, precise assessment should be that it offers immediate feedback. If students get quick, specific, corrective feedback, they are more likely to continue the task successfully (Sousa, 1995).

Students feel more accountable for the material if they know they can expect some sort of assessment often, and are more likely to persevere. However, if the assessment becomes predictable, such as true-false questions, or fill-in-the-blank quizzes that test only rote memory, students will stop processing the ideas and applying them. Assessments must be creative and varied in order to create a learning climate that results in improved student performance. Here are some assessments that could be given during a reading exercise that could be done and corrected quickly, that appeal to different learning styles, and test a variety of more complex thinking skills:

- Compare the relationship of these two characters to a relationship in a song you've heard or a poem you've read.
- Contrast this chapter with the previous chapter, using a Venn diagram.
- Pretend you're the author, and explain why you chose the title of this book.
- Draw a time line of what events have occurred so far in this story.
- Draw a series of cartoons to show what has happened to the main character in this chapter.
- Fill in a job application for the main character.
- Compare where you live with the village in this story.
- Would you like to have this character as a friend? Explain.

When students have done one of the above activities, there is a variety of ways to correct, reinforce success, and give immediate feedback. One way is to pick all the products up and then discuss what elements they should have contained (the standard method). This gives feedback, but mostly tells students what they have done wrong, and some will immediately tune out. There are several alternate ways I prefer to handle these assessments.

One is called Think/Pair/Share, discussed previously. Because the student has already done the thinking part when creating his or her product, you then pair the student, and have the pairs share products. To create a positive atmosphere, specify that they may only give compliments to each other (but, in seeing someone else's product, they may see missed ideas or errors that have been made). Give students time to review and revise their product, and then collect them. You may even wish to put two pairs together for a four-way sharing session. Using this method, you will see fewer mistakes to correct: Students are more likely to put forth more effort if their peers are going to see and/or hear their work. In addition, students will review the material several times in reading or looking at each other's products (another chance to learn), and they will be involved in each other's success (team building). But, you say, students can cheat, and coast along on someone else's coattails? Don't let students with no product participate in the sharing sessions. The student who has produced a product, even if it wasn't a superlative product to begin with, is reading several other products and evaluating the ideas contained therein, and revising his or her product. If an initially poor product becomes better in the process, learning *is* taking place. Remember that on Glasser's scale (see Figure 1.2, p. 7), students who teach each other have the greatest level of retention.

A similar method, but without the verbal discussion aspect, is called Roam Around the Room. Students place their products out on their desk, and silently, taking paper and pencil to jot down ideas, look at each other's work, returning to their own desk to reexamine and revise their product before handing it in. Seeing an idea another classmate has written often makes a bigger impression than hearing the teacher say it. Again, there will be fewer corrections for you to make, and any misapprehensions that survive a cooperative activity like this should be discussed the following day.

GIVE CHOICES

Because students have different learning styles give them choices when assessing them. For example, instead of the "Compare where you live with the village in this story," allow students to choose one of these activities:

- Draw a map of the village in this story.
- Write a script or a brochure for a walking tour of this village.
- Make up a poem/song/rap about the village in this story.
- Discuss the items found in this village that are not found in our town.
- Make a page for a phone book, listing businesses found in this town.
- Compare this village to one you saw on TV or in a movie.

The student can choose a product that would be easiest for him or her to do, but the information to be included in each is virtually the same.

VARY PROJECTS

Consider using a project as a final assessment, rather than the standard multiple-choice test. Figure 6.2 contains a long list of project ideas for a literature final.

Again, give students a choice of projects, such as:

- Design a book cover for your book, or a poster for the film made from this book.
- Draw a comic strip version of this book.
- Do an interview: You are the author. Tell what you were trying to say in this book, as well as which portion was the most fun to write.

FIGURE 6.2. ALTERNATIVE ASSESSMENTS

Kinesthetic Products	*Written Products*	*Visual Products*	*Oral Products*
ballet/dance	advertisement	advertisement	anecdote
card game	autobiography	album	audio recording
ceramics	book report	anagram	ballad/rap/ song
charade	booklet/brochure	animation	book report
clothing	business letter	annotated bibliography	campaign speech
collage	celebrity profile	area graph	choral reading
demonstration	checklist	artifact collection	comedy act
device	comic book	award	comparison
diorama	commercial (script)	banner	debate
display	comparison	blueprint	dialogue
dramatization	computer program	book jacket	discussion
equipment	creative writing	booklet	documentary
etching	description	book mark	dramatization
experiment	dialogue	bullet chart	explanation
field trip	diary/journal	bulletin board	fairy tale/myth
finger puppets	fact file	calendar	free verse
food	fairy tale/myth	cartoon	interview
furniture	field manual	chart	jingle
gadget	glossary	checklist	job interview
game	guidebook	collage	joke
gauge	handbook	collection	lecture
hat	headline	comic book	lesson
instruments	interview script	costume	limerick
jigsaw puzzle	job description	crossword puzzle	monologue
kite	joke	diagram	narration
learning center	law	diorama	newscast
machine/invention	lesson plan	display	panel discussion
macrame	log	drawing	rhyme
marionette	lyrics	fabric	riddle
mime	magazine article	film	role-play
mobile	metaphor	flag	seminar
model	new story ending	flannel board	speech
movement game	oath	flash card	

Kinesthetic Products	*Written Products*	*Visual Products*	*Oral Products*
observation	observation sheet	flip chart	
origami	outline	flowchart	
	parody	graphic organizer	
	pen pal letter	greeting card	
	petition	hieroglyphic	
	prediction	illustration	
	puppet show	imprint	
	questionnaire	jigsaw puzzle	
	quiz	map	
	recipe	mask	
	report	mobile	
	review	mosaic	
	rewritten ending	mural	
	riddle	newscast	
	scroll	outline	
	short story	painting	
	skit	pattern	
	slogan	photo essay	
	speech	photograph	
	story problems	pie chart	
	telegram	playing card	
	travel log	poster	
	vocab list	rebus story	
	yearbook	scrapbook	
		scroll	
		slide show	
		stencil	
		storyboard	
		time line	
		transparency	
		travel log	
		video	
		wall hanging	
		weather map	
		word search	

- Using the *Reader's Guide* find an article that criticizes this book, and agree or disagree with it.
- You are the prosecutor at the trial of (villain in the book or story). Write or speak (live or on video) your final summation to the jury, reviewing the character's misdeeds, and asking for whatever punishment you feel is fair.
- Write a letter to the author and tell him or her what you think of the book/story.

INVOLVE STUDENTS DIRECTLY IN CREATING RUBRICS

Choice alone is not enough to get a good project from your students. Enlist their help in preparing a rubric for each choice you have given them. Rubrics are a fixed scale, usually from 1 to 4, with a list of characteristics that describe the performance expected, showing the distinction between A, B, C, and D performances (or, if you prefer, exemplary, proficient, in-progress, and unsatisfactory performances). Rubrics should be based on national, state, and local standards, and should involve students who see examples of products or performances. Students, together with the teacher, should then:

- Determine the essential parts of the product, using terms that are understood by all.
- Define the qualities of each part.
- Assign point value or otherwise designate the parts that are most important.

For the map, for example, bring out three maps. Ask students which one is the best, and why. As they point out the good qualities, list them on the board. When you get a complete list—for example, use of color, print big enough to read across the room, detail in drawings, lots of buildings, overhead perspective, not messy (or whatever the students like)—then announce that an A map must have all those listed. Have students also help decide what elements a B must have, and so on. This only takes a few minutes, and the dividend is tremendous: not only do more students remember what elements the map must have, but they feel ownership for the grading scale. Parents will not question your grading of a child's product because the child will not question it, and students won't be able to validly claim they didn't know you wanted them to do such-and-such. And finally, you will have a student-written rubric that you can use for grading. All you do is circle an element such as "Only has one street depicted" and you are justified in giving the project a C or D on that basis, because the students helped you decide.

Figure 6.3 is a rubric students helped me create for a project we did while reading *Candide,* a novel whose main character travels the world, always with a sidekick, and always having some negative experience that impels him to leave and go somewhere else. Students were given the choice of writing a story, a poem, a postcard; drawing a storyboard; or suggesting an alternative of their own devising. The first time I did this assignment, of course, I had no samples to show the students, but we did look at three postcards, short stories, and narrative poems and discuss which was best and why. In subsequent years, of course, we looked at the products from the first year. Using rubrics, the products get better every year.

FIGURE 6.3. RUBRIC: POSTCARDS

An "A" postcard:	Has a detailed color illustration, not necessarily hand-drawn Has a salutation and closing, with signature* Has a destination address and addressee indicated Has at least five sentences Uses descriptive adjectives and colorful verbs Is written in French, with no major errors in grammar and no more than one spelling error Indicates clearly Candide's opinion of this place Mentions Candide's companion and his/her actions
A "B" postcard:	Has a scene pictured that is generic or difficult to identify Has a closing with signature, but no salutation Has only four sentences Has one or two major grammar errors and more than one spelling error Describes Candide's actions only Does not describe the place visited Is vague or unclear about Candide's opinion of this place
A "C" postcard:	Has a black-and-white picture on card Has only three sentences Has no salutation or signature Has more than two serious errors in grammar Has no description of the scene or a generic "Having fun, wish you were here" type message Does not give Candide's opinion of this place
A "D" postcard:	Has incomplete illustrations Has incomplete sentences Has handwriting that is difficult to read Has serious errors in grammar or spelling Provides very little information about the destination
An "F" postcard:	Has words in English Is illegible Has many serious errors Has less than three sentences

*NOTE: All postcards are from Candide, so put your initials on the illustration!

GIVE NOTEBOOK QUIZZES

To encourage students to take notes on discussions and come prepared to class, try impromptu "notebook quizzes." These should be, as stated previously, brief, easy to correct, and unannounced. These take approximately 10 minutes, and may be graded by the teacher or the students. The first time, you may wish to give one as a "practice" to let students know the value you place on preparedness and organization, and use Pair/Share or Roam Around the Room so they can see each other's organization methods, answers, and so forth.

A typical notebook quiz might ask students to quote from a handout they were given in class and were supposed to keep or from notes on projects and reports given by classmates. It might also have them translate a vocabulary word discussed in class, ask or answer a question as practiced in class, give examples of a concept (grammar or cultural) practiced in class, or simply give the answer to a specific question from a homework assignment, quiz or test that was checked or reviewed in class (a good way to check that a student corrected his or her paper as you went over the correct answers in class). Anything a student should have in notes or on a paper he or she should have kept would be material for a brief quiz. The "brief" timed aspect of the quiz also is to encourage the student to organize the notebook. If a student cannot find the material easily, then it is of little value to the student, as too much time would be spent searching for information.

A notebook quiz is a wonderful way to review for a test. Give students a quiz that is very similar to what the test will be, and have them fill it out, using only their notes and not the text. This may be done on an individual basis, or use Team Test (see the next section).

I use notebook quizzes as part of students' Participation grade. Some students' quizzes mirror their achievement on tests. Others score better on these than on tests, whether it is due to test anxiety or not memorizing enough things, but these quizzes help their overall average a little. The ones who get low scores and care enough, upon seeing their grade drop, begin to modify their behavior and organize their notes.

TEAM TEST

In Team Test, after dividing the students into groups of mixed ability level, give each person a copy of the test, and have them discuss and answer each question, but only write on one copy. Designate the student with the lowest ability as the secretary for the group. Everyone on the team must agree on the answer before it is written down. If this is review for a test, correct these in class, either by supplying an answer sheet, with students discussing why they got the wrong answer, and how to do better next time, or through class discussion of the answers, using Numbered Heads.

In Numbered Heads, students in each group have a number, and the teacher calls out a question and a number, and the student in each group who has that number says the answer. Next, a student picked at random from those responding must explain the group's answer. If that student cannot do so, the group loses a point, as they did not make sure everyone in the group understood the answer. This method forestalls a group from simply writing down whatever the brightest student in the group says, because each member is responsible for knowing every answer. Peer coaching, according to Glasser's scale (Figure 1.2, p. 7) encourages long-term memory storage of information.

Team Test is also a really good follow-up when most of the class has performed poorly on an assessment. Instead of teacher-led review, put the students in teams, and, as a team, have them take exactly the same test as the day before. This time, they all contribute their answers and discuss what to write. Once they have all done this (and learned their mistakes), give back the tests. I have never had a single question about a grade when I have used this method. If you give "retake tests" (correctives), they have all just reviewed for the retake, and that could be given immediately.

Give More Oral Assessments

With the new emphasis on being able to communicate, it is important to incorporate the listening and especially the speaking aspect in every unit. I like to use learning stations to practice what we are studying, and one station each time is my tape recorder. Once there, students would be asked to do a brief speaking activity. Here are some examples:

- The student reads the times pictured on four clocks.
- The student looks at four pictures of reflexive verb activities, accompanied by a subject pronoun, and says the correct verb for each, using the correct reflexive pronoun and ending.
- The student picks up a card with four questions on it in English asking, for example, the day, the date, the time, or his or her birthday, favorite food, or whatever is in the unit. The student answers the questions.
- While looking at a picture, the student makes up a short story about it.
- While looking at a picture, the student narrates a short story about it, using the past tenses.
- Given a picture of a room, the student names objects seen in the picture.
- The student looks at a picture of a place. He or she names the place, says he or she is going there, and what they are going to do there.

Journals

Journals are useful tools for the foreign language classroom. Students must think, translate, consider grammar issues, and write their thoughts for others to read. Journal entries could be reflections on what is being read in class, or discussion of issues that pertain to what will happen in the next section of the reading, such as cultural differences or values (e.g., "Which is more important, family or friends?"). Having students reread their own journal entries is also reading practice.

MEMORIZATION

Perhaps it is my age speaking here, but I see value in having students memorize pertinent quotations or short poems. Not only do they gain a small bit of cultural literacy that will stay with them, but they will practice the pacing, rhythm, and flow of the target language.

PORTFOLIOS

In recent years, more schools are being asked to have students prepare portfolios, usually for math and English, but occasionally across the curriculum. Literature projects make really good additions to portfolios, as the projects usually require reflection, research and creativity, and, because students usually enjoy them, they choose these projects to put in their portfolio.

Portfolio items are also good things to have on hand to show parents at conference time. When a student accompanies his or her parent to the conference, I always hand the portfolio to the student, and have him or her go through the portfolio, showing and commenting on each item to the parent, as I sit by. Students enjoy doing this, and parents are impressed.

However, portfolios are also excellent to use as a means of assessment, especially as part of a semester grade. Here is a partial list of items to have students put in their portfolio:

- Brief statement, perhaps in English (depending on the level), that the student writes the first day stating why he or she is taking the class, and goals for this year
- Periodic self-evaluations such as that in Figure 6.4, and at least two of these:
  - Video or audio recordings of a speech, skit, or presentation made especially for the portfolio
  - An A paper, quiz, or test
  - A drawing they have done as part of an assignment
  - Their favorite creative writing assignment, all errors corrected, and recopied for the portfolio

In addition to the student's work, a self/peer/teacher assessment could be included, such as that in Figure 6.5.

Some colleges are beginning to require portfolios. They are good to review at the end of a year's studies to see what was accomplished and how much progress has been made.

FIGURE 6.4. SELF-EVALUATION QUESTIONNAIRE

Name ______________________________

Rate yourself on a scale from 0 to 4.

0 = can't do
1 = rarely
2 = sometimes
3 = often
4 = easily

I can tell you the following in French:

my first and last names	1	2	3	4
my birthday	1	2	3	4
where I live	1	2	3	4
about my family	1	2	3	4
about things I like	1	2	3	4
about my city	1	2	3	4
about my country	1	2	3	4
the time, day, and date	1	2	3	4
the weather	1	2	3	4
what we are wearing	1	2	3	4
about a typical day in my life	1	2	3	4

I can understand and answer questions about:

sports	1	2	3	4
my leisure activities	1	2	3	4
food I would like to order	1	2	3	4
things I want to buy	1	2	3	4
how I feel	1	2	3	4
school studies	1	2	3	4

I can ask questions that:

ask directions (where things are)	1	2	3	4
ask someone to repeat a word	1	2	3	4
ask someone to define a word	1	2	3	4
invite someone	1	2	3	4
ask what someone else likes	1	2	3	4

I can:

write a letter about myself	1	2	3	4
agree or disagree with someone	1	2	3	4
understand a short conversation	1	2	3	4
read a short paragraph (about school, friends, sports)	1	2	3	4

Grammar:				
I can write the correct endings on verbs.	1	2	3	4
I can correctly use gender with nouns.	1	2	3	4
I can correctly use adjectives.	1	2	3	4
Behavior:				
I came to class on time.	1	2	3	4
I came to class prepared.	1	2	3	4
I was courteous to classmates.	1	2	3	4
I asked others for help, not answers.	1	2	3	4
I helped others participate.	1	2	3	4

FIGURE 6.5. SELF/PEER/TEACHER ASSESSMENT

Steuben County Tourism
Brochure Assessment Sheet

Check that each element is present and completed.

Element	*Self*	*Peer (Initials__)*	*Teacher*
Cover illustration & logo	____	____	____
Map (locates county)	____	____	____
Description of county	____	____	____
List of attractions	____	____	____
List of activities	____	____	____
Complete sentences	____	____	____
Verb endings correct	____	____	____
No gender errors	____	____	____
Pleasing layout/look	____	____	____
Additional information given	____	____	____

Each element is worth 10 points for a total of 100 points. Consult rubric for grading information.

7

INCORPORATING TECHNOLOGY

Technology for teaching foreign languages has gone far beyond the language laboratory, though the use of these is still recommended. Modern laboratories have many more capabilities than labs did 10 years ago due to computers. The computer currently reigns supreme in education, with lots of grants available for the purchase of equipment and for training in its use. Not only are computers available, but schools are feeling a lot of pressure from their communities and from industry to require use of them, and train students in the various uses—"integrating technology" is the latest buzzword, and the Internet is its focus. If you aren't yet comfortable with technology, I strongly urge you to get some basic training in its use, as computers have a lot to offer foreign language educators.

INTERNET USE

Here are some general guidelines for using the Internet:

- Pick your lesson plans carefully.

Not all lesson plans lend themselves to Internet lessons. Look for lessons that involve:

- Research on a particular topic such as Gothic cathedrals, types of food, holidays, particular cities or regions, art and artists, authors, or news events.
- A topic that involves comparison and contrast of the target country and our own, such as educational systems, monetary systems, government structures, fashion, and/or shopping.
- The opportunity to gather information from human sources, such as a keypal exchange with another class, or consultation with other students or experts on a topic of opinion.
- The opportunity to conduct a survey using a questionnaire, for example to find out German stereotypes about Americans/

American stereotypes about the French, or to compile a list of students' suggestions on the best ways to get an "A" in a foreign language class.

Caution: Be careful not to have students go online just for the sake of going online. The novelty will wear off quickly. Lesson plans that require students to go online for information that they could find in one-eighth the time by pulling an encyclopedia off the shelf defeats the purpose of using the Internet.

- Check the Net carefully.

Of course, the only way to find out if a lesson plan will work on the Internet is to get on-line and search for information on the subject. For some plans you will only need a site or two, but for others, you will want a topic with many sites available.

But don't stop there: visit every portion of every site. Often, just because a search engine finds a site does not mean that the site still exists (a screen often appears with the message "Site not found") or that your school's filter/blocking/censor system allows students to access the site. Because most schools now use filters, it is also imperative to do the search at school, using the system the students will use. It is very important to explore the sites you plan to have students access. Discovering unpleasantries, dead ends, or inappropriate links before sending the class on an online mission will head off a lot of problems. I can tell you that a search using the word "French" will turn up a lot of pornographic sites. I can also vouch for the "inappropriate links" portion. I have my students check out Mardi Gras each year, but only after informing them of all the dire consequences that would ensue if they visit links I specifically tell them to avoid due to pornographic content. Another way of filtering such sites is to copy the site, minus those portions, onto a diskette, and have the students access only the portions that you want, instead of going directly onto the Internet (called "whacking" a site). Whacking would enable you to preserve material for viewing the following day.

- Do a dry run of the lesson beforehand.

Do a "dry run" of the lesson to make sure you've allocated enough class time for the activity. With the Net you can never be sure. A particular site that presented no problems one day can be hard to get into when twenty students are trying to access it at once. Also keep in mind the time of day, and try to access the site at the time the students would check it. With the Mardi Gras sites, I watched a parade one afternoon and had my students access the site the next morning only to find the camera showing an empty, trash-strewn street. A site overseas may be easier to access in the afternoon, when overseas users have gone to bed, than it is in the morning, when it is only early evening in Europe.

- Make students accountable.

Having students simply retrieve a document is much less important than what they actually do with it after they've downloaded it. There are several ways to do this. A simple one is to construct a cloze activity (fill-in-the-blank) based on the site. For example:

> A ticket to the Eiffel tower costs: ________ to the first floor ________ to the second floor ________ to the top.

Another easy way is to have students list/log their Internet travels, as in Figure 7.1.

FIGURE 7.1. INTERNET LOG

Date ________________________

Name________________________

SITE accessed: Name ________________________

Internet address: ________________________

Type of site (education, travel, game, etc.) ________________________

Describe/list subheadings/options found at this site: ________________________

____

Option explored: ________________________

Summary of information found there: ________________________

Did you learn anything? List ideas/vocabulary that were new for you:

Rate this site on a scale of 1 to 10 (10 being the best) for the following:

Educational value ______ Easy to understand & navigate ______

Entertaining/interesting ____ Looks/attractively presented ______

Below, write a critique of this site. Did you like it? Would you visit it again? Why or why not?

A third way is to have students report on what they have found. I have a Valentine's Day activity in which students locate a love poem and find out information about who wrote it. They then present their poem to the class and lead a discussion on it. Assess any work in the same way you would any other class activity, and if students learned what you wanted, it's a lesson you can use again.

- Take full advantage of networking you can do with other teachers.

Have another teacher who is familiar with the Internet look over your plan (even better if they also have some knowledge of your subject area, of course). You can also post your lesson plan on various newsgroups for advice: FL-TEACH is a good one, or k12.chat.teacher, or on a mailing list such as EdNet. And don't forget to look in the various lesson plan stockpiles, to find out if someone else already has a lesson plan on that topic, before you spend a lot of time creating one on your own. See the list of sites in this chapter.

The Internet changes daily. The Web sites that follow in this chapter were all valid and usable as of November 1998.

GENERAL SITES FOR TEACHERS

These sites have Internet lesson plans for all subject areas, including foreign languages:

Ron MacKinnon's Educational Bookmarks, my favorite starting point.
http://juliet.stfx.ca/people/stu/x94emf/bookmark.html

Blue Web'n—a library of learning sites that includes Web-based lessons, tutorials, and projects.
http://www.kn.pacbell.com/wired/bluewebn

Free Online Unit Studies—originally created for home-schooled students
http://www.alaska.net/~cccandc/free.htm

Armadillo's K–12 WWW Resources
http://chico.rice.edu/armadillo/Rice/k12resources.html

Schoolnet Integrating Technology Library—go to the section "Classroom Projects"
http://schoolnet.carleton.ca

Take your classes to play educational games that you create especially for them (or use one someone else has posted) at
http://www.quia.com

Puzzlemaker WWW site (this site is *very* busy during school hours!)
http://www.puzzlemaker.com

These sites are specifically foreign language sites, but for all languages:

The absolute best thing on the Net is FLTEACH—dialogue with ideas from thousands of other FL teachers (but if you subscribe, expect over 100 postings every day)
http://www.cortland.edu/www_root/flteach/flteach.html

The new FLTEACH frequently asked questions (FAQ) files include: Advice to the New Teacher, Accent Marks, the Alphabet, Art Projects, Class Size, Classroom Discipline, Classroom Management, Dictation, Foreign Language and/or International Clubs, Individual Student Whiteboards, Oral Participation, Pronunciation, Accent, Language Melody, Student Journals, Student Portfolios, Student Teaching, Total Physical Response (TPR) and TPR Storytelling (TPRS) http://www.cortland.edu/flteach/flteach-FAQ.html

The California Foreign Language Project has a Web site on using the Internet in the foreign language classroom. It includes strategies for writing lessons, suggestions for hardware and software, popular sites for foreign language teachers, and sample lesson plans.and hints for the neophyte. The address is
http://members.aol.com/maestro12/web/wadir.html

Information on cities and countries all over the world
http://www.city.net/countries

Jennifer's Language Page—basic phrases in 275 languages
http://www.elite.net/~runner/jennifers

The CIA World Factbook: shows every country's flag, map, and basic info on just about everything, including current government and political problems
http://www.odci.gov/cia/publications/factbook

Library of Congress—Country Studies on 85 countries, including photos, bibliographies, glossaries, and other tidbits.
http://lcweb2.loc.gov/frd/cs/cshome.html

Circle of Friends has information on seven children from around the world and a quiz afterward. Also lists holidays such as Oktoberfest, so it's worth checking periodically.
http://www.circle-of-friends.com/fun.htm

World Surfari picks a new country monthly to spotlight with history and "fun facts" about it, and also keeps links to a few of the "older" spotlighted countries
http://www.supersurf.com

Six hundred dictionaries in 150 different languages.
http://www.facstaff.bucknell.edu/rbeard/diction.html

Phone books around the world
http://www.contractjobs.com/tel/

Open-air markets all over the world, with photos and descriptions
http://www.openair.org/opair/twebmar.html

Internet projects and activities for foreign language classes, including 200 minilesson plans
http://www.geocities.com/Athens/Crete/4634/methods.html

Foreign Languages on the Web: a culture-specific site of links for approximately 20 languages
http://www.itp.berkeley.edu/~thorne/HumanResources.html

Vocabulary Training Exercises—drills, verbs, and other grammar in Spanish, English, French, and German
http://www.vokabel.com

Tongue twisters in 48 languages
http://www.uebersetzung.at/twister/index.htm

The Interagency Language Roundtable Scale contains the guidelines of the government and the American Council on the Teaching of Foreign Languages (ACTFL) guidelines, both with critical introductions
http://fmc.utm.edu/~rpeckham/ilrhome.html

Colonel Craig's Language Links: something for everyone
http://www.isu.edu/~nickcrai/frenlinx.html (French)
http://www.isu.edu/~nickcrai/man.html (German)
http://www.isu.edu/~nickcrai/jpnlinx.html (Japanese)
http://www.isu.edu/~nickcrai/russlinx.html (Russian)
http://www.isu.edu/~nickcrai/spanlinx.html (Spanish)

TrackStar has some interactive Internet lessons for foreign languages
http://scrtec.org/track/index/flanguage.html

Janel Brennan (a teacher) made this Web site with links to other foreign language teachers' sites, plus art and culture sites
http://www.erols.com/jbrennan/janel.htm

Another teacher site, with many languages and a search engine
http://www.geocities.com/~lagringa

Here is an excellent site regarding everything imaginable to do with foreign language education (FLED)
http://www.cal.org/ericcll/digest/marcos02.html

Global Schoolhouse has a variety of projects and programs; membership is free
http://www.gsn.org/join

Ethnologue Languages of the World—information on 6,500 languages
http://www.sil.org/ethnologue/

Foreign Language for Travelers—vocabulary and sound files in over 60 languages
http://www.travlang.com/languages

Subways all over the world
http://metro.jussieu.fr

Helpful site for students of English, French, German, Italian, and Spanish
http://www.geocities.com/~oberoi/language.html

University of Wisconsin's Language Links
http://polyglot.lss.wisc.edu/lss/lang/

Amazon Books & Music has books and music in many languages
http://www.amazon.com

And don't forget that the publisher of your textbook probably has a Web site, too!

STARTING A KEYPAL PROGRAM FOR YOUR STUDENTS

Keypals are the Internet equivalent of pen pals, and have the same benefits and drawbacks. Benefits include getting to know a native speaker of the language being studied, being able to ask questions about cultural differences, and being able discover the similarities between the two corespondents. The drawbacks are that some students will respond more often than others, and that keypals may misspell, use incorrect grammar, or mislead their American counterpart.

Some guidelines: To avoid potential problems, however minimal, students should not give personal information such as address and phone number. This also shows that you are taking precautions on behalf of students, which parents will appreciate.

Collect the students' letters and mail them from your (the teacher's) address as one large unit, allowing the teacher to distribute the letters and thus supervise the exchange, as well as to verify that students are sticking to the agreed-upon exchange topic, instead of asking for money or other things.

Another solution that provides you with the most "distance" is to make a handout telling students how to sign up for a keypal themselves, from home, on their own time, which is like making up a book list of suggestions for optional outside reading.

Even better, perhaps, than having keypals is conversing using the new videoconferencing that seems to be gaining popularity. Programs such as CUSeeMe are offered inexpensively for the classroom, and enable similarly equipped classrooms to meet, see each other, and talk. More information about this program may be had by calling (619) 433-3413 or found on the Internet at http://www.gsn.org/cu.

KEYPAL SITES

Tells how to structure keypal usage, and gives lesson plans
http://www.vcu.edu/cspweb/,icp/ipi.html

Tandem Keypals matches keypals by language being studied
http://www. slf.ruhr-uni-bochum.de

British group that connects students individually
http://www.ling.lancs.ac.uk/staff/visitors/kenji/keypal.htm

International Penfriend Club
http://www.advertising-america.com/club.htm

Intercultural E-mail Classroom Connection
http://www.stolaf.edu/network/iecc/

A wonderful site with tips and many links to brand new sites for keypals
http://www.kyoto-su.ac.jp/~trobb/keypals.html

This one has mostly links to keypals and projects for elementary school programs
http://www.eduplace.com/projects/keypals.html

Keypal Sites Specifically for Spanish

http://www.inetworld.net/eac/penpal.htm
http://www.cyberramp.net/~mdbutler/flaglinks.html
http://www.lingolex.com/ceespf.htm

Nueva Alejandria, based in Argentina but schools from Chile, Peru and Spain subscribe
http://www.nalejandria.com/clases-gemelas/listado.htm

Keypal Sites Specifically for French

"Café électronique" du Quartier français du village planétaire:
http://www.richmond.edu/~jpaulsen/gvfrench.html

Specific Target Language Sites

Arabic

Information on Arab countries and culture
http://www.bgsu.edu/departments/greal/Arabic.html

Arab Net: food, art, and information on Arab countries and culture
http://www.arab.net/arabnet_contents.html

French

Tennessee Bob's Famous French Links: the number one site for French, though it lacks a search engine! There are three ways to get to it
http://www.utm.edu/departments/french/french.html
http://192.239.144.18/departments/french/french.html
http://www.utm.edu:80/departments/french/french.html

The "site officiel de Paris" is
http://www.paris-france.org/

Another good one is
http://www.pariscope.fr/

A site with some beautiful postcard views of Paris to send that will make the students want to read the language (and you could always have them send each other a card)
http://www.abeille-cartes.com

Paris Match magazine has a great site with color photos
http://www.parismatch.com

Visit the Global Village French Quarter. Try the Bureau de Tourisme
http://www.richmond.edu/~jpaulsen/gvfrench.html

or this one
http://www.francetourism.com

or
http://www.franceway.com

or the official French government site
http://www. Fgtousa.inter.net

Pariscope: everything that's happening in Paris at
http://www.pariscope.fr/

Les Sources d'informations environmentales
http://www.imt-mrs.fr/transfert/CLUB/source1.html

Cinéfil is a Web site that describes current and upcoming films to hit the movie theaters in France, Belgium, and Switzerland
http://www.online.fr/cinefil/

Lively, yet everyday French conversation can be found at Bienvenue a La Causerie
http://www2.hawaii.edu/~herve/cause/causerienet.htm

Le Quid 99, encyclopedia in French
http://www.quid.fr

France Telecom has created a site for educators, in French, on how to use the Internet
http://www.edu.francetelecom.fr/

French Civilization WWW pages at
http://www.cortland.edu/flteach/civ/

Forum Francais (books, teacher resources, etc.)
http://www.forumfrancais.com

A French high school site, created by and for kids from any country, in French or English
http://perso.infonie.fr

The "Terrain des Sports du Quartier français" has listings, current sporting event updates, lexiques
http://www.richmond.edu/~jpaulsen/sportjeu.html

A series of activities using WWW pages with these topics: les Catalogues et les magasins, les Routes, le Mariage, les Réservations SNCF, la Météo, la Cuisine, la Télévision, Médecins sans frontières
http://snycorva.cortland.edu/~ponterior/fre102/

France Pratique: a Web site that has a search feature and lots of info about everyday life in France. It has information about getting marriage and driver's licenses, so it has great potential as authentic reading documents that are in a question/answer format
http://www.pratique.fr:80/recherche.html

Proverbs and explanations (also traditional folk songs and fables)
http://www.canalmedia.com/fdt/F/Proverbes/F5.html

Version Francaise (CDs, books, movies—with and without subtitles)
http://www.francevision.com

"Decouvrons le Canada" has many links and treasure hunts for teachers and students of French
http://www.geocities.com/Paris/Bistro/7445/index.html

An online practice test for the written exam of the French road test is at
http://www.volga.fr

The site for the Quebec daily newspaper, useful for want ads, film information, or current events, is at
http://www.lesoleil.com

DEDALE—history, geography, civics, science, math, and arts in French
http://www.interpc.fr/mapage/dedale/index.htm

Pages Zoom— the phone book (yellow and white pages) in French
http://www.pageszoom.com/files/nojava/francais/commun/sommaire.html

French language lesson plans
http://scrtec.org/track/index/flanguage.html

SNCF (Société Nationale des Chemins de Fer)-Les TGV for train schedules
http://www.sncf.fr/co/materiel/tgv/index.htm

The official site for the French arm of CBC Radio in Canada, with news in French
http://radio-canada.ca/

Tic-tac-toc—play it on line, in French, and it taunts you if you lose
http://www.mediom.qc.ca/~gbegin/ttt0.htm

Learn from Francophone TV and radio at Globe-Gate
http://globegate.utm.edu/french/globegate_mirror/radiotv.html

Adopt An Escargot, a humorous site with stories, pictures, jokes, and more
http://www.busprod.com/pokesfan/escargot.htm

If you like to introduce students to poetry, this is a good French-language site; some poems have sound and there is a search engine if you can only remember a line or two of the poem
http://Poesie.webnet.fr

Shopping
http://www.galerieslafayette.com/fb/home/gbhome.html
http://quiquoiou.wanadoo.fr/quiquoiou/html/qqo_shopping.html

Food shopping
http://www.telemarket.fr

This page has 79 French tongue twisters
http://www.uebersetzung.at/twister/fr.htm

Or try this Web site
http://www.geocities.com/Athens/8136/tonguetwisters.html

Clicnet— resources for many French activities and links to other sites
http://clicnet.swarthmore.edu/fle.html

Premiers Pas Sur Internet: has a huge supply of nursery rhymes and "comptines" (like jump rope rhymes)—perfect for FLES classes
http://www.momes.net/

GERMAN

To subscribe to the American Association of Teachers of German (AATG) listserv: send a message to listserv@listserv. iupui.edu, and type subscribe aatg as the message. German teachers share ideas on this listserv.

The GermanWay Forum (discussion group)
http://www.onelist.com/subscribe.cgi/germanway

The German Way Web site address
http://www.german-way.com/german/germany.html

The German-American Home Page—pictures, links, lots of beautiful sites
http://www.angelfire.com/il/wd9gng

Deutsche Internet Chronik—Internet exercises, and more
http://www.uncg.edu/~lixlpurc/GIP/german_units/UnitsCover.html

Another site with Internet exercises
http://www.tricounty.esu6.k12.ne.us/german/WebIntro.htm

German shopping URLs
http://www.neukauf-weissmann.de
http://www.shop.de
http://www.edwin-jeans.de
http://www.homeshop.at (Austria)
http://www.OnkelEmma.de/oekat/oekat.htm (Germany)

German politics
http://www.agora.it/politic/germany.htm

Here's a site with materials for beginning students and their teachers
http://www.ualberta.ca/~german/lehrer.htm

ITALIAN

E.L. Easton's Italian pages: Grammar, readings, art, movies and music at
http://www.geocities.com/Athens/Crete/4634/italian.html

JAPANESE

KC/J 2.0 (Vocabulary, Kanji, Conjugation Exercise in Japanese) is now available for noncommercial educational use at
http://www.sla.purdue.edu/fll/JapanProj

Kids' Window to Japan: learn origami, Japanese phrases (and listen to them pronounced), and look at a food menu
http://www.homeworkcentral.com/toplinks/228.html

Links to hundreds of sites about Japan and its language
http://fmc.utm.edu/~rpeckham/JAPAN.HTM

LATIN

Classics students can explore the city of Rome (150 A.D.) at VROMA, a project supported by the National Endowment for the Humanities. VROMA includes images, maps, texts, and links to other sites related to the ancient city. Students can access VROMA through the

Web or a MOO, in which educators may conduct real-time courses, give lectures, and collect and share resources. For information, see
http://vroma.rhodes.edu/

Take a look at songs in Latin, vocabulary, and several sites which are directly related to teaching younger children Latin, especially the Texas Classical Association and Young Children's Latin Page at
http://www.geocities.com/Athens/Crete/4634/latin.html

Forum Romanum, all about ancient Rome
http://www.geocities.com/Athens/Forum/6946/rome.html

LATINTEACH is an e-mail discussion forum for Latin teachers. Conversations include (but are certainly not limited to) pedagogy, teaching methodology and techniques, use of conversational Latin in the classroom, textbooks, incorporation of Roman culture into the curriculum, projects, and lessons. Best of all, it's free. All you need is an e-mail address. To subscribe, send the message subscribe latinteach username@domain to majordomo@mlists.net

Latin Dictionary and Grammar Aid: type in word stems or endings then peruse a list of Latin words with the same elements, translate words from English to Latin, discover the meanings of 6,000 Latin words, and use a Latin Grammar Aid.
http://www.nd.edu/~archives/latgramm.htm

Latin-L information
http://www.n2h2.com/KOVACS/CD/1823.html

And a form that helps you subscribe to Latin-L
http://wsrv.clas.virginia.edu/~dew7e/anthronet/subscribe/latinl.html

RUSSIAN

To subscribe to RusTeach listserv, please send e-mail to RusTeach-L@design.techpromotion.com. Use Subscribe in the subject field. The first line of your message text must contain your e-mail address.

Russian pictures site
http://www.middlebury.edu/~beyer/RT/pages/signs/picthtml/pict1.shtml

From here one can click on the right arrow or change the number in the URL for another picture
http://www.middlebury.edu/~beyer/RT/pages/signs/picthtml/pict34.shtml

SPANISH

A pilot project at International House in Barcelona that integrates the use of the Internet with the Spanish classroom can be seen at
http://www.ihes.com/mar/index.htm

TeachSpanish includes lesson plans at
http://www.teachspanish.com/

You Too Can Learn Spanish (weekly lessons)
http://www.willamette.edu/~tjones/Spanish/lesson1.html

WWW for Spanish Teachers
http://www.niles-hs.k12.il.us/north/depts/forlan/sp/sp.html

Spanish links
http://globegate.utm.edu/spanish/span.html

EspanOle, with pages on Hispanic language, literature, history, heritage, food, countries and peoples
http://www.yourlink.net/kappa/espanole/principal.html

An interactive online grammar tutorial
http://www.studyspanish.com

Another grammar site, Verb Conjugator, is at
http://csg.uwaterloo.ca/~dmg/lando/verbos/con-jugador.html

Visit a site with a search engine at
http://www.spanishconnection.com.

Hola Amigos Web site (supplements an elementary Spanish class broadcast on TV in West Virginia)—vocabulary, culture, and links to other sites
http://kcs.kana.k12.wv.us/holaamigos.

LatinoWeb search engine with links to many sites featuring Latino culture, jobs, and so forth
http://www.latinoweb.com

The Hispanic Pages in the United States—very good information on bullfights, famous Hispanics, country links, and more
http://coloquio.com/index.html

El Tiempo en sus Manos: Spain's weather Web site
http://www.inm.es

A good link for finding Spanish song lyrics
http://www.musica.org

Mondo Sonoro—interviews, concerts, and info on the world of music
http://www.mondosonoro.es

Intercine (Spanish movie site)
http://www.intercine.com

More movies, music, and children's sites
http://www.ozu.com/

Juegos de Pelicula, a Spanish-language a site with quizzes and info on movies
http://www.elcine.com

Nuestro Cine (Spanish Ministry of Education site)
http://www.mcu.es/cine

Mexican cooking and recipes from the University of Guadalajara
http://mexico.udg.mx/cocina/home.html

More recipes at
http://www.masterstech-home.com/The_Kitchen/Recipes/Recipe_Indices/

Cocina Espanola, with the history of the potato
http://www.iponet.es/~jlpolo

The Lost Cities Adventure—a site where, if you have QuickTime 3 loaded, you can visit important sites in Peru. It has many panoramic photos, where you can click and spin around in a picture to see it in 360 degrees.
http://www.studio360.com/lostcities.htm

Try these—rompecabezas
http://www.geocities.com/Athens/Forum/2867/23.htm
http://www.geocities.com/Athens/Forum/2867/24.htm

TRAVEL

Discover Spain
http://www.ozemail.com.au/~spain/overview.htm

Spain Undercover
http://ibgwww.colorado.edu/~gayan/Spain.html

Information on Latin America as well as over 700 links to other pages about Latin America at
http://www.latinamericatravel.com

A complete course on Central and Southern America
http://uts.cc.utexas.edu/~gwk/courses/grg319/topics/LAtopics.html

Welcome to Mexico (big link page in English and Spanish)
http://info.pue.udlap.mx/mexico-info.html

Pictures of Venezuela (English)
http://venezuela.mit.edu/pictures/

Discover the Spanish World has lots of links
http://www.geocities.com/Paris/Bistro/7445/spanish.html

Clark Net's Spanish Speaking Countries (links page)
http://www.clark.net/pub/jgbustam/heritage/heritage.html

University of Texas Latin American countries page (in Spanish)
http://edb518ea.edb.utexas.edu/html/LatinAmerica.html

Agencia de empleo—tells how to get a job, in Spanish
http://www.lalinea.com/trabajo.htm

Instituto de empleo
http://www.inem.es

El doctor en casa
http://ecomedic.com

La biblioteca nacional
http://www.bne.es

Diccionarios en español
http://www3.anaya.es/diccionario/diccionar.htm

La Reforma, a good Mexico City newspaper online is at
http://www.reforma.com.mx

SHOPPING

Ibermercado (shopping online in Spanish)
http://www.cybercentro.com

La Tienda En Casa, an online shopping Web site in Spain
http://www.readysoft.es/latiendaencasa/nouindex.html

ART

Guadalajara-Centro Universitario Arte Arquitectura y Deseno (site has stunning graphics, audio files)
http://udgftp.cencar.udg.mx/

A Virtual museum for Chicano/Latino art, customs, music, and artifacts
http://latino.sscnet.ucla.edu/MUSEUM.HTML

Mexico—Arte, Cultura y Folklore: music, painters, and paintings, all in Spanish
http://www.udg.mx/cultfolk/mexico.html

TECLA archives (an Hispanic world cultural magazine)
http://www.bbk.ac.uk/Departments/Spanish/TeclaHome.html

Guide to Mexican Culture (folklore, chat room, search engine)
http://mexicanculture.miningco.com/

Rabbit in the Moon, an English-language site about various aspects of Mayan culture and language
http://www.halfmoon.org/

LESS COMMONLY TAUGHT LANGUAGES

The LCTL project includes mailing lists and a virtual picture album with sample exercises for approximately 300 languages from Afrikaans to Zulu
http://carla.acad.umn.edu/LCTL

OTHER COMPUTER APPLICATIONS

POWERPOINT

PowerPoint is a Microsoft software product and is an alternative way of presenting information in a multimedia context on your computer or on your computer that is linked with a television screen. When it is used correctly it can greatly contribute to students' learning. PowerPoint is a presentation software program, which is basically a slide show with pictures (scanned from books, photographs, art, or taken off the Internet) that are combined with music or sound effects (that you record yourself, or from CDs or the Internet), and moving parts (from movie clips to computer graphics). A similar presentation without PowerPoint (or another presentation software program) would require a slide projector, a movie projector, a screen, a tape recorder, an overhead projector, transparencies, and a stack of books! You can create the PowerPoint presentation yourself, or assign them to students as an assessment for a unit.

To effectively use this method, a person must first boil down the unit to its basics, and figure out the best order in which to present them. The slides for the presentation can also be printed and used as an outline for taking notes, or for review of the ideas presented. If you put them on the school Web site, they are accessible to students for review purposes long after you have finished a unit. Many students access these while studying for final exams, for example, and some even visit and pull them up from their college computer for a brief review.

PowerPoint has many applications:

- Instead of holding up flash cards, do it using the computer and show it on the TV screen (good for verbs or vocabulary).
- Instead of showing slides of foreign sites, pulled from containers and stuffed into a tray, make a permanent slide show that can be edited as needed, and that is available at a moment's notice. When you

use PowerPoint, in addition to merely showing a picture, you can program information about that site to pop onto the screen, a bonus for visual students, for whom an oral presentation is not beneficial.

- Make a PowerPoint presentation from a series of pictures and construct a rebus story that students must narrate as they view it (or write a story that goes with the illustrations).
- Use PowerPoint to show how pronouns replace nouns, having them literally do that on screen.
- Make a presentation of just pictures of people, and use them over and over. Ask "How would you greet this person (formal vs. informal)?" "How would you ask his or her name or age?" "Describe this person." If the picture shows the person at work, ask "What is his or her profession?" "What did he or she study in school?" and so on.
- Using a digital camera, take pictures of the students to demonstrate action verbs, emotions, relationships, or even use the pictures to make a "comic strip" that the students narrate.

USING VIDEOS IN THE FOREIGN LANGUAGE CLASSROOM

In addition to the obvious benefits of a travel video, almost any video may be used as a classroom exercise. Try some of these:

- Show any video (even in English) with the *sound off,* and have students describe in the target language what they see taking place, or write possible dialogue for the people they see. Have students focus on the gestures they see, or any other cultural detail you wish them to focus on.
- Stop the video and have students predict what will happen, either orally or in writing.
- Have students list all the words they hear that they know, and the English meaning of the words.
- Have student reenact scenes from the video, using props if possible. This is good speaking and listening practice, as well as a great way to review the plot of the movie.
- Assign each student a specific character to look for. After viewing all or part of the video, have them come forward, and have the class play Twenty Questions, asking yes/no questions to determine who the character is, until they guess.
- Write out a plot summary of the video, leaving out key words that they must listen for (a cloze activity). Make sure the words are either already in the students' vocabulary, or are repeated often—or list the possibilities at the top of the page.

- Hold a trial for an evil character in a video—for example, Papet in *Jean de la Florette.* Assign students to prosecute, defend, or act as witnesses or jury.
- Assign portions of the story for students to illustrate and explain.
- Use a video in the target language as a grammar exercise: Give students a list of verbs to listen for during the video. Ask them to listen for those verbs, and write down either the form they heard (subject and tense) or the situation in which they heard it used. This can also be done with pronouns or a particular verb tense ("Write down examples of the subjunctive tense you hear in this video."). I have also, as students watched a video, written examples of phrases using a verb tense on the board, and afterward, they read these, and told me where they were in the video, a good review of the video's content as well as the verb tense.
- Another way to watch a video is with Jigsaw. Divide the students into groups, and each takes notes on one aspect of the video: one looks at architecture, another looks at food/dining, another at historical information, another at clothing, another at transportation, and so on. As students watch the video, each takes notes on what he or she sees about their assigned topic. After the video, have the students compare notes within their groups. Then put the students in new groupings with one from each expert group, and have them each give a short report on their topic to their new group. There are many ways to assess this type of activity. It could be something creative like a poster or a poem (or a rap) created by the group. You could have each student write a postcard from that area, showing what they have learned. You could have each group write a quiz about the video, and then have them take turns taking each other's quiz—the possibilities are endless.
- Have students write a critical review of the video, using the vocabulary (director, setting, dialogue, screenplay, special effects, etc.) that film critics use. Give students a critical review of the movie in the target language or have them agree or disagree with it.

Get a book that lists videos by category, such as *VideoHound's Golden Movie Retriever 1998* (ISBN: 1-57859-024-8, $19.95). It is nearly 2,000 pages with listings by actor, director, and category, as well as content warnings for language, nudity, and so on, which are especially helpful on unrated foreign films. This can be very helpful when you need a movie about a certain topic; for example, if you are doing a unit on the environment, you will find several listings such as *Medicine Man* that, though in English, are filmed in Central or South America.

I have found the Old Poster Peddler to be a wonderful resource for visuals for my classroom. The latest catalog, for example, offers not only art reproductions but actual Metro maps, movie ads, official road maps, and also videos on the TGV train, Fiesta de los Muertos, and Mexico City's metro. No poster costs over $5; maps and videos cost a bit more. The Old Poster Peddler, 2820 Villageside Drive, Santa Rosa, CA 95405.

Let's not forget about making videos, as well. Have students make a video to illustrate reflexive verbs; for example: their mom saying "I wash the dishes" and then little sister in the tub, saying "I wash myself." Our school has a video exchange with two other schools in France; we make one or two videos each year to show them our school, jobs, holidays, homes, and other topics of interest. I use a video project form (see Figure 7.2) when doing any video project, both to divide the assignment into small steps, each with a due date and point value, and to evaluate the final video.

FIGURE 7.2. VIDEO PROJECT ON REFLEXIVE VERBS

1. List of the verbs you will be filming, due ________________________.
2. List of the verbs, as well as the actors and where it will be filmed, due _________________.
3. The script for the video, due ______________________ for proof-reading in class.
4. List of equipment needed, and date to be used: __________________.
5. Final video, with script due: _________________.

****

EVALUATION:

RANK YOURSELF by circling a number from 1 to 4, with 4 as the highest/best score:

CONTENT: Video contained enough information, presented accurately

Student	Teacher
1 2 3 4	1 2 3 4

PREPARATION: Completed each step on time, was on task

Student	Teacher
1 2 3 4	1 2 3 4

CREATIVITY: Showed verbs in a unique way

Student	Teacher
1 2 3 4	1 2 3 4

ORGANIZATION: Presented ideas clearly

Student	Teacher
1 2 3 4	1 2 3 4

What improvements could be made?___________________________

What would be a good follow-up for this activity?

REFERENCES

BOOKS

Campbell, L., Campbell, B., & Dickinson, D. (1996). *Teaching and learning through multiple intelligences*. Needham Heights, MA: Allyn & Bacon.

Canady, R. L., & Rettig, M. D. (1995). *Block scheduling: A catalyst for change in high schools*. Larchmont, NY: Eye on Education.

Canady, R. L., & Rettig, M. D. (1996). *Teaching in the block: Strategies for engaging active learners*. Larchmont, NY: Eye on Education.

Gardner, H. (1983). *Frames of mind*. New York: Basic Books Inc.

Gardner, H. (1993). *Multiple intelligences: the theory in practice.* New York: Basic Books Inc.

Hoye, A. G. (1991). Interaction of students and teachers with the learning environment. In *Foreign language education: A reappraisal*. National Textbook Company, 259–290.

Hunter, M. C. (1982). *Mastery teaching*. El Segundo, CA: T.I.P. Publications.

Kagan, S. (1995). *Cooperative learning: Resources for teachers*. San Juan Capistrano, CA: Resources for Teachers, Inc.

Lazear, D. (1992). *Teaching for multiple intelligences*. Fastback 342. Bloomington, IN: Phi Delta Kappan Educational Foundation.

Morie, E. D. (1996). Simulations. In R. L. Canady and M. D. Rettig (Eds.), *Teaching in the block* (pp. 141–160). Larchmont, NY: Eye On Education.

Postovsky, V. A. (1981). The priority of aural comprehension in the language acquisition process. In W. Harris (Ed.), *The Comprehension approach to foreign language instruction* (pp. 170–186). Cambridge, MA: Newbury House Publishers.

Rosensline, B., & Stevens, R. (1986). Teaching functions. In M. C. Wittrock (Ed.), *Handbook of research on teaching* (3rd ed., pp. 376–391). New York: Macmillan.

Rost, M. (1991). *Listening in action: Activities for developing listening in language teaching*. New York: Prentice Hall.

Sousa, D. A. (1995). *How the brain learns*. Reston, VA: National Association of Secondary School Principals.

ARTICLES

Begley, S. (1998, November 2). Talking with your hands. *Newsweek*, 69.

Berne, J. E. (1995). How does varying pre-listening activities affect second language listening comprehension? *Hispania, 78*, 316–329.

Danesi, N. (1990). The contribution of neurolinguistics to second and foreign language theory and practice. *System, 3*, 373–396.

Ebbinghaus, H. (1885). The forgetting curve. In L. A. Lefton (Ed.), *Psychology* (5th ed., p. 226). Needham Heights, MA: Paramount Publishing.

Gardner, H., & Hatch, T. (1989). Multiple intelligences go to school: Educational implications of the theory of multiple intelligences. *Educational Researcher, 18*(8), 4–9.

Perkins, D. N., & Salomon, G. (1998, September). Teaching for transfer. *Educational Leadership.*

Secules, T., Herron, C., & Tomasello, M. (1992). The effect of video context on foreign language learning. *The Modern Language Journal, 76*, 480–490.

Slavin, R. E. (1991, February). Synthesis of research on cooperative learning. *Educational Leadership.*

Willis, B. D., & Mason, K. (1994). Canciones en la Clase: The why and how of integrating songs in Spanish by English-speaking and bilingual artists. *Hispania, 77*, 102–109.